D1267820

# The White Response
# to Black Emancipation

# The
# White
# Response

### Second-Class Citizenship
### in the United States
### Since Reconstruction

# to
# Black
# Emancipation

## Sig Synnestvedt
*State University of New York, Brockport*

THE MACMILLAN COMPANY/NEW YORK
COLLIER-MACMILLAN LIMITED/LONDON

To all the young people in America
but especially
to
Barbara, Nancy, Suzanne, Jeanette, and Steven,
who will soon,
I fervently hope,
be able to live out their lives in a nation
which has completely eliminated the evil practice of racism
in all of its ugly detail.

The Macmillan Company
866 Third Avenue, New York, New York 10022

Collier-Macmillan Canada, Ltd., Toronto, Ontario

Library of Congress catalog card number: 75–161429
First Printing

# Preface

This book contains reflections on the racial contest in the United States during the past century. This struggle has pitted minority blacks against a vast white majority which, for the most part, does not even realize that it is involved in an ethnic war. Whites in America live in a white world, as do blacks. This situation provides blacks with endless opportunities to judge whites, but the reverse does not take place to anywhere near the same degree. Whites generally go about their lives with only occasional, inconclusive, and confusing insights into the lives and thoughts of their fellow black citizens. The militant tone of the black revolution during the past decade has begun to change social assumptions in many quarters, but the pace and degree of alteration which seems breathlessly, even aggressively, rapid to many whites strikes most blacks as ridiculously, even gallingly, slow.

In spite of many white assumptions to the contrary we continue to suffer from the errors and injustices of the past. The legacies of the slave system, the era of Jim Crow, the line of violence called lynching, placed American blacks in a subservient status. Early attempts to escape this position led by individuals and groups, both black and white, failed to achieve the goal. An immense internal migration followed, during which blacks sought to change their status by moving to the north or west, but these geographical shifts merely served to make the race problem a nationwide phenomenon. The United States fought World Wars I and II in the name of extending freedom over the globe, but blacks found it impossible to ignore the fact that Americans had by no means put the home front in proper order.

During and after World War I, race relations in the United States descended to their lowest point. World War II began with little improvement in the status of blacks in spite of a decade of social reform under the New Deal. But the turmoil of the second great war period of the half century provided, at last, initial opportunities to mobilize activists for the ultimate assault upon the nation's ancient tradition of according inferior treatment to blacks. The equal-rights revolution of the 1950's and 1960's has set trends in motion which will compel final solution of America's racial confrontation. The outcome, however, remains in doubt.

It is hoped that the synthesis provided in this book may prove to be of value in separating historic reality from the confused, contradictory mixture of ignorance, anger, and myth characteristic of the racial equation in the United States.

In writing a book of this type an author acquires an immense debt to persons who have previously supplied monographs, biographies, autobiographies, and other statements on the subjects under review. A work of synthesis could not possibly be presented unless numerous books of more precise focus existed to supply the necessary source materials, analyses, and insights. Without mentioning any specific persons, I wish to express my appreciation to all of my fellow authors who have contributed so much to whatever of merit this book may contain. It goes without saying, of course, that limitations of judgment, errors of syntax, and aberrations of style are my own responsibility.

My warm thanks also to Shirley Maranda, Sue Weatherby, Nancy Synnestvedt, and Sandy Hamilton for the typing, proofing, and xeroxing of numerous manuscript drafts, and to Diana Wedel for secretarial support services such as the above, plus the organization, screening, and decision making vital to the operation of any departmental office.

I have benefited greatly from contacts with hundreds of students of all colors. They have made it possible for me to test out my ideas in a real context. Particularly, I would like to mention Chris Merkle, Grace Murabito, Sherry Smith, and Ross Reisinger, who have spent a good many hours tracing down this or that book, article, or quotation. I would especially like to thank Paige Gorham, who has rendered endless service as my research assistant, much of it quite beyond my ability to support financially.

Finally, and most especially, I thank my wife Nadine.

Sig Synnestvedt
*Brockport, New York*

# Contents

# Introduction

1

THE white response to black emancipation did not begin, of course, until the Civil War ended. Consideration of events prior to 1865 would require a different title, such as *The History of Race Relations in the United States* or *American Slavery and Its Aftermath*. The study at hand deals primarily with events since Reconstruction, but no historical focus can escape the influences of the past.

This book might have started with the first contacts between white English explorers and blacks from western Africa. Winthrop Jordan describes these initial meetings in the following words: "English contact with Africans did not take place primarily in a context which prejudged the Negro as a slave, at least not as a slave of Englishmen. Rather, Englishmen met Negroes merely as another sort of men. . . . The most arresting characteristic of the newly discovered African was his color. . . . The powerful impact which the Negro's color made upon Englishmen must have been partly owing to suddenness of contact. . . . The impact of the Negro's color was the more powerful upon Englishmen, moreover, because England's principal contact with Africans came in West Africa and the Congo where men were not merely dark but almost literally black; one of the fairest-skinned nations suddenly came face to face with one of the darkest peoples on earth. . . . And for Englishmen this juxtaposition was more than a curiosity. . . . White and black connoted purity and filthiness, virginity and sin, virtue and baseness, beauty and ugliness, beneficence and evil, God and the devil."[1]

This book might also have started with the first arrival of black servants in Virginia in 1619. A score of persons stepped off

---

[1] Winthrop D. Jordan, *White Over Black* (Baltimore: Penguin Books, 1969), pp. 4–7.

the ship at Jamestown into indentured servitude and into history. One writer has re-created the situation in these words: "Southerners did not create the slave system all at once in 1619; rather, they built it little by little, step by step, choice by choice, over a period of many years; and all the while most of them were more or less blind to the ultimate consequences of the choices they were making. . . . When a 'Dutch man of warre' brought the first cargo of twenty 'negars' to Virginia in 1619, John Rolfe and his neighbors sanctioned a trade and tapped a source of labor that had been familiar to some Europeans for nearly two centuries."[2]

Or this book might have started in Philadelphia during the Constitutional Convention of 1787. Several topics had threatened to split the delegates, all of whom were white, but none contained social dynamite equivalent to the question of the future of the slave system. The compromise effected has been termed one of "brutal expediency." Catherine Drinker Bowen concludes: "The Northern states agreed that Congress should not pass any navigation law by a mere majority, but must have two-thirds vote of each house; agreed also that the import tax on slaves would not exceed ten dollars a head; that slaves would be counted, for purpose of representation and taxes, in the proportion of five slaves to three free white inhabitants—the 'federal ratio.' In return, the Southern states conceded that the importation of slaves would cease in the year 1808.

"Hamilton said later that without the federal ratio 'no union could possibly have been formed.' It was true, and true also that the Constitution could not have gone through without the slavery compromise. The question before the Convention was not, shall slavery be abolished? It was rather, Who shall have the power to control it—the states or the national government."[3]

Or this book might have begun with the story of the acquisition of great pieces of potential slave territory from Mexico in the 1840's, with the supposedly permanent Compromise of 1850, with the Dred Scott decision which insisted that slavery must be accepted everywhere in the nation, with the Lincoln decision to issue the Emancipation Proclamation in 1863, or with the Confederate surrender to Grant at a tiny crossroads village in western Virginia in the spring of 1865. The decision to concentrate on the period following Reconstruction stems partly from the fact that my professional training has been mostly with twentieth-century

---

2 Kenneth M. Stampp, *The Peculiar Institution* (New York: Vintage Books, 1956), pp. 6 and 18.
3 Catherine Drinker Bowen, *Miracle at Philadelphia* (Boston: Little, Brown, 1966), pp. 200–201.

materials and partly from various personal experiences of more recent date.

The original idea of this study entered my thinking six or seven years ago during three days of reflecting upon an acid criticism leveled at me by the charming wife of a former colleague. She, also white, had become active in a local open housing effort. The community and the county involved were lily-white, affluent, and unconcerned. She and others began the painful process of effecting social change through education, persuasion, and, where necessary, confrontation. After talking a bit about the project, she asked me directly, "And what are you doing to improve race relations?" My rather pompous response indicated that I was speaking out firmly against racism wherever I found it. She replied, "Isn't that grand! You live in an all-white community, teach in an all-white school, and socialize only with white persons. When exactly does your tolerant stance go into action?" I found her remarks irritating and after several days told her I thought she was correct. I determined to start doing something other than pontificate.

In a typically white, paternalistic state of mind I set upon the idea of teaching a course in "Negro history." Much reading, considerable reflection, and some contact with blacks in a variety of new situations led me to realize that the original idea needed severe modification. I determined instead to develop a course, and eventually a book, on "white history" with emphasis upon the means by which whites in America have imposed second-class citizenship upon their black fellow citizens. My determination to move in this direction received support when I observed that white colleagues who tried to teach "Negro history" experienced varying degrees of failure.

A basic awkwardness is present whenever a professor, who happens to be white, attempts to teach black history. Students, both black and white, view his efforts with skepticism, and the end experience may well be both uncomfortable and depressing. In the present emotion-laden social context, any white professor who attempts to teach black history will probably generate adverse responses. The reasons are obvious but often overlooked.[4]

For more than three hundred years white professors took no interest in black history. Textbooks and monographs consistently omitted or underplayed the black contribution to American culture by presenting negative stereotypes of nonwhites. But now that black history has become current, white faces appear in class-

[4] The analysis which follows is taken largely from my own article, "White Faces and White Studies," *Commonweal*, May 8, 1970, pp. 182–83.

rooms all over the nation, teaching courses in black history. White authors write books on black history and deliver them to white publishers. White speakers give lectures on black themes. Many of these efforts are born of genuine desire to do good. Yet I cannot see how any self-aware black could be other than cynical and negative about this sudden quickening of scholarly, white interest in an area so long neglected. Although there are some dedicated white students of black history, all whites who present themselves for assignment in the field deserve close, skeptical scrutiny.

In my own work I have tried to avoid the problem by shunning the assignment. I do not teach black history; I teach race relations history. I do not attempt to present the black contribution to American culture, nor do I attempt to interpret "the black experience in America" or provide insight into some other minority group perspective for which I have only a secondhand knowledge. In a course that I teach, "The White Response to Black Emancipation," I concentrate on the central aspects of white majority control of the black minority with emphasis on the political, economic, judicial, and social crisis points at which attempts to change the caste system in America have been blunted or turned aside.

During the first week of classes, and at any other suitable opportunity, I stress the fact that I am not teaching black history. I advance alternate titles to the course such as "The Means by Which Second-Class Citizenship Is Sustained in the United States," "White Racism at Work," or simply "The White Problem in America."

One white professor who tried to teach "Negro history" at a major mid-western university suffered through a single semester of friction and concluded that "The educational goal of courses in Afro-American history . . . becomes strictly utilitarian, a highly selective sifting of the past to yield information and to produce attitudes that together will support programs of radical action. This is the 'racial and cultural identity' such courses are expected to help achieve."[5] I do not know this to be a fact, although scattered evidence suggests it may be true in some circumstances. Perhaps matters will trend in this direction for some time to come, until the power equation in America comes into better balance largely through the efforts of militant, educated blacks. There are aspects to such trends which I, along with other "detached," "objective" scholars, deplore and even, to an extent, fear.

---

[5] Merton L. Dillon, "White Faces and Black Studies," *Commonweal*, January 30, 1970, p. 477.

But if we are to avoid a racial holocaust in America, immense social change must take place rapidly. Most of this change must come in the minds of white Americans who presently enjoy numerous benefits from the white racist policies of the past which have become socially institutionalized. White students, not black, require the greatest amount of attention because they are the ones who need most to change. In this process of attitude change, I believe that the white professor, like the white leader in any white community, plays an indispensable role.

At one point in his autobiography, Malcolm X recalls telling a white college girl who desperately wants to "do something to improve race relations" that there is nothing she can do that would be meaningful. Later, he comes to feel that whites can do much, but not by joining or "hovering" around black organizations. This salves white consciences, but does nothing to solve America's racist problem. As Malcolm saw it, "Where the really sincere white people have got to do their 'proving' of themselves is not among the black *victims,* but out on the battle lines of where America's racism really *is* . . . among their own fellow whites."[6]

In teaching white students about race relations history in America, the white teacher has a certain advantage over his black colleague. Subconsciously perhaps, but almost inevitably, most American whites discount indictments of the American racial record advanced by blacks. Malcolm X, Stokely Carmichael, H. Rap Brown, Eldridge Cleaver, even a relatively bland critic like Martin Luther King, Jr.—are all considered to be biased in varying degrees. A white observer, on the other hand, usually obtains a fairer hearing. If he exposes the ugly details of the white problem in America, he makes a significant contribution.

This "strategy of truth," as Kenneth B. Clark has called it, must be the basis for genuine social change. Clark concedes truth to be "abstract," "nebulous," and sometimes ineffective, especially when it opposes strongly vested interests which can, in a short-run contest, place truth on the defensive. But he insists that "the search for truth, while impotent without implementation in action, undergirds every other strategy in behalf of constructive social change. None could proceed toward democratic ends without it."[7]

Thousands of white teachers are needed to study the real story of race relations in America and then present it to students

---

6 Malcolm X, *Autobiography* (New York: Grove Press, 1965), pp. 290 and 382.
7 Kenneth B. Clark, *Dark Ghetto: Dilemmas of Social Power* (New York: Harper & Row, 1967), p. 221.

at every level of education. The effort calls for massive involvement. It may not be enough, but those who participate may take
satisfaction from the thought that they will be committing themselves to the greatest social need in America today—re-educating
whites of all ages to the stark realities of the exploitative reject-
tion of black humanity which has marred this nation from its
beginning.

I doubt whether these prospective teachers will meet any
opposition or hostility from blacks who know only too well where
the real changes must take place. Whites who so commit themselves will be attacking the social problem which former Chief
Justice Earl Warren has described as the one which "approaches
more closely to the limit of insolubility than any other."[8] Finally
they will contribute to the two noble necessities which James
Weldon Johnson saw so clearly two generations ago shortly after
he had investigated a particularly brutal lynching of a black
man by a number of gleeful whites. "The race question," he
wrote, "involves the saving of black America's body and white
America's soul."[9]

8 *New York Times,* November 23, 1970, p. 49.
9 James Weldon Johnson, *Along This Way* (New York: Viking, 1943), p. 318.

# Slavery and Reconstruction

## 2

No clear definition of the word *race* exists. Because human groupings are in a constant state of change, future efforts to find a precise meaning for this expression will doubtless fail as well. Ashley Montagu and others insist that race is man's "most dangerous myth" and advocate dropping the term.

Obviously, some differences between ethnic groups are noticeably real. Height, weight, head shape, eye color, skin color, hair, and so forth establish varieties of humankind. All such physical features are traceable to genetic combinations scientifically predictable within limits. Some evidence suggests that these biological differences contribute to a group's ability to flourish in a particular area, and indeed may have resulted from generations of life there. For example, mountain people like the Sherpas in the Himalayas or Peruvians in the Andes have larger lung capacities. Eskimos carry additional layers of fat for cold winters, and dark-skinned Africans can better stand prolonged exposure to bright sun.

But other traits commonly associated with ethnic groups, such as loud or quiet behavior, propensities for certain occupations, desires to travel or stay at home, moral practices, habits of marriage and family, crime records, amounts of intellect or brain power, and so forth have never been scientifically traced to genetic factors. Most, if not all, such differences seem to have cultural or environmental origins. And no traits can be traced to the blood. All human species carry varying percentages of the same basic blood types.

The idea of race is relatively recent in origin. Probably Georges Buffon, an eighteenth-century French naturalist, first introduced the word *race* into scientific writings. The concept of racial superiority and inferiority has stemmed chiefly from white,

Western culture as it has permeated the world during the past 250 years. Slavery and colonialism, two central features of the nineteenth century, fostered a racist climate of opinion. Most overt racial antagonism has stemmed from white, Western writers, like Joseph Arthur de Gobineau, Houston Stewart Chamberlain, Richard Wagner, Friedrich Nietzsche, Alfred Rosenburg, Charles Carroll, Madison Grant, Robert Shufeldt, and others. Modern politicians like Hitler and Mussolini caused racial considerations to become one of the chief origins of twentieth-century violence.

Endless tracts have appeared attempting to establish the superiority or inferiority of one or another ethnic group. And the effort of some whites to sustain second-class citizenship for blacks by proving inborn inferiority goes on. De Gobineau judged blacks to be ugly, animal-like, passionate, gluttonous, capricious, cowardly, weak-reasoned, cruel, and dishonorable, a race which belonged at the bottom of the human scale. He found whites beautiful, intellectual, honorable, and superior to other ethnic groups. De Gobineau predicted little future for the black race because, he concluded, an "animal character" which "appears in the shape of the pelvis, is stamped on the Negro from birth, and foreshadows his destiny. His intellect will always move within a very narrow circle." On the other hand, de Gobineau argued that history demonstrated all genuine civilization emanated from the white race, the "most illustrious" section of humanity.[1]

De Gobineau had contempt for blacks as leaders, insisting that they only cared to chew tobacco, drink, disembowel their enemies, conciliate their sorcerers, and sleep. He liked the cutting aphorism which defined a black as "an animal who eats as much, and works as little, as possible."[2]

In the United States, white racist authors opened the present century with a series of crude books presenting blacks in a viciously distorted image. Charles Carroll's *The Negro a Beast,* published in 1900, argued that blacks were subhumans designed by the creator to serve whites. "All scientific investigation," Carroll wrote, "proves the Negro to be an ape; and that he simply stands at the head of the ape family, as the lion stands at the head of the cat family. . . . The Negro is the only anthropoid, or man-like ape; and . . . the gibbon, ourang [*sic*], chimpanzee and gorilla are merely negro-like apes." He particularly despised the mixed-blood products of cross racial intercourse and de-

---

[1] Joseph de Gobineau, "Essays," in Louis L. Snyder, ed., *The Idea of Racialism* (Princeton, N.J.: D. Van Nostrand, Inc., 1962), pp. 128, 130.
[2] Joseph de Gobineau, *The Inequality of Human Races* (New York: G. P. Putnam's Sons, 1915), pp. 49, 180.

scribed mulattos as "dung" and "monstrosities" who had "no rights, social, financial, political or religious that man need respect; they have no rights that man dare respect—not even the right to live."[3] On the other hand, Carroll judged whites to be flashing, energetic, courageous, humane, and civilized.

R. W. Shufeldt followed Carroll in 1907 with *The Negro: A Menace to American Civilization.* He considered the black presence in the United States to be the greatest danger the nation faced and favored forcible migration, mandatory emasculation, and even genocide as the ultimate means by which American whites must protect themselves from degeneration. Shufeldt variously termed blacks apelike, nonmoral, savage, superstitious, cannibalistic, odoriferous, criminally inclined, lewd, brutal, and bestial. He particularly liked to depict blacks as "skunks" and "snakes" who threatened to halt American cultural progress.[4] Whites, of course, emerged as pure and noble creatures whom God destined to rule the earth.

Madison Grant, a brilliant Yale graduate, published his polemic *The Passing of the Great Race* in 1916. He particularly deplored the mixing of races, having concluded that hereditary factors governed everything. His influence spread, carried by the erudite language imbedded in a twisted patriotism. He worried that America was "doomed to receive in these later days the least desirable classes and types from each European nation now exporting men." Such types would add themselves to the debasing influence of the blacks and force the country into further decline. He asserted that "maudlin sentimentalism" had led America to pride itself on being a haven for the underprivileged, but that the "melting pot" was being allowed to "boil without control."[5]

Professor Carleton S. Coon's relatively high-toned *Origin of the Races* appeared in 1962. A well-known scholar, he nevertheless presented his theories in a form which encouraged the racists to conclude that irrefutable scientific evidence in favor of white superiority had been presented.

Carleton Putnam, perhaps the most widely read white supremacist writing in America today, published *Race and Reason: A Yankee View* in 1961 and followed it with *Race and Reality* in 1967. Putnam, who gained notoriety during the 1950's with

3 Charles Carroll, *The Negro a Beast* (Miami, Florida: Mnemosyne Publishing Co., 1900), 87, 99, 161, 210, passim.

4 Robert W. Shufeldt, *The Negro: A Menace to American Civilization* (Boston: R. G. Badger, 1907), pp. 11, 40, 41, 54, 90, 112, 124, 125, 128, 145, 160, 161, passim.

5 Madison Grant, *The Passing of the Great Race* (New York: Charles Scribner's Sons, 1918), pp. 77, 211, 218, 263, passim.

his "open letters" published in many newspapers across the country, has a high ability to present racist judgments in a manner which appeals to a broad cross section of American whites who possess varying degrees of antiblack bias. He is particularly adept in the use of pseudoscientific "evidence" and delights in denigrating egalitarian authors with emotion-packed words loaded to favor his interpretation. His books are a powerful mix of personal experience, apparently dispassionate judgment, and blatant racism. His summary conclusions, however, reveal a Nazi-like outlook. For example, after asserting that blacks have inferior intelligence and a "vastly lower creative record throughout history," he opposes racial mixing because absorption of "twenty million largely uncreative Negroes into our White gene pool" will bring about a product which "may be expected to lack the combination of qualities (insight, foresight, intelligence, and drive) necessary to maintain and advance American civilization."

At another point he describes the "difference between the Congo and Germany under Hitler" thus: ". . . the behavior of the rebels in the Congo is standard procedure when the Negro is left to his own devices under similar circumstances, whereas the behavior of the Germans under Hitler was an exception to the rule among White men."[6]

Arthur Jensen, a professor at the University of California, Berkeley, as recently as the winter 1969 issue of the *Harvard Educational Review,* published a lengthy, scholarly article which supplies further ammunition for those who wish for "scientific" support to their racial biases. Jensen's language leans to fancy and involuted expressions which take some effort to unravel. However, the real meaning of phrases like the following seems clear: "Certain census statistics suggest that there might be forces at work which could create and widen the genetic aspect of the average difference in ability between the Negro and white populations in the United States, with the possible consequence that the improvement of educational facilities and increasing equality of opportunity will have a *decreasing* probability of producing equal achievement or continuing gains in the Negro population's abil-

---

[6] Carleton Putnam, *Race and Reality* (Washington, D.C.: Public Affairs Press, 1967), pp. 100, 124, passim. Putnam's books have had a wide vogue in white racist circles. An illustration can be seen in the account of one of the Freedom Riders who was jailed in Alabama in 1961. His group sang and prayed to pass the time, but when they asked for reading matter the only book they received (in addition to the Bible) was a copy of Putnam's *Race and Reason.*

ity to compete on equal terms."[7] In simple language, blacks have inferior genetic potential, and improved educational opportunities will only cause the whites to get even further ahead.

The white racist argument has long centered upon concern for physical differences. It seeks to establish that these differences demonstrate racial superiority. One of the most common arguments involves the size of the brain. Biological studies indicate that on the average, the brains of blacks are slightly smaller in size than those of whites. The normal black brain has a capacity of 1,350 cc. or about 50 cc. less than the average white. The conclusion becomes inescapable: whites have more brains and must be superior.

However, further considerations suggest the entire concept of brain size as an important factor in racial "advancement" to be highly questionable. For example, other studies show that the Amahosa tribal groups of Africa have a brain capacity of 1,490 cc., the Buriat tribal group, 1,496 cc., the Iroquois Indians 1,519 cc., the Eskimos 1,563 cc. and the Mongols, 1,570 cc.; all possess "more brains" than whites. Furthermore, Neanderthal man who lived more than 50,000 years ago had a brain capacity of 1,550 cc., some 150 cc. greater than the average modern white.[8]

Another line of argument holds that the black man is nearer to the jungle, more primitive, in brief, closer to the apes in the line of evolution. Examination, however, shows apes to have straight hair, not kinky; much body hair, not little; thin lips, not thick; and white skin, not dark.

Still another white racist view holds blacks to be physically less attractive than whites. Long facial features, straight hair, blue eyes, and light skin are equated with beauty. Thick lips, broad noses, kinky hair, and dark skin are viewed as aesthetically substandard unless modified by "white blood" to produce more attractive half-breeds. But whites who hold such a view might note that blacks do not accept it. The idea that "black is beautiful" has been expressed in various ways, perhaps none better than in the words of John S. Rock, a nineteenth-century black biologist. "When I contrast the fine, tough, muscular system, the rich beautiful color, the full broad features of the Negro," Rock wrote, "with the delicate physical organization, wan color and lank hair of the Caucasian, I am inclined to believe that when the white

---

7 Arthur R. Jensen, "How Much Can We Boost IQ and Scholastic Achievement?" *Harvard Educational Review*, Vol. 39, No. 1, Winter 1969, p. 95.

8 Ashley Montagu, *Man's Most Dangerous Myth: The Fallacy of Race* (Cleveland: World Publishing Co., 1964), pp. 105, 106. My treatment of race developed in this chapter owes much to Montagu's classic study.

man was created, nature was pretty well exhausted."[9] Culturally imposed attitudes determine physical attraction rather than any elements of intrinsic beauty.

The people of one culture rarely establish standards of style or beauty for another culture. An examination of a set of the *National Geographic* magazine suggests that physical beauty encompasses a seemingly endless assortment of human practices, including ear and nose splitting, lip piercing, teeth filing, feet binding, and face and body painting. The head hair has been worn very short, short, medium, long, very long. One hundred years ago, many males in America allowed their facial hair to grow; fifty years ago scarcely any did so. Today many males in America allow their facial hair to grow.

White supremacists have long argued that blacks have a distinct and unpleasant odor. R. W. Shufeldt insisted that the body odor of blacks is "sometimes so strong that I have known ladies of our own race brought almost to the stage of emesis when compelled to inhale it for any length of time."[10] In 1950 this common white racist assumption was tested in an experiment in which two blacks and two whites served as the objects to be identified. Fifty-nine persons were tested in 715 experiments in which no possibility existed of recognition of person, other than by body odor. In 190 cases blindfolded volunteers judged the whites and blacks correctly. However, on 368 occasions no difference could be detected, and in 157 cases wrong judgments were made. In 73.3 per cent of the cases a failure of choice resulted, creating a negative correlation, because random choice should bring 50 per cent success.

The entire argument for racial superiority could be stretched endlessly. Regrettably, in the matter of finding scapegoat creatures of contempt, the human race has long demonstrated tremendous abilities. Were the entire subject of racism not so horrible in most of its aspects, amusing endeavors could be enjoyed. For example, various American state legislatures have gone to ludicrous lengths simply trying to define a racial black.

Florida's lawmakers once identified Negroes as persons with one-eighth black blood; more cautious Kentuckians settled upon those with one-sixteenth black blood; legislators in Arkansas and Mississippi went further and stated that a black is "any person who has in his or her veins any Negro blood whatever." Georgia's congressmen approached the matter differently when

[9] Speech of John S. Rock, Boston, March 5, 1958, in Benjamin Quarles, *Black Abolitionists* (New York: Oxford University Press, 1968), p. 234.
[10] Robert W. Shufeldt, *The Negro: A Menace to American Civilization* (Boston: Gorham Press, 1907), p. 33.

they stated: "No person, any one of whose ancestors has been duly registered with the State Bureau of Vital Statistics as a colored person or person of color, shall be deemed to be a white person."[11] Scientifically speaking, no blood samples could have demonstrated any of such nonsense. Yet as recently as World War II, federal authorities segregated blood plasma by race, and in 1958 Louisiana passed a law requiring the segregation of blood to be used for transfusions in public hospitals.

Voltaire has written that "as long as people believe in absurdities they will continue to commit atrocities."[12] The significant minority of American whites who have the idea of innate superiority in their own group, perpetuate the concepts through successive generations of indoctrination. The following comments, all made by American whites within the past six years, may not represent the majority of white opinion, but they do reflect the thinking of those who are genuine bigots. Such views keep the nation burdened with its awful white problem.

"People . . . just don't realize all the things we do for the Negroes. We don't hate them at all. We're always untangling their problems which is anything but easy, for after all, they're animals, simply animals."

"The best way to understand how people . . . feel is to put it the way my daddy put it; the nigger has no soul. He is like a duck, a chicken, or a mule. He just hasn't got a soul."

"Let's face it; the nigger is a high-class beast."[13]

In the presidential election of 1968 George Wallace and his thinly veiled white racist appeal received twelve million votes. How many other white Americans secretly applauded his views? A partial antidote to bigoted nonsense can be found in a story like one told by Mary White Ovington, one of the founders of the NAACP. She was talking to an Irish housewife who said in all seriousness: "Do you know, yesterday I dined wid a naygur. Little did I ivir think I wud do sich a thing, but it was this way. You know my man is sixretary of his union, and the min are on strike, and who should come to the door at twelve o'clock but a big black naygur. 'Is Brother O'Neill at home?' says he. 'Brother O'Neill,' thinks I; 'well, if I'm brother to you I'd better have stayed in Ireland.' But I axed him in, and in a minute my man

11 Excerpts from various state laws in John H. Franklin and Isidore Starr, eds., *The Negro in 20th Century America: A Reader on the Struggle for Civil Rights* (New York: Vintage Books, Random House, 1967), pp. 4–7.

12 F. M. A. de Voltaire, in Ashley Montagu, *Man's Most Dangerous Myth: The Fallacy of Race* (Cleveland: World Publishing Co., 1964), p. 374.

13 Various citizen comments in Walter Lord, "Mississippi: The Past That Would Not Die," *American Heritage*, Vol. XVI, No. 4, June 1965, p. 98.

comes and he shakes the naygur by the hand, and he says, 'You must stay and ate wid us.' So I puts the dinner on the table and I sat down and ate wid a naygur."

"Well," said Mary Ovington "how did he seem?"

"To tell you the truth," she said, "he seemed just like anybody else."[14]

When all other considerations have been answered, the racial bigot invariably returns to the matter of racial mingling. "You wouldn't want your sister to marry one, would you?" The best answer would appear to be: "She did, you know." The argument against racial equality rests upon the belief that racial mixing will become widespread and the "superior" race will be diminished by the "inferior." However, no sociological evidence convincingly demonstrates that racial mixing has indeed brought about decline of anything. And contrary evidence from royal families and small isolated societies suggests that lack of variety in family or ethnic groups, rather than mixing, creates genuine danger of biological decline. A large amount of scientific data demonstrate that hybridization, or crossbreeding, improves plant and animal strains. No mass testing of humans has ever taken place and doubtless never will be conducted, but the examples from plants and animals are rather suggestive.

The weight of evidence indicates that the human race descended from a single origin; we are all extensively interconnected as well as endlessly varied. Differences within groups seem as great or greater than the variance between the physical averages of ethnic strains. Franz Boas, one of the greatest of modern anthropologists, wrote that "if we were able to select the most intelligent, imaginative, energetic and emotionally stable third of mankind, all races would be represented." Thomas Young observed that "A man who has formed intimacies and friendships with inhabitants of different parts of the globe will find enough to love and to disapprove among every people; and perhaps one who has acquired the faculty of communicating his thoughts with equal ease and pleasure to the individuals of several nations, will find himself as much at home in the one as in the other. Certainly one who is totally destitute of this attainment can never be admitted to judge with impartiality of the character of any country."

Yet racist confusion persists. Lancelot Hogben concludes: "Geneticists believe that anthropologists have decided what a race is. Ethnologists assume that their classifications embody principles

---

[14] Story told by Mary White Ovington, in Sterling D. Spero and Abram L. Harris, *The Black Worker* (New York: Atheneum, 1968), p. xiii.

which genetic science has proved to be correct. Politicians believe that their prejudices have the sanction of genetic laws and the findings of physical anthropology to sustain them." Ashley Montagu believes: "In reality, none of them have any such grounds, but those which spring from their prejudices, for such beliefs."[15]

A distinguished international group of scholars has termed the idea of "race" a "social myth" rather than a "biological phenomenon." They correctly condemn racism because it "stultifies the development of those who suffer from it, perverts those who apply it, divides nations within themselves, aggravates international conflict and threatens world peace."[16]

For all purposes in this book, the word *race* supplies a convenient symbol for identifying members of castes. Racial appearances are an easy way for one caste to establish and maintain advantage over another caste. The racial equation in America since Reconstruction has nothing to do with the superiority or inferiority of white over black in any genuine physical or mental sense. Skin color has allowed whites to create and sustain two classes of citizenship. A common aphorism among American blacks declares, "If you're white you're right. If you're brown stick around. If you're black stay back."[17] Although somewhat oversimplified, the central thrust of the aphorism remains accurate. Justice Holmes once said that the Constitution was color blind, but the individuals who make up the social structure built upon it continue to apply standards of color. In this one sense *race* means a great deal in twentieth-century America.

White groups and individuals have, from time to time, found themselves suffering under the adversities of a second-class citizenship not dissimilar to that applied to American blacks. The difference has been that social and economic escape hatches have been open *simply because the convenient identification mechanism of black skin has been missing*. If one traces one's ancestry fifteen generations back one will have to account for more than 65,000 persons. The best of us would find a fantastic variety of saints, devils, and clowns in the messy package.

The United States has suffered a multitude of adversities resulting from the slave system. The nation's many successes—victories in foreign wars, peaceful acquisitions of rich territories, creation

---

15 Boas, Young, and Hogben, in Ashley Montagu, *Man's Most Dangerous Myth: The Fallacy of Race* (Cleveland: World Publishing Co., 1964), pp. 24, 228, 267.

16 Department of Mass Communication, UNESCO, *What Is Race?* (Paris: United Nations, 1952), p. 78, and same source *Statement on Race* (Paris: United Nations, 1967), p. 50.

17 Charles E. Silberman, *Crisis in Black and White* (New York: Vintage Books, Random House, 1964), p. 11.

of the most productive industrial society in human history—
have, until recent times, obscured some of the more painful
aspects of the suppression of its black citizens. But the national
character has been deeply marred by the slave experience.

The monetary cost of the Civil War was approximately fifty
billion dollars. Compensated emancipation on the British pattern,
in which the government used tax money to purchase freedom
for all slaves, would have cost only about one and a quarter
billion dollars. Illustrations of the folly of warfare seem endless.
W. E. B. Du Bois, the great sociologist and one of the giant
leaders of American blacks, has written, "War is murder, force,
anarchy, and debt. Its end is evil, despite all incidental good."[18]
The Civil War also destroyed approximately a half million American lives. The southern section of the nation was physically and
economically ruined, and there were intangible moral losses
which always characterize brutal epochs.

But the legacy of slavery bore most heavily on the black freedmen. Approximately three and one half million blacks emerged
illiterate and unskilled into an industrial society. The system
had physically brutalized endless numbers of human beings; all
the happy tales of contented slaves come from white sources.

Virtually any sampling of slave narratives reveals emotional
accounts of humiliating and abusive practices which degraded
and divided the helpless slave population. For example, an
artisan who eventually ran away recounted the following: "Some
dispute arose one morning between the overseer and one of the
farm hands, when the former made at the slave with a hickory
club, the slave taking to his heels, started for the woods; as he
was crossing the yard, the overseer turned, snatched his gun
which was near, and fired at the flying slave, lodging several shots
in the calf of one leg. The poor fellow continued his flight, and
got into the woods; but he was in so much pain that he was
compelled to come out in the evening, and give himself up to his
master thinking he would not allow him to be punished as he had
been shot. He was locked up that night; the next morning the
overseer was allowed to tie him up and flog him; his master then
took his instruments and picked the shot out of his leg and told
him, it served him just right.

"My master had a deeply pious and exemplary slave, an
elderly man, who one day had a misunderstanding with the
overseer, when the latter attempted to flog him. He fled to the

---

[18] W. E. B. Du Bois, *Black Reconstruction in America* (New York: Atheneum, 1969), p. 55.

woods; it was noon; at evening he came home orderly. The next morning, my master, taking one of his sons with him, a rope and cowhide in his hand, led the poor old man away into the stable, tied him up and ordered the son to lay on thirty-nine lashes, which he did, making the keen end of the cowhide lap around and strike him in the tenderest part of his side, till the blood sped out, as if a lance had been used.

"While my master's son was thus engaged, the sufferer's little daughter, a child six years of age, stood at the door, weeping in agony for the fate of her father. I heard the old man articulating in a low tone of voice; I listened at the intervals between the stripes, and lo! he was praying!

"When the last lash was laid on, he was let down; and leaving him to put his clothes on, they passed out of the door, and drove the man's weeping child away!"[19]

Another slave described the actions of a master who often stayed away for long periods but whose return brought dreadful scenes:

"He sometimes ordered all the slaves to assemble at the house, when he would whip them all round; a little whipping being, as he thought, necessary, in order to secure the humble submission of the slaves.

"Sometimes he forced one slave to flog another, the husband his wife; the mother her daughter; or the father his son. This practice seemed very amusing to himself and his children, especially to his son, John, who failed not to walk in his father's footsteps, by carrying into effect the same principle, until he became characteristically a tyrant.

"When at home from school, he would frequently request his grandmother's permission, to call all the black children from their quarters to the house, to sweep and clear the yard from weeds, &c., in order that he might oversee them. Then, whip in hand, he walked about among them, and sometimes lashed the poor little creatures, who had on nothing but a shirt, and often nothing at all, until the blood streamed down their backs and limbs, apparently for no reason whatever, except to gratify his own cruel fancy.

"This was pleasing to his father and grandmother, who accordingly, considered him a very smart boy indeed! Often my mother, after being in the field all day, upon returning at night, would find her little children's backs mangled by the lash of John

---

[19] James W. C. Pennington, "The Fugitive Blacksmith," in Arna Bontemps, ed., *Great Slave Narratives* (Boston: Beacon Press, 1969), p. 213.

Wagar, or his grandmother; for if any child dared to resist the boy, she would order the cook to lash it with a cowhide, kept for that purpose.

"I well remember the tears of my poor mother, as they fell upon my back, while she was bathing and dressing my wounds. But there was no redress for her grievance, she had no appeal for justice, save to high heaven, for if she complained, her own back would be cut in a similar manner.

"Sometimes she wept and sobbed all night, but her tears must be dried and her sobs hushed, ere the overseer's horn sounded, which it did at early dawn, lest they should betray her. And she, unrefreshed, must shake off her dull slumbers, and repair, at break of day, to the field, leaving her little ones to a similar, or perhaps, worse fate on the coming day, and dreading a renewal of her own sorrows the coming evening. Great God, what a succession of crimes! Is there no balm in Gilead; is there no physician there, that thy people can be healed?"[20]

A third runaway summarized the black view of slavery in these words: "I was raised a house servant, and was well used, but I saw and heard a great deal of the cruelty of slavery. I saw more than I wanted to—I never want to see so much again. The slaveholders say their slaves are better off than if they were free, and that they prefer slavery to freedom. I do not, and never saw one that wished to go back. It would be a hard trial to make me a slave again. I had rather live in Canada, on one potato a day, than to live in the South with all the wealth they have got. I am now my own mistress, and need not work when I am sick. I can do my own thinking, without having any one to think for me— to tell me when to come, what to do, and to sell me when they get ready. I wish I could have my relatives here. I might say a great deal more against slavery—nothing for it."[21]

The slave system psychologically emasculated the black male. A man's self-image is rooted in his ability to earn, love, and care for job, wife, and children. The system denied him all of these and tended to disrupt the entire black family structure. Although the black female emerged in many situations as the family leader, she too suffered psychological depression, prey as she was to the whim, lust, and injustice of the white owner. His economic interests were best served through increase in the numbers of the

---

20 John Thompson, *The Life of John Thompson* (New York: Negro Universities Press, 1968), pp. 20–21.
21 Statement of Mrs. Christopher Hamilton in Benjamin Drew, *The Refugee: A North-Side View of Slavery* (Reading, Mass: Addison-Wesley Co., 1969), p. 124.

slaves he owned. A child born to a slave mother represented substantial financial return to the master whether the baby was pure
black or of mixed blood. Rarely in human history has economic
advantage so directly coincided with personal lechery. As he
mounted a helpless slave girl, a master's conscience regarding the
violation could be eased with the rationalization that slave breed-
ing brought handsome long-term rewards.

Finally, the slave system as practiced in America fixed the concept of racial superiority in the mind of the white majority.
Slavery practiced in other cultures defined a slave as one who
had suffered bad luck, usually in war; the American creed, beginning with the Declaration of Independence and the doctrine
that all men are created equal, required a different rationale.
Obviously slavery and the basic national documents were contradictory. Assumption of innate racial inferiority of black people
emerged as the only satisfactory explanation for chattel slavery in
a nation committed to individual freedom. From these cursed
legacies of a monstrous system America suffers yet.

Much has been written about the Reconstruction period
following the Civil War. Early scholarship misconceived the era.
This profile, supplied as it was almost entirely by white authors,
painted the freedmen as dangerous primitives who took over
the states of the Confederacy and worked varying degrees of injustice upon the helpless whites who had lost the war. This view
gained emotional strength after the turn of the twentieth century
through the powerful film "The Birth of a Nation," derived
from the racist tracts of Thomas Ryan Dixon. It received further
thrust in the scholarly world with the publication of Claude G.
Bowers' *Tragic Era* in 1929. Bowers, and earlier white authors,
emotionally but effectively insisted that the governments in the
Southern states during Reconstruction failed partly because
Lincoln's assassination and Andrew Johnson's awkward flailing
at Congress undermined the great emancipator's "lenient plan"
for restoring the nation to political health. Bowers' thesis also
heavily criticized self-seeking carpetbaggers, scalawags, and their
black allies who allegedly oppressed the mass of Southern whites
while robbing the public treasury and ruining the area's economic
recovery. The "redemption" of the Southern state governments
by the whites following the Compromise of 1877 constituted a
period of improvement as seen by the white perspective on this
vitally important era in American history.

Subsequent scholarship has substantially reversed this inac-
curate view. W. E. B. Du Bois' *Black Reconstruction,* which
appeared in 1934, contributed impressive contrary evidence which

led eventually to reinterpretation of the Reconstruction period. Although Du Bois' book was partially discounted by whites consistent with the general American tendency to look down on the scholarship of blacks, it had a lasting influence and remains one of the great works on the period. More recent studies by C. Vann Woodward, John Hope Franklin, Kenneth Stampp, and others have further redressed the balance, although the earlier white hero view continues to permeate history courses in schools through all parts of the country.

The record indicates that the freedmen played an important and constructive role during the Reconstruction period. As early as the end of April 1862, the Union army of occupation in New Orleans faced practical questions regarding the government of both blacks and whites in the defeated territories. Neither the Lincoln nor the Johnson plans for Reconstruction paid sufficient attention to the status of the freedmen. The so-called Radicals in Congress, led by Thad Stevens of Pennsylvania and Charles Sumner of Massachusetts, fought to have the federal government recognize the central nature of this question. Generally speaking they lost to the white supremacists and the silent majority which quickly became discouraged with efforts to solve the complex problem.

Contrary to popular belief, national authorities left no great number of Union soldiers in the South after the war. By late 1865 the army had been drastically reduced in size and increasing numbers of the soldiers were sent to the Western states to guard against the "Indian menace." By 1866 only a skeleton force remained stationed in the South.

Congress created the Freedmen's Bureau and placed General O. O. Howard, a white, in charge of official efforts to incorporate the ex-slaves into the nation's life. But General Howard received practically no funds with which to accomplish the task. In spite of this shortsighted action, Howard's understaffed Bureau established more than forty hospitals, distributed thousands of tools and rations (but very little land or mules), supported large numbers of schools and colleges (Howard, Hampton, Atlanta, and Fisk are well-known modern descendants of the Bureau's efforts), and conducted many other useful activities designed to redress the wrongs of common people.

The Bureau deserves much credit; few public agencies prior to the twentieth century faced such profound challenges; none met them better. But the Bureau became a political issue between President Johnson and the Congress and faced increasingly insurmountable obstacles to the completion of its assigned task. Despite the noble efforts of General Howard and his dedicated co-workers, white and black, the Bureau scarcely began to affect the immense social needs of the post-Civil War era.

Already frustrated by contacts with the Freedmen's Bureau, the black man became even more frustrated by the actions of his own state government during 1865, 1866, and 1867. Most of the states continued under the control of former white leaders who enacted "Black Codes" to keep the freedman in his place and salvage the "Lost Cause." In addition, state officials either led or acquiesced in allowing organized bands to commit endless outrages against the relatively helpless freedmen. Groups variously known as Regulators, Jayhawkers, Black Cavalry, and others terrorized the countryside.

The national Congress tried to relieve the situation with a series of laws including the Civil Rights Act of 1866, the first statute passed specifically with intent to support the civil rights of minority group citizens. President Johnson vetoed the bill and Congress overrode his veto; however, the law was not enforced.

As the national congressional leaders emphasized their belief in one class of citizenship and demonstrated their willingness to make such a reality in the South, Southern whites sought increasingly violent means to block these efforts. For example, in Memphis, Tennessee, during the period April 30 to May 2, 1866, white mobs joined white police officers in assaulting the black population of the city. Federal troops succeeded in restoring order but forty-six blacks had been killed and more than eighty seriously wounded. In addition mobs burned four black churches and twelve black schools and destroyed other property owned by blacks. One white man was seriously injured.

The figures underscore a racial generalization: whites commit disproportionate amounts of violence against blacks. Repeatedly in American history, riots have marred the racial scene. Nearly always, contrary to the stereotype held by the white of the black as a razor-wielding danger, race riots have resulted in a preponderance of death and injury to blacks. The congressional committee that investigated the Memphis riot concluded that the white mob had exhibited a "deadly hatred of the colored race" and committed acts almost without comparison in their cruelty.[22]

In New Orleans, on July 30, 1866, a white mob attacked blacks wherever they appeared, killing thirty-four and injuring more than two hundred. Four white mobsmen were killed and ten white policemen sustained injuries. General Sheridan, in

---

[22] Report of special investigating committee, U.S. House of Representatives, in John Hope Franklin, *Reconstruction After the Civil War* (Chicago: University of Chicago Press, 1961), p. 63.

charge of the federal troops there, reported: ". . . an absolute massacre by the police . . . a murder which the mayor and police . . . perpetrated without the shadow of necessity."[23]

Despite its ferocity, the fight for political control in the South drew scant attention in the North. Aside from militants like Douglass, Sumner, and Stevens, few Northern leaders took any initiative to protect the rights of blacks. Indeed, during 1867 alone Ohio, Connecticut, Pennsylvania, New York, New Jersey, and Maryland explicitly or implicitly refused even the vote to blacks. Michigan, Minnesota, and Kansas similarly restricted suffrage to whites at various times in the postwar era.

But the militants insisted that the question of suffrage for blacks be faced and the Reconstruction Act of 1867 provided federal registrars for the South. When the registration process was completed more blacks than whites were qualified to vote in the region. The figures raised questions about the common white assumption that freedmen were incapable of self-government, partly because they were uninterested in the process. In Alabama, Florida, Louisiana, Mississippi, and South Carolina blacks held voting majorities. Upon this new base, "Black Reconstruction" began. Blacks quickly demonstrated a strong desire to better themselves through wise use of the political structure. But some white observers and historians, burdened with ideas of racial superiority, advanced jaundiced views of minority contributions during Black Reconstruction.

James S. Pike's highly colored *Prostrate State*, for example, told of buffoonery, chicanery, and corruption in South Carolina and gave the freedmen credit only for somewhat less crass motives than their carpetbagging white allies. Pike described one session of the legislature in these words: "The Speaker orders a member whom he has discovered to be particularly unruly to take his seat. The member obeys, and with the same motion that he sits down, throws his feet on to his desk, hiding himself from the Speaker by the soles of his boots. In an instant he appears again on the floor. After a few experiences of this sort, the Speaker threatens, in a laugh, to call 'the gemman' to order. This is considered a capital joke, and a guffaw follows. The laugh goes round, and then the peanuts are cracked and munched faster than ever; one hand being employed in fortifying the inner man with this nutriment of universal use, while the other enforces the views of the orator. This laughing propensity of the sable crowd is a great cause of disorder. They laugh as hens cackle—one begins

---

[23] Comment of General Philip Sheridan to congressional committee in ibid., p. 64.

and all follow.''[24] At other times, Pike presented the blacks as imitative, ludicrous, and thieving.

Yet during Reconstruction a remarkable number of capable blacks served in a broad variety of ways to upgrade public and private life in the South. Hiram Revels entered the U.S. Senate from Mississippi and served with distinction. He was the first black member of the U.S. Congress. Later, Blanche K. Bruce also sat in the Senate representing Mississippi. Joseph Rainey became a distinguished congressman from South Carolina. Richard Cain and Robert Smalls joined him in the House, as did John M. Langston of Virginia and Jefferson Long of Georgia. Jonathan C. Gibbs, a Dartmouth College graduate, was Secretary of State in Florida, and Francis Cardoza held the same office in South Carolina. J. J. Wright served on the Supreme Court of South Carolina and John Roy Lynch became speaker of the House in Mississippi. P. B. S. Pinchback, one of the most able as well as most colorful leaders of Black Reconstruction, served as lieutenant governor of Louisiana and also, for a short time, as governor of that state. He was elected a U.S. senator, but the Senate refused to seat him because of his color. Eventually Pinchback held more public offices than any black in American history and showed great ability and courage throughout his career. Robert B. Elliot held a variety of public offices in South Carolina. A brilliant speaker, master of five languages, and owner of a large private library, Elliot deserves recognition as one of the most talented men of American history. Few textbooks even mention his name. Dozens of blacks, some educated highly, some with practically no formal training, served in Southern governments. They helped to rewrite the constitutions of the Southern states and did a great deal to develop public education in an area of the country where it had never flourished before.

A few black officials were corrupt. Some permitted unscrupulous scalawags and carpetbaggers to use them. But the vast majority distinguished themselves and accomplished remarkable changes in a short period of time. All competent modern scholars, black and white, now agree to this generalization.

To their further credit, these black leaders carried out their responsibilities with virtually no animosity or injustice toward whites. Black public officials worked to establish equal suffrage and equal rights. James Rapier, a black delegate to the Alabama constitutional convention, later elected to Congress, sponsored

---

24 James S. Pike, *The Prostrate State: South Carolina Under Negro Government* (New York: Harper & Row, 1968), p. 20. (Originally published in 1874.)

the congressional resolution to lift the political disabilities of Southern whites who had served with the Confederate forces. In Jackson, Mississippi, a white-owned Democratic newspaper said of black participation in the state government: "The Negroes have shown consideration for the feelings of the whites. . . ."[25] Blacks for the most part judged their future to lie in the South. Although they conceded nothing in matters of equal suffrage and rights, they sought to avoid vengeful actions. Blacks took a humane and conciliatory attitude because they believed that only a cooperative society would last.

Lerone Bennett, Jr., notes the views of Sir George Campbell, a white member of the British House of Commons who visited the area during this period and wrote the following interesting commentary: "Before I went south I certainly expected to find that the Southern States had been for a time a sort of pandemonium in which a white man could hardly live. Yet it certainly was not so. . . . When I went to South Carolina I thought that there at least I must find great social disturbances; and in South Carolina I went to the county of Beaufort, the blackest part of the State in point of population, and that in which black rule has been most complete and has lasted longest. It has the reputation of being a sort of black paradise, and per contra, I rather expected a sort of white hell. . . . To my great surprise I found exactly the contrary. . . . White girls go about as freely and pleasantly as if no black man had ever been in power. . . ." Campbell went on, "the Negroes have had a very large share of political education. . . . It is, I think, wonderful how beneficial this education has been to them, and how much these people so lately in the most debased condition of slavery, have acquired, independent ideas and, far from lapsing into anarchy, have become citizens with ideas of law and property and order."[26]

Actually, blacks did not control the governments of the Southern states during Black Reconstruction, although they heavily influenced the history of the period. The peak of black strength occurred in South Carolina where, in the 1873 state house, eighty-seven blacks outnumbered forty whites. However, the state senate remained white controlled, as did the governor's office throughout the period. In Mississippi, although black voters outregistered whites, the legislature was never more than one third black. In Florida, Virginia, Arkansas, Texas, and North Carolina

---

25 Jackson, Mississippi, *Clarion,* in John Hope Franklin, *Reconstruction After the Civil War* (Chicago: University of Chicago Press, 1961), p. 90.
26 George Campbell, *White and Black: The Outcome of a Visit to the United States* (New York: Negro Universities Press, 1969), pp. 131, 176, 177. (Originally published 1879.)

little black representation occurred. Taking the South as a whole, 771 whites and only 268 blacks rewrote the state constitutions.

The Gilded Age was not one much given to modern concepts of social planning. It was a laissez-faire era in which corruption flourished to add to the problems created by the war. Yet the matter of the increasing public debt of the Southern states under black rule deserves more objective consideration than it has sometimes received. State debts did go up during the period; for example, Louisiana went from $17 to $29 million, South Carolina from $15 to $22 million, and Alabama from $8 to $25 million; other states of the former Confederacy showed similar increases. However, during this era public debt over the entire nation expanded rapidly. The Southern state governments were attempting to carry forward the social reconstruction for which the federal government refused to take responsibility.

Actually, the money did much good in the field of public education. The freedmen of all ages and both sexes flocked to the new schools. In 1868 approximately 30,000 students attended 400 schools with 500 teachers across the South. By 1876, at the end of the Black Reconstruction period, 123,000 students attended nearly 3,000 schools with more than 3,000 teachers, one third of them black. In some cases, the blacks received better education than the whites and worked more diligently to get the maximum benefit from it. Blacks emerged rapidly into manhood in spite of the generations of neglect which characterized the slave era. The mass of freedmen pursued their goals with neither undue deference nor hostility toward their former white masters.

During the era of Black Reconstruction, from almost any angle one views the period, blacks demonstrated uncommon interest and ability in the field of self-government. Yet not until the 1960's, with the election of Carl Stokes in Ohio, Andrew Hatcher in Indiana, Kenneth Gibson in New Jersey, Charles Evers in Mississippi, and more than a dozen black congressmen, did black power receive even a modest chance in the most successful democracy in the world.

Whites sought continuously for means to undermine the political power of blacks and "redeem" the South. The doctrine of white supremacy was too deeply rooted to be eradicated easily. As W. E. B. Du Bois put it, "Whites esteem the blacks their property by natural rights, and however much they admit that the individual relations of masters and slaves have been destroyed by the war . . . they still have an ingrained feeling that . . . blacks at large belong to . . . whites at large."[27] Lerone Bennett, Jr.,

---

27 W. E. B. Du Bois, *Black Reconstruction in America* (New York: Atheneum, 1969), p. 136.

adds, many whites "hated black people largely because they had been taught to hate black people but also because hate dignified and gave meaning to their lives."[28] Racism can be termed a "faith." But the racist doctrine, contrary to most religious faiths, seeks to attract adherents by convincing them that uplift of their spirit depends upon derogation of others.

Whites began with verbal denigration of everything black officials had done. They called the state constitutional conventions and state legislative assemblies the "Convention of Kangaroos," the "Black Crook" convention, the "Congo" meeting, and the "Bones and Banjo" convention. In addition, white spokesmen diligently presented blacks through negative stereotypes. John Hope Franklin lists seven basic categories: the contented slave, the wretched freedman, the comic Negro, the brute Negro, the tragic mulatto, the local-color Negro, and the exotic primitive.[29]

Beyond the verbal denigration, whites, wherever possible, used crass political maneuvers to reduce black influence, black representation, and eventually black voting itself. In Georgia, as soon as Union troops had been reduced in number, the white majority in the state legislature voted to expel black legislators, all of whom had been properly elected. They allowed four blacks who were almost white to retain their seats. Considerations of race alone brought about the expulsion action. Even Georgia may have progressed. In 1967, when the legislature denied Julian Bond his seat, the grounds were not that he was black, but that he had expressed opposition to the Vietnam War.

Henry McNeal Turner, the first black chaplain in the U.S. Army, denounced his Georgia colleagues in the following moving words: "Cases may be found where men have been deprived of their rights for crimes and misdemeanors; but it has remained for the state of Georgia . . . to call a man before the bar and there charge him with an act for which he is no more responsible than for the head which he carries upon his shoulders. The Anglo-Saxon race, Sir, is a most surprising one. . . . I was not aware that there was in the character of the race so much cowardice, or so much pusillanimity. . . . It is very strange, if a white man can occupy on this floor a seat created by colored votes, and a black man cannot do it. Why, Gentlemen; it is the most shortsighted reasoning in the world. . . . You have all the elements of superior-

---

28 Lerone Bennett, Jr., *Black Power USA: The Human Side of Reconstruction* (Chicago: Johnson Publishing Co., 1967), p. 65.
29 John Hope Franklin, *Reconstruction After the Civil War* (Chicago: University of Chicago Press, 1961), pp. 200–201. Franklin attributes the categories to Sterling Brown.

ity upon your side; you have our money and your own; you have our education and your own; you have our land and your own, too. We, who number hundreds of thousands in Georgia, including our wives and families, with not a foot of land to call our own—strangers in the land of our birth; without education, without aid, without a roof to cover us while we live, nor sufficient clay to cover us when we die! It is extraordinary that a race such as yours, professing gallantry, chivalry, education, and superiority, living in a land where ringing chimes call child and sire to the Church of God—a land where Bibles are read and Gospel truths are spoken and where courts of justice are presumed to exist; it is extraordinary, I say, that with all these advantages on your side, you can make war upon the poor, defenseless black man."[30]

Turner's plea, and those of others, caused the U.S. Congress to delay Georgia's return to the Union until its legislature readmitted the expelled blacks. However, within a year the legislature reversed itself and Georgia was "redeemed."

But the most shocking means by which whites destroyed black power in the South involved a full range of violent repressions. Black Reconstruction, or black power, was hammered out of existence, largely by illegal and inhumane attacks on persons. The Ku Klux Klan emerged as the chief instrument of this violence. The Klan, formed in 1865 in Tennessee with race and "redemption" overtones from the beginning, tried to conceal its real nature in claims that the members merely sought social companionship and fun. In 1867 the Klan, which included many of the leading whites of the South, selected ex-Confederate General Nathan Bedford Forrest, a former slave trader, as its leader. The organization then began to make its record as the most brutal and unjust organization which has ever disgraced the American scene. Many lesser organizations, like the Knights of the White Camellia, the White Line, the Society of the White Roses, the Pale Faces, the Bushwackers, the Innocents, and the Knights of the Rising Sun, contributed their measure to Klan-led violence. The Klan described itself as a group devoted to "chivalry, humanity, mercy and patriotism," but from the beginning weeks of its existence it dedicated itself to the separation of black and white and renewed suppression of the black. All blacks, and any whites with the wrong ideas, were subject to its brutality.

The record of violence during the early 1870's will probably never be completed. Far too much of it went on in secret and at

---

30 Speech of Henry McNeal Turner as quoted in Lerone Bennett, Jr., *Black Power U.S.A.: The Human Side of Reconstruction, 1867–1877* (Chicago: Johnson Publishing Co., 1967), pp. 294–95.

night. Too many white officers of public safety were involved in it; too many blacks were intimidated and effectively silenced. Certainly no less than several thousand persons were beaten, whipped, shot, and lynched between 1868 and 1876.

John Hope Franklin, one of the most distinguished historians of the Reconstruction period, summarized the Klan-led violence of the 1870's in these words: "It involved the murder of respectable Negroes by roving gangs of terrorists, the murder of Negro renters of land, the looting of stores whose owners were sometimes killed, and the murder of peaceable white citizens. On one occasion in Mississippi a member of a local gang, 'Heggies's Scouts,' claimed that his group killed 116 Negroes and threw their bodies into the Tallahatchie River. It was reported that in North Carolina the Klan was responsible for 260 outrages, including 7 murders and the whipping of 72 whites and 141 Negroes. In one county in South Carolina 6 men were murdered and more than 300 were whipped during the first six months of 1870. Meanwhile, the personal indignities inflicted upon individual whites and Negroes were so varied and so numerous as to defy classification or enumeration. There were the public whippings, the maimings, the mutilations, and other almost inconceivable forms of intimidation."[31]

The perpetrators aimed to retake the centers of power in the South through any means. A special committee of the National Congress investigated the 1875 election in Mississippi and concluded that "force, fraud and intimidation" characterized the contest with supremacist-minded whites winning out. The Democratic organization operated on a paramilitary basis using force to break up meetings, intimidate and threaten leaders, compel candidates to withdraw from electoral contests, turn voters away from the polls, cow election officials into resignations or falsification of ballots, and, in a few cases, to foment riots which led to the deaths of between thirty and forty persons.[32]

The Democratic candidate for governor in Louisiana stated publicly: "We shall carry the next election if we have to ride saddle-deep in blood to do it." An Alabama editor wrote, "We must render this either a white man's government or convert the land into a Negro man's cemetery."[33]

---

[31] John Hope Franklin, *Reconstruction After the Civil War* (Chicago: University of Chicago Press, 1961), p. 157.

[32] Senate Reports, No. 527, 44th Congress, 1st Session, "Mississippi in 1875: Report of the Select Committee to Inquire into the *Mississippi Election of 1875*," in Robert W. Johannsen, ed., *Reconstruction 1865–1877* (New York: The Free Press, 1970), pp. 173–82.

[33] Both quoted in Lerone Bennett, Jr., *Black Power U.S.A.: The Human Side of Reconstruction, 1867–1877* (Chicago: Johnson Publishing Co., 1967), p. 356.

Some blacks fought back. Charles Caldwell, a courageous and outspoken state senator from Hinds County, Mississippi, said what he thought. Whites feared him for his unflinching demeanor; in addition he was a crack shot. The white "leaders" in the area decided that he must be killed. They arranged to lure him in for a drink with a white acquaintance. On Christmas Day, 1875, in the town of Clinton, they hid in wait. Caldwell at first refused the invitation, but finally entered the meeting place. When the two men clinked glasses, those outside shot Caldwell through the door. A crowd of white men gathered quickly, most of them carrying rifles. Caldwell, gravely wounded, asked to be taken outside into the air. He stood erect, bleeding profusely, looked his assassins in the face as he said: "Remember, when you kill me you kill a gentleman and a brave man. Never say you killed a coward. I want you to remember it when I am gone." The crowd opened fire and according to one eyewitness the bullets "grotesquely turned his body completely over by the impact of innumerable shots fired at close range."[34]

Albion W. Tourgee, a white politician, described the period in these words: "Of the slain there was enough to furnish forth a battlefield, and all from those three classes, the Negro, the scalawag, and the carpetbagger, all killed with deliberation, overwhelmed by numbers, roused from slumber at murk midnight, in the halls of public assembly, upon the river-bank, on the lonely woods roads, in simulation of the public execution, tortured beyond conception. And . . . the wounded in this silent warfare were more thousands than those who groaned upon the slopes of Gettysburg."[35]

As Lerone Bennett, Jr., eloquently summarized the era of Black Reconstruction: ". . . white Southerners hurled themselves with a bloody spasm against the ramparts of black power. The struggle, which was waged by political assassination, midnight massacres, and repeated coups d'état, raged for more than ten years and completely changed the political climate of America. It was a cruel and unequal struggle."[36]

The famous Hayes-Tilden election of 1876 with disputed returns from three Southern states—Florida, Louisiana, and South Carolina—has long received close attention from political historians. When the special commission to determine the outcome

---

34 Ibid., pp. 328–29. See also John Hope Franklin, *Reconstruction After the Civil War* (Chicago: University of Chicago Press, 1961), pp. 159–60.

35 Albion W. Tourgee, *A Fool's Errand* (Cambridge, Mass.: Harvard University Press, 1961), pp. 251–52. (First published in 1879.)

36 Lerone Bennett, Jr., *Black Power U.S.A.: The Human Side of Reconstruction* (Chicago: Johnson Publishing Co., 1967), p. 330.

deliberated the case it did so against a background of increasing white apathy to the entire "problem of the Negro." As President Grant put it when asked for more troops to guard the polls in Mississippi, "The whole public are tired of the annual autumnal outbreaks in the South."[37] He then refused the request. Mississippi had been "redeemed."

The Compromise of 1877 involved a series of meetings between representatives of Hayes and white Democratic leadership in some of the Southern states. They arranged the final meeting at the Wormley House, later the Willard Hotel in Washington, D.C. Southern Democratic opposition to Hayes' presidency would end with the final withdrawal of the few remaining federal troops in the South and the granting of the concept of "home rule" to the still "unredeemed" areas. The intricate compromise arrangements included Northern Republican assurance to the Southern Democratic leaders, that federal assistance to the Southern railroad building program would be forthcoming in Congress. On their part, the white "gentlemen" of the South assured the Republicans that the proper interests of the region's blacks would be guarded.

In the context of barter, compromise, and sellout of the freedmen's interests, Senator Sumner of Massachusetts pushed tirelessly for a civil rights law which would assure the rights of all citizens. He drafted the bill and fought for it brilliantly. His health failing, Sumner, still suffering from the physical damage given him by Preston Brooks of South Carolina during their famous fight on the Senate floor, failed to gather sufficient support. Opponents from North and South defeated the measure in both 1872 and 1874. Sumner did not live to see his bill become law. On his deathbed, surrounded by prominent supporters including the greatest black leader of the nineteenth century, Frederick Douglass, Sumner gasped, "You must take care of the civil rights bill . . . don't let it fail."[38]

Black congressman Robert Brown Elliott, one of the most effective proponents of the law, finally led its passage on March 1, 1875, after conservatives eliminated the sections barring segregation in schools and churches. The law nevertheless contained some impressive items. Ironically, the Civil Rights Act of 1964 closely follows some of the provisions of the Act of 1875.

The 1875 law was actually one of a series of civil rights bills

---

[37] Statement of President Ulysses S. Grant in John Hope Franklin, *Reconstruction After the Civil War* (Chicago: University of Chicago Press, 1961), p. 150.
[38] Statement of Charles Sumner in Moorfield Storey, ed., *American Statesmen*, Vol. XXX, "Charles Sumner" (Boston: Houghton Mifflin, 1900), p. 430.

passed during the era. In addition, three constitutional amendments similarly sought to protect minority rights. But all of the measures ran into presidential and judicial opposition, plus flagrant violation by the majority of American whites.

The law of 1875 stated in part,

"Whereas it is essential to just government we recognize the equality of all men before the law, and hold that it is the duty of government in its dealings with the people to mete out equal and exact justice to all, of whatever nativity, race, color, or persuasion, religious or political; and it being the appropriate object of legislation to enact great fundamental principles into law: Therefore:

"Be it enacted, That all persons within the jurisdiction of the United States shall be entitled to the full and equal enjoyment of the accommodations, advantages, facilities, and privileges of inns, public conveyances on land or water, theaters, and other places of public amusement: subject only to the constitution and limitations established by law, and applicable alike to citizens of every race and color, regardless of any previous condition of servitude. . . .

"That no citizen possessing all other qualifications which are or may be prescribed by law shall be disqualified for service as grand or petit juror in any court of the United States, or of any state, on account of race, color, or previous condition of servitude."[39] The law provided both fines and imprisonment for offenders.

Like many other laws, it was entirely clear in its import. But no written law effects social change unless it is enforced. Majority opinion opposed the measure and public officials responsible for enforcement made few efforts to overcome this opposition.

The burden of bringing action lay largely upon the generally impoverished blacks. A few interesting situations developed, but the freedmen lacked organization. No NAACP, SNCC, CORE or more militant group existed to assist individuals. Federal district attorneys responsible for enforcing the law experienced difficulty getting copies of the act because the Attorney General's office took little interest in the matter.

In New York City, a black journalist tried to enter the opera house accompanied by a quadroon lady friend. Although she had purchased the tickets that morning, the doorman told them they were no good. The journalist went back to the street, paid a white to buy him two more tickets, and returned to the entrance. This

---

39 Civil Rights Act, March 1, 1875, in Henry Steele Commager, ed., *Documents of American History*, Vol. I to 1898, Seventh Edition (New York: Appleton-Century-Crofts, 1963), p. 536.

time the ticket taker told him that the lady, who looked almost white, could come in but the black journalist could not. The journalist brought legal suit against the opera house manager but was unable to get any satisfaction. The *New York Times* vigorously editorialized against the law while condemning the entire idea of racial mixing in public places.

Public inns, hotels, restaurants, and bars, almost entirely owned by whites, ignored the law; many made fun of it. One Virginia saloon owner put up a sign to discourage black customers, indicating all drinks cost $5, with liberal discounts extended to friends. "Presumably," as John Hope Franklin notes, "the proprietors had no Negro friends."[40] In North Carolina, a black had a saloonkeeper arrested for refusing to serve him a drink, but authorities dismissed the case on the grounds that the law did not apply to barrooms because they were not specifically mentioned in the Act. A similar case involved an ice cream parlor. The *New York Times* said the Act was ludicrous and predicted that it would be "utterly routed by laughter and ridicule."[41] Southern leaders openly called the Act a dead letter and boasted that it would never be enforced in their area. Events demonstrated them to be correct.

The North and West established no better record. The law brought some integration in public schools, but white students often abused the minority blacks. Widespread incidents led white parents to call for exclusion of blacks, for the blacks' own good and safety. This rationalization supported segregation with the comfortable words of thoughtfulness and charity when the real need was courageous adherence to the principles of justice.

A series of court cases ensued, and the decisions steadily undermined the Sumner law. In *U.S.* v. *Cruikshank* (1876) the Court held that the Fourteenth Amendment only guaranteed the citizen against actions of the states and not those of private individuals. Thus, the Court blunted the thrust of all equal-rights legislation because most violations resulted from individual prejudice. In 1877 black plaintiffs brought five suits against private owners who had violated provisions for equal treatment in public accommodations. Two suits involved efforts to register for rooms at hotels, two involved efforts to be seated in theaters (one in New York and one in San Francisco), and one involved a suit against the Memphis and Charleston Railroad for denying a woman a seat in the ladies' car on the grounds that she was "of African

---

[40] John Hope Franklin, "The Enforcement of the Civil Rights Act of 1875," unpublished paper, p. 6. I am indebted to the author for a copy of this paper from which I have summarized the reactions to the law.
[41] *The New York Times*, March 7, 1870, p. 2.

descent." The cases dragged slowly toward a decision. Finally, after six years of delay, the Supreme Court called the Act of 1875 "not corrective legislation; it is primary and direct; it takes immediate and absolute possession of the subject of the right of admission to inns. . . ." Refusal by an inkeeper or theater owner to grant equal access "has nothing to do with slavery or involuntary servitude. . . ."

In writing the majority decision, Justice Bradley stated: "There were thousands of free colored people in this country before the abolition of slavery, enjoying all the essential rights of life, liberty and property the same as white citizens; yet no one, at that time, thought that it was any invasion of his personal status as a freeman because he was not admitted to all the privileges enjoyed by white citizens, or because he was subjected to discrimination in the enjoyment of accommodations in inns, public conveyance and places of amusement. Mere discriminations on account of race or color were not regarded as badges of slavery."[42] Recourse, the justices concluded, must be through the laws of states; they declared Sumner's Act unconstitutional.

Associate Justice John Marshall Harlan objected in a tone which prophesied his ringing dissent in *Plessy* v. *Ferguson* thirteen years later: "Railroad corporations, keepers of inns, and managers of places of public amusement," Harlan wrote, "are agents or instrumentalities of the State, because they are charged with the duties to the public and are amenable in respect of their duties and functions, to governmental regulation. . . .

"The nation has been confronted with class tyranny, which a contemporary English historian says is, of all tyrannies, the most intolerable, 'for it is ubiquitous in its operation, and weighs . . . most heavily on those whose obscurity or distance would withdraw from them the notice of a single despot.' Today, it is the colored race which is denied, by corporations and individuals wielding public authority, rights fundamental in their freedom and citizenship. At some future time it may be that some other race will fall under the ban of race discrimination. . . .

"The supreme law of the land has decreed that no authority shall be exercised in this country upon the basis of discrimination, in respect of civil rights, against freemen and citizens because of their race, color, or previous condition of servitude. . . . Congress has been invested with express power to carry such protections into effect."[43]

---

42 Mr. Justice Bradley, Supreme Court of the United States, 109 U.S. 3 (1883) in Albert P. Blaustein and Robert L. Zangrando, eds., *Civil Rights and the American Negro, A Documentary History* (New York: Washington Square Press, 1968), pp. 269–76. Copyright © 1968, by Washington Square Press, Inc. Reprinted by permission of WSP, Inc., division of Simon & Schuster, Inc.

43 Associate Justice Harlan dissenting, ibid., pp. 276–81.

A long time passed before Harlan's dissent became the majority view. American whites seemed entirely comfortable with
the Court's support of second-class citizenship. Rayford Logan
has noted that as late as 1922, Charles Warren, in his authorita-
tive *The Supreme Court in United States History,* favored the
Court's views. Warren wrote of the civil rights decisions of the
period: "Viewed in historical perspective now (1922) . . . there
can be no question that the decisions in these cases were most
fortunate. They largely eliminated from national politics the
Negro question which had so long embittered Congressional
debates; they relegated the burden and the duty of protecting the
negro to the states, to whom they properly belonged; and they
served to restore confidence in the National Court in the Southern States."[44]

Not until 1957 did the Congress of the United States consider
and pass another piece of civil rights legislation. President
Nixon's attempt to appoint Haynsworth of South Carolina and
Carswell of Florida in 1969 and 1970 were designed to "restore
confidence in the national court" in the minds of Southern
whites. Truly the "Lost Cause" cannot be said to have been entirely lost.

Laws are important. Morals *can* be legislated, or to be more
precise, can be decidedly influenced by legislation. Human behavior can be curbed by law, when the preponderant majority
of the citizens uphold the law in both letter and spirit. The Civil
Rights Act of 1964, so like its sister act passed years before, could
well be rendered as dead as the Act of 1875 if a substantial percentage of the citizens come to wish the matter to end this way.
The law and the citizen must be closely allied. Because law is
inanimate, the entire burden of support falls upon the individual
citizen.

The Reconstruction era has rightly been termed one of the
most crucial periods of American history. Of the Civil War era,
John Hope Franklin has written: "The Union had been pre-
served and human slavery had been abolished; but these were
achievements of the war. In the postwar years the Union had not
made the achievements of the war a foundation for the healthy
advancement of the political, social and economic life of the
United States."[45] A recent observer of the nation's racial ills has
written of the Reconstruction period: "After the victory of the
North, a vindictive Congressional majority tried first to solve with

44 Charles Warren, *The Supreme Court in United States History,* Vol. II,
1836–1918 (Boston: Little, Brown, 1922), p. 608.
45 John Hope Franklin, *Reconstruction After the Civil War* (Chicago:
University of Chicago Press, 1961), p. 227.

force a moral and sociological problem and then gave up. The People of the United States through their duly elected representatives in Congress acquiesced for generations in the establishment of a tight caste system as a substitute for Negro slavery. A majority of the Supreme Court struck down what attempts were made to use federal power to loosen bonds of race prejudice and supported a doctrine of equal but separate facilities."[46]

How united the nation might be today, had we as a people, white and black together, faced the race problem one hundred years ago and created an integrated society. A century of justice could have avoided most of the pressing problems which now threaten to destroy us. But only in very recent years has the majority begun to face the greatest social question of our national experience. White America's slow response has caused much suffering and the end has not been reached. In addition, the tragic waste of human creativity which second-class citizenship imposes not only on the minority but on the strength of the country as a whole has cut deeply into the nation's ability to surmount its current crisis. Keeping the black man "in his place" is unquestionably the greatest folly America has ever entered upon.

# The Coming of Jim Crow

# 3

A TERRIBLE inconsistency marred the national record during the nineteenth century. While Americans as a whole gradually enjoyed increased political freedom, the submerged black minority suffered agonies of injustice. Peaks of hope and depths of disappointment succeeded each other. During the 1840's and 1850's abolitionists, white and black, stirred the country deeply and eventually forced the slavery issue with the Civil War. Issuance of the Emancipation Proclamation in 1863 raised the hope of blacks; the settlement at Appomattox resolved the slave question and an era of true freedom seemed to beckon. Yet within a few months whites began to turn away from concern for equal rights and a period of disillusionment for blacks began. Most whites were to some degree believers in the innate superiority of their own species and exhibited little interest in making certain that their public representatives enforced equal justice for people of all races. Even the ardent abolitionists tended to view ʾheir task as ended and increasingly left the freedmen to struggle alone. Black leaders like Frederick Douglass, Hiram Revels, Blanche K. Bruce, Robert Brown Elliot, and P. B. S. Pinchback fought racism against great odds. As the century waned, the condition of American blacks became increasingly desperate.

For a time, from the passage of the Reconstruction Act in 1867 to the Compromise of 1877, federal centers of social power seemed committed to the protection of equal rights. But beginning with the administration of President Rutherford Hayes, the national government, regardless of party leadership, largely ignored the white problem.

In 1889 Frederick Douglass, then in the twilight of his career, posed the question bluntly: Will "American justice, American liberty, American civilization, American Law, and American

Christianity . . . be made to include and protect alike and forever all American citizens in the rights which . . . have been guaranteed to them by the organic and fundamental laws of the land?"[1]

Douglass was still asking, in different form, the question he had asked before the war. Invited to speak at a July 4th celebration in Rochester, New York, he said: ". . . why am I called upon to speak here today? What, to the American slave, is your fourth of July? I answer; a day that reveals to him, more than all other days in the year, the gross injustice and cruelty to which he is the constant victim. To him, your celebration is sham; your boasted liberty an unholy license; your national greatness, swelling vanity; your sounds of rejoicing are empty and heartless; your denunciation of tyrants, brass-fronted impudence; your shouts of liberty and equality, hollow mockery; your prayers and hymns, your sermons and thanksgivings, with all your religious parades and solemnity, are to him, mere bombast, fraud, deception impiety and hypocrisy—a thin veil to cover up crimes which would disgrace a nation of savages. There is not a nation on the earth guilty of practices, more shocking and bloody, than are the people of these United States. . . . Search where you will . . . for revolting barbarity and shameless hypocrisy, America reigns without a rival."[2]

In 1876 Rutherford B. Hayes received the Republican nomination for president after the corruption of the Grant administration had brought the integrity of the American system of government into question. Hayes' reputation for integrity, coupled with his demonstrated competence in executive positions, pointed toward a successful and honest administration. This promise included the field of racial equality, for his earlier record indicated he was a man of vision. In 1867, while running for the governorship in Ohio, he said of the rights of black people: "The plain and monstrous inconsistencies and injustice of excluding one-seventh of our population from all participation in a Government founded on the consent of the governed in this land of free discussion is simply impossible."[3]

But once in the White House, Hayes found his ability to act in the South crippled by the 1877 compromise and his time taken up with the hordes of office seekers which plagued every

---

1 Speech titled "The Nation's Problem," in Howard Brotz, ed., *Negro Social and Political Thought* (New York: Basic Books, 1966), p. 314.
2 Speech of Frederick Douglass in Herbert J. Storing, ed., *What Country Have I? Political Writings by Black Americans* (New York: St. Martin's Press, 1970), pp. 31–35.
3 Speech of Rutherford B. Hayes in Rayford W. Logan, *The Betrayal of the Negro* (New York: Collier Books, 1968), p. 24. The analysis of presidential practices which follows owes much to Logan's treatment.

president from the introduction of the spoils system onward. In addition, it was easier to be on good terms with the white majority of the population who wanted to ignore or suppress the black man.

On the day of Hayes' acceptance speech a lynch-riot erupted in Hamburg, South Carolina; many blacks died or suffered serious injury. A few months later a similar event occurred in Ellentown, South Carolina. Whites, determined to block the exercise of rights by black citizens, presented the president with a clear decision. When the difficult choice arose Hayes verbally reaffirmed his desires to "require absolute justice and fair play to the negro." But in the same speech he expressed his basically racist conviction that this could most surely be accomplished by "trusting the honorable and influential southern whites."[4]

In September of 1877 the president made a "good will" tour of the South. Reporters questioned him about the purposes of the trip and his reasons for statements apparently designed to placate white sentiment. Hayes replied, "I considered the situation of things in the South; how impossible it seemed to restore order and peace and harmony; saw the violence and bloodshed at their elections; how white Republicans as well as black were shot down during their political contests, and I asked myself why is it, and how long must this continue. Those men down South—*the white educated citizens*—are as good men as you or I; they are Christians; not thieves, nor cutthroats; nor bandits. . . ."[5] Hayes decided that restoration of internal calm depended upon returning to Southern whites the political power they had previously enjoyed. Law and order, in place of justice, emerged as the more pressing consideration.

In the interests of immediate domestic peace, he came to rely almost exclusively on the hope that education of blacks would solve the white problem. Hayes succeeded in getting Congress to appropriate the first significant amounts of federal aid to education. He also vetoed eight bills which would have further undermined civil rights for blacks. But the president's over-all racial record was poor. Rayford W. Logan's summation seems accurate: "However well intentioned Hayes may have been . . . White Supremacy was more securely entrenched in the South when he left the White House than it had been when he entered it."[6] Most Northern whites wanted to be free to pursue their own concerns; letting Southern whites handle the "Negro problem" contributed to this end. The problem of protecting minority rights,

4 *Ibid.*, p. 26.
5 *Ibid.*, p. 33.
6 *Ibid.*, p. 45.

therefore, devolved upon the unlettered blacks, who were in the weakest position to accomplish the task. The South had been left to deal with the freedmen but, lacking powerful allies, how was the freedman to deal with the South?

James A. Garfield had only a few months of presidential power, but like Hayes he entered with a record of promise. As a congressman from Ohio, he supported Thad Stevens and his program of vigorous federal defense of equal justice for citizens of all colors. In 1866 Garfield said, "I will never so long as I have any voice in political affairs, rest satisfied until the way is opened by which these colored citizens, so soon as they are worthy, shall be lifted to the full rights of citizenship."[7] And in his Inaugural Address he said that "under our institutions there ... [is] no middle ground for the negro between slavery and equal citizenship. There can be no permanent disfranchised peasantry in the United States."[8]

Garfield might have done much had he lived, but even a few months of national responsibility had reduced his resolve. Shortly before his assassination, he wrote that "time is the only cure for the Southern difficulties. In what shape it will finally come, if it comes at all, is not ... clear."[9] It seems unlikely that he would have reintroduced federal power on a scale sufficient to redress the increasingly adverse power balance then swinging against Southern blacks.

Chester A. Arthur came to office without making a single comment on the freedmen in his initial address. In his first annual message to Congress he spent far more time on Indian problems than on the sufferings of blacks. His one brief reference simply accepted the idea that illiteracy rates among blacks justified their temporary disfranchisement by the state governments. The Arthur administration followed a policy of continued neglect of black rights.

During his initial term in the presidency Grover Cleveland told worried blacks that the first Democrat in the White House since the Civil War would not allow freedmen's rights to be harmed. He appointed blacks to the traditional "Negro positions" of Ambassador to Haiti, Ambassador to Liberia, and Recorder of Deeds in the District of Columbia. But he took no real action to insure racial justice and consistently dedicated himself to the concept of negative government for which he became famous.

Their defeat by Cleveland in 1884 caused the Republicans to

---

7 Speech by Garfield in Burke A. Hinsdale, ed., *The Works of James A. Garfield* (Boston: James R. Osgood, 1882), Vol. I, p. 114.

8 Garfield Inaugural Address in Rayford W. Logan, *The Betrayal of the Negro* (New York: Collier Books, 1968), p. 49.

9 Ibid., p. 54.

rejuvenate their profreedmen policies of the immediate postwar era. In their 1888 platform they committed themselves to protecting "the supreme and sovereign right of every lawful citizen, rich or poor, native or foreign born, white or black to cast one free ballot in public elections and to have that ballot duly counted."[10] Partly supported by black votes, Benjamin Harrison recaptured the White House. Republican leaders then attempted to sustain their platform promise by the introduction of two new laws.

The first of these bills was designed to supply significant amounts of federal aid to education on an equal, although segregated, basis. The Senate killed the measure after a one-sided debate. The author of this bill, Senator Henry Blair of New Hampshire, a white, had long championed the cause of equal rights. Possessed of a biting wit he once advocated that the so-called colored problem in America be solved by sending "10,000 judiciously selected white people" to Africa. "I really believe," he added, that the "race problem exists in the excited imaginations and . . . ineradicable prejudices of a few white men. . . ."[11]

Henry Cabot Lodge, Sr., introduced a second law, which came to be called the Force Bill. It was designed to insure black voting in the South through the use of federal registrars and federally supervised election procedures. Ironically, the so-called Force Bill, which provided for very little in the way of force, is strikingly similar to the Voting Rights Act of 1965, which has finally made it possible for Southern blacks to vote and hold office. The Force, or Lodge, Bill also died in the Senate.

The death of these two bills ended the Harrison administration's efforts to pass equal-rights legislation. Ironically, the ineffectual problack efforts by the majority Republicans during and after the election of 1888 led to white supremacist initiatives for further reducing civil rights for blacks. The Force Bill stirred the bigots to renewed action. Defiance became the order of the day. Senator George of Mississippi said that "it will never come to pass in Mississippi, in Florida, in South Carolina, or any other state in the South, that the neck of the white race shall be under the foot of the negro, or the Mongolian, or of any created being." Senator Vest of Missouri concurred with the thought that the "tiger blood" of the white race could never be "tamed or chained." And Senator Pasco of Florida insisted that the black race was not fit to govern, asserting that "in every quarter of the

---

10 Francis Curtis, *The Republican Party* (New York: G. P. Putnam's Sons, 1904), p. 188.

11 Speech of Henry W. Blair in *Congressional Record*, 51st Congress, 1st Session, January 16, 1890, p. 630.

world where . . . [the white] has been placed side by side with people of other races he has ruled."[12] Colonel Pat Donan, editor of the Lexington, Missouri, *Tribune,* put the matter more crudely, "No simian-souled, sooty-skinned, kink-curled, blubber-lipped, prehensile-heeled, Ethiopian gorilla shall pollute the ballot box with his leprous vote."[13]

The Democratic Platform of 1892 denounced the Lodge Bill and not surprisingly Grover Cleveland took no new initiatives for racial justice during his second administration. Unfortunately, Cleveland's rigidly negative view of governmental responsibility kept him from taking needed actions, although his unquestioned personal courage can be demonstrated in many of his moves to deny venal access to the public treasury. Modern critics who seek to weaken the American government even as they denounce the nation for racial bias might ponder the Cleveland record and ask themselves whether government is really the enemy. Can justice be established without extended actions by public officials? Is not abdication of responsibility just as detrimental as misuse of power?

William McKinley, whose administration ended the nineteenth century, demonstrated no concern for improvement of race relations. His failures in the field of equal rights simply conformed to the dismal showing of his predecessors. Post-Civil War America produced no strong national leader to uphold the rights of all citizens, although a half million Americans had died to accomplish this objective. Southern white leadership determined the black man's "proper place," and Northern whites calmly acquiesced in the brutal suppression.

As majority whites regained full political control in the black belt areas of the South, Ben Tillman of South Carolina introduced a new tempo to the exploitation process. Tillman not only scorned and ridiculed the black man as any good bigot will do, he also heaped sarcastic abuse on the white moderates. He crudely pushed them aside in the struggle for power. The "Red Necks" entered upon a full revolt; the "Crackers" and "Church Burners" found a champion.

When Tillman became the governor of South Carolina in 1890 he made his position clear: "Democracy has won a great victory unparalleled," he said. "The triumph of . . . white supremacy over mongrelism and anarchy is most complete!" Later, when Tillman had been elected to the U.S. Senate, he proudly noted that blacks had been entirely removed from political action in his

---

12 Rayford W. Logan, *The Betrayal of the Negro* (New York: Collier Books, 1968), pp. 77–78.
13 Ibid., p. 44.

home state. "We have done our level best," he said. "We have
scratched our heads to find out how we could eliminate them. . . .
We stuffed ballot boxes. We shot them. We are not ashamed of
it."[14] "How did we bring it about?" he asked. "Every white man
sunk his personal feelings and ambitions. The white people of the
State, illustrating our glorious motto, 'Ready with their lives and
fortunes,' came together as one. By fraud and violence, if you
please, we threw . . . off [black] rule. In 1878 we had to resort to
more fraud and violence, and so again in 1880. Then the Registration Law and eight-box system was evolved from the superior
intelligence of the white man to check and control this surging,
muddy stream of ignorance and to tell it to back up and since
then we have carried our elections without resort to any illegal
methods, simply because the whites were united. If we were to
remain united it would still be desirable that we should guard
against the possibility of this flood, which is now dammed up,
breaking loose; or, like the viper that is asleep, only to be
warmed into life again and sting us whenever some more white
rascals, native or foreign, come here and mobilize the ignorant
blacks. Therefore, the only thing we can do as patriots and statesmen is to take from them every ballot that we can under the laws
of our national government."[15]

The Registration Law of 1882 set a number of restrictions on
black voters. The eight-box system to which Tillman referred was
an ingenious fraud. Election officials used eight boxes to receive
votes but refused to count those placed in an incorrect box. They
instructed the white voters but not the blacks, who frequently
put ballots in the wrong place.

When the Congress considered passing an antilynching bill,
Tillman said he would even renounce the Constitution if it in-
terfered with the lynching of rapists. Tillman also favored warp-
ing state constitutions to maintain white supremacy. When
South Carolina rewrote its constitution in 1895 Tillman argued
for total disfranchisement of black citizens. His words for the suppression of freedom through constitutional establishment of
second-class citizenship for blacks ironically rang with all of the
clichés for freedom's support. "Can we not rise," he said, "to the
necessities of the occasion and put into this Constitution such an
Article in reference to suffrage as will guarantee, as far as the law
can guarantee, to future generations that they shall have the

14 Speech of Benjamin Tillman, *Congressional Record*, 56th Congress, 1st
Session, February 26, 1900, pp. 2243, 2245.

15 Journal of the Constitutional Convention of the State of South Carolina,
in Gilbert Osofsky, *The Burden of Race: A Documentary History of Negro-
White Relations in America* (New York: Harper & Row, 1967), p. 167.

blessings of Anglo-Saxon civilization and liberty in this State? How pitiable, how puerile, how ineffably, unutterably contemptible appear the personal ambitions and petty spites of men alongside of this grand and glorious purpose!"[16]

Increasingly, during the 1870's and 1880's, protection for the civil rights of minority group citizens, which had been guarded during the era of Black Reconstruction, diminished. No effective white leadership rose to block the establishment of second-class citizenship for nonwhites. Black militants like Frederick Douglass fought on but enfeebled by age and increasingly alienated from white majority opinion, they accomplished little. Booker T. Washington emerged to speak for many blacks and his almost instant success with whites insured a type of black leadership which contributed to the decline of black rights.

Obviously, Washington had no idea that his approach would harm fellow blacks. An extremely hard-working and creative man, he built a great school at Tuskegee and, during his long career, assisted numbers of poor blacks to a somewhat better existence. But he worked in the South when whites systematically reduced blacks to a position not substantially different from slavery. Thus his options were severely limited.

Washington believed that education—especially practical education—would solve the race problem. In his lifetime, direct political participation by blacks had been tried during the Reconstruction period. Whites put this movement down with violence; a new approach was needed. Blacks remained a minority; stripped of political power might they yet "earn" their way into acceptance by whites through other means? Washington thought so and convinced many persons of both races that his view was correct. He supported his stand with carefully reasoned arguments.

But in spite of all possible rationalizations, one cannot review Washington's Atlanta Exposition speech of 1895 without a feeling of agonized regret. Washington's initiative delayed the black revolution for two generations and caused endless injustice. Social change cannot be purchased by abdication of minority rights; majority views merely hardened against the blacks and the delay probably rendered the necessary changes more difficult to accomplish.

Rayford W. Logan calls Washington's Atlanta Exposition Address of September 18, 1895, "one of the most effective pieces of political oratory in the history of the United States. It deserves a place," he added, "alongside that in which Patrick Henry proclaimed 'Give Me Liberty or give me death,' and that in which

---

[16] Ibid., p. 168.

William Jennings Bryan portrayed the 'Cross of Gold.' "[17] But the outcomes, Logan observes correctly, worked to the painful disadvantage of those Washington most earnestly hoped to help. Washington had lobbied in the national capital for a congressional appropriation for the Cotton States Exposition to be held in Atlanta. He was the most "successful" Southern black since the war and a logical choice to be given a prominent speaking place by the business committee sponsoring the Exposition.

Washington, the only black speaker on the program, strongly desired to advance the status of minority group citizens. He had been fighting for racial harmony and betterment of blacks since he established Tuskegee in 1881. Frederick Douglass still insisted that blacks should be given absolutely equal treatment before the law, but Washington set forth a different view. Some of his words have been quoted so often as to have become trite, but they are worth recalling because the white reaction made them the national racial policy for the next two generations. When the program chairman introduced Washington he received only scattered applause from the whites, while the blacks in the crowd cheered him loudly. Soon the blacks fell silent and the whites began cheering.

"No race can prosper," Washington said, "till it learns that there is as much dignity in tilling a field as in writing a poem. It is at the bottom of life we must begin, and not at the top. Nor should we permit our grievances to overshadow our opportunities." Washington urged whites to use black labor instead of European immigrants. He predicted that if white employers did so they and their "families will be surrounded by the most patient, faithful, law-abiding, and unresentful people that the world has ever seen."

"As we have proved our loyalty to you in the past, in nursing your children, watching by the sick-bed of your mothers and fathers, and often following them with tear-dimmed eyes to their graves, so in the future in our humble way, we shall stand by you with a devotion that no foreigner can approach, ready to lay down our lives, if need be, in defense of yours, interlacing our industrial, commercial, civil and religious life with yours in a way that shall make the interests of both races one. In all things that are purely social we can be separate as the fingers, yet one as the hand in all things essential to mutual progress. . . ."

Then Washington climaxed his appeal with the words: "The wisest among my race understand that the agitation of questions

---

[17] Rayford W. Logan, *The Betrayal of the Negro* (New York: Collier Books, 1968), p. 276.

of social equality is the extremest folly, and that progress in the enjoyment of all the privileges that will come to us must be the result of severe and constant struggle rather than of artificial forcing. No race that has anything to contribute to the market of the world is long in any degree ostracized. It is important and right that all privileges of the law be ours, but it is vastly more important that we be prepared for the exercise of these privileges. The opportunity to earn a dollar in a factory just now is worth infinitely more than the opportunity to spend a dollar in an opera-house.

"In conclusion," Washington said, ". . . nothing in thirty years has given us more hope and encouragement, and drawn us so near to you of the white race, as this opportunity offered by the Exposition . . . I pledge that in your effort to work out the great and intricate problem which God has laid at the doors of the South, you shall have at all times the patient, sympathetic help of my race. . . ."[18]

Former Governor Bullock rushed over to shake his hand as did other whites on the platform. Tributes poured in by letter and telegram. President Cleveland congratulated Washington. Harvard University gave Washington an honorary doctorate, the first time a black received one in New England. The nation's press commented in an overwhelmingly favorable tone; most editors called the speech the hit of the entire Exposition. The Charleston, South Carolina, *News and Courier* called Washington one of the great men of the South. The editor added with typically galling white condescension, "His skin is colored, but his head is sound, and his heart is in the right place."[19]

The Chicago *Inter-ocean* said, Washington "has done more for the improvement of the negro in the South than has been accomplished by all the political agitators. . . . The possession of a vote does not always insure respect, but the possession of a good character, a good home and a little money reserve always insures respect. . . . If every southern state had such an institution as that at Tuskegee, Alabama, presided over by such a man as Professor Washington, the race question would settle itself in ten years."[20]

In addition to praise, Washington's speech brought him a vast outpouring of philanthropy, mostly from successful Northern whites who agreed with Washington's self-help approach. Wash-

18 Atlanta Exposition Address, by Booker T. Washington, September 18, 1895, in *Negro Social and Political Thought, 1850–1920*, edited by Howard Brotz, © 1966 by Basic Books, Inc., Publishers, New York, pp. 356–59.
19 Rayford W. Logan, *The Betrayal of the Negro* (New York: Collier Books, 1968), p. 281.
20 Ibid., p. 285.

ington had bargained away black rights and, at least tacitly, accepted second-class citizenship, in return for economic opportunity in menial functions and support for black education. Many blacks accepted Washington's formula.

However, some blacks did not approve Washington's view. W. E. B. Du Bois led the opposition and eventually broke Washington's monopoly on "solutions" to the race problem. But Du Bois found his job to be a formidable one. In his words, "Not only did presidents of the United States consult Booker Washington, but governors and congressmen; philanthropists conferred with him, scholars wrote to him. Tuskegee became a vast information bureau and center of advice. It was not merely passive in these matters but . . . suave and far seeing; active efforts were made to concentrate influence at Tuskegee. After a time almost no Negro institution could collect funds without the recommendation or acquiescence of Mr. Washington. Few political appointments were made anywhere in the United States without his consent. Even the careers of rising young men were very often determined by his advice and certainly his opposition was fatal."[21]

Washington's 1895 Atlanta address opened numerous possible initiatives for white action to restrict further the freedom of black people. Many individuals availed themselves of the opportunity presented. In 1896 the Supreme Court of the United States heard a case, a just decision on which could have reversed the national trend. But the Court determined to solve the racial problem in America with increased oppression of the black minority. Before the Civil War the Court's antiblack Dred Scott decision had not proved popular. At that time abolitionist sentiment ran strong and the "irrepressible" conflict approached. But after the war, in 1883, whites readily accepted Supreme Court destruction of the Civil Rights Act of 1875.

Circumstances in the 1890's paralleled those in 1883; most whites had become thoroughly tired of the entire question of the rights of blacks. Washington's speech gave them a partial out. The Supreme Court supplied them with further welcome relief.

During the decade of the 1880's the federal courts moved to curb black rights. Between 1882 and 1888 lower courts ruled on four different occasions that separate facilities met all constitutional provisions for protection of citizen rights. And, parallel to the courts' trend, the Interstate Commerce Commission made three rulings in 1887, 1888, and 1889, which approved the doctrine of separate facilities on common carriers.

The specific case, *Plessy* v. *Ferguson,* originated in Louisiana

---

21 W. E. B. DuBois, *Dusk of Dawn: An Essay Toward an Autiobiography of a Race Concept* (New York: Schocken Books, 1968), p. 73.

where an octoroon broke a state law requiring separate railroad cars for the races. He deliberately sought arrest by sitting in a "white" car; the case became a classic miscarriage of justice when Henry B. Brown, speaking for the majority, wrote: "A statute which implies merely a legal distinction between the white and colored races—a distinction which is founded in the color of the two races, and which must always exist so long as white men are distinguished from the other race by color—has no tendency to destroy the legal equality of the two races or to reestablish a state of involuntary servitude." The Court held that the Thirteenth and Fourteenth Amendments "could not have been intended to abolish distinctions based upon color, or to enforce social, as distinguished from political, equality, or a commingling of the two races upon terms unsatisfactory to either. Laws permitting, and even requiring their separation in places where they are liable to be brought into contact do not necessarily imply the inferiority of either race. . . ."

The majority opinion went on, "We cannot say that a law which authorizes or even requires the separation of the two races in public conveyances is unreasonable or . . . obnoxious.

"We consider the underlying fallacy of the plaintiff's argument to consist in the assumption that the enforced separation of the two races stamps the colored race with a badge of inferiority. If this is so, it is not by reason of anything found in the act, but solely because the colored race chooses to put that construction upon it.

"If the two races are to meet on terms of social equality it must be the result of natural affinities, a mutual appreciation of each other's merits and a voluntary consent of individuals. . . . Legislation is powerless to eradicate racial instincts or to abolish distinctions based upon physical differences, and the attempt to do so can only result in accentuating the difficulties of the present situation. . . . If one race be inferior to the other socially, the Constitution of the United States cannot put them upon the same plane."[22]

When the Court finally spoke in reverse of this obnoxious doctrine the jurists altered all of the original rationalization. But that did not take place until 1954. Wrong decisions can vastly increase the ability of a majority to inflict injustice upon a minority. The majority of American whites, north and south, supported the *Plessy* v. *Ferguson* decision and gave the matter little further thought.

---

22 *Plessy* v. *Ferguson*, 163 U.S. 537, 1896 in Henry Steele Commager, ed., *Documents of American History*, Vol. I, Seventh Edition (New York: Appleton-Century-Crofts, 1968), pp. 628–29.

The author of the Supreme Court ruling, Henry B. Brown, a Republican from the state of Michigan, might have been expected to render a less biased opinion. John Marshall Harlan, a Democrat from Kentucky, again supplied the lone voice of opposition. He presented one of the great dissents in Supreme Court history when he wrote, "The Constitution of the U.S. does not . . . permit any public authority to know the race of those entitled to be protected in the enjoyment of . . . rights.

"Every true man has pride of race, and under appropriate circumstances, when the rights of others, his equals before the law, are not to be affected, it is his privilege to express such pride and to take such action based upon it as to him seems proper. But I deny that any legislative body or judicial tribunal may have regard to the race of citizens when the civil rights of those citizens are involved. . . .

"The Judgment this day rendered will, in time, prove to be quite as pernicious as the decision made by this tribunal in the Dred Scott case. . . .

"We have yet . . . a dominant race, a superior class of citizens, which assumes to regulate the enjoyment of civil rights, common to all citizens, upon the basis of race. The present decision . . . will . . . stimulate aggressions, more or less brutal and irritating upon the . . . rights of colored citizens. . . .

"Sixty millions of whites are in no danger from the presence . . . of eight millions of blacks. The destinies of the two races in this country are indissolubly linked together, and the interests of both require that the common government of all shall not permit the seeds of race hate to be planted under sanction of law. What can more certainly arouse race hate, what more certainly create and perpetuate a feeling of distrust between . . . races, than state enactments which . . . proceed on the ground that colored citizens are so inferior and degraded that they cannot be allowed to sit in public coaches occupied by white citizens? That, as all will admit, is the real meaning of such legislation.

"We boast of the freedom enjoyed by our people above all other peoples. But it is difficult to reconcile that boast with a state of the law which practically puts the brand of servitude and degradation upon a large class of our fellow citizens. . . . The thin disguise of 'equal' accommodations for passengers in railroad coaches will not mislead anyone, or atone for the wrong this day done. . . ."[23]

But Justice Harlan's eloquent opinion failed to persuade either his colleagues or his fellow citizens. White sentiment favored the

---

[23] Mr. Justice Harlan's dissent, ibid., pp. 629–30.

view expressed in the Court majority and black rights suffered further reduction.

The segregation decision in *Plessy* v. *Ferguson* climaxed, rather than initiated, the long, post-Reconstruction decline of the rights of black people. After the political Compromise of 1877 the South gradually moved toward a system of complete public and private segregation. Jim Crow did not come all at once, immediately upon the end of Reconstruction. The process was a slow and deliberate one with a significant number of Jim Crow restrictions being established in the decade of the 1890's and after the turn of the century.

C. Vann Woodward, the most informed historian of the Jim Crow movement, says that the origins of the phrase *Jim Crow* as applied to restrictions on blacks cannot be easily traced. The term, in use as early as the 1830's, was derived from an Uncle Tom-like character in a popular song. In 1841 at least one railroad in Massachusetts publicly listed seats for blacks in "Jim Crow" cars. The Jim Crow system came to full maturity in the post-Civil War South, but its prewar invention centered in the North. While majority opinion subjected Northern "free" blacks to a wide variety of Jim Crow and segregationist practices, during the same period in the South, blacks and whites intermingled relatively freely. For example, Boston whites in 1847 boasted that they allowed no colored families to live among them. Boston's black district was called "Nigger Hill"; in Cincinnati it was "Little Africa." New York and Philadelphia had black ghettos, but these as yet did not exist in the cities of the South.

And, in the newer, "more democratic" frontier states of the West, whites applied restrictions even more harshly. Indiana, Illinois, and Oregon passed laws against black immigration; other Northern and Western states required free blacks to post public bond for their good behavior before allowing them to settle. De Tocqueville wrote, "The prejudice of race appears to be stronger in the states that have abolished slavery than in those where it still exists; and nowhere is it so intolerant as in those states where servitude has never been known."[24] The observant Frenchman thus early noted the predilection of American whites for "solving" the white problem not by altering the source—their own racist views—but by ridding society of blacks.

Removal of the freedman as a voting force supplied the basic

---

24 Alexis de Tocqueville in C. Vann Woodward, *The Strange Career of Jim Crow* (New York: Oxford University Press, 1966), p. 20. The following summary of Jim Crow practices draws heavily on Professor C. Vann Woodward's analysis. See especially Chapter III, "Capitulation to Racism," and Chapter IV, "The Man on the Cliff," pp. 67–148.

precondition for the coming of Jim Crow. South Carolina accelerated the disfranchisement process in 1882 with the eight-box system of voting already mentioned. During the 1880's, whites applied increasingly complex registration laws which helped to reduce the number of black voters. Louisiana and Mississippi joined South Carolina in applying the most imaginative disfranchisement schemes. Final elimination of blacks from Southern voting lists followed the Supreme Court decision in *Williams* v. *Mississippi* in 1898. The Court upheld Mississippi practice which removed blacks from polling lists on the basis of the poll tax, gerrymandering, and subjective judgments regarding literacy. Prior to the 1890's blacks continued to vote in significant numbers, although subjected to intimidation and manipulation. As late as 1890, sixteen blacks sat in the Louisiana state legislature. Following Reconstruction ten blacks served in the U.S. Congress, the same number as had been elected during the Reconstruction period.

But the Mississippi approach became popular all over the South. Restrictions on voting lay against illiterate whites as well as blacks, but biased local officials breached these restrictions for whites through "understanding clauses," "grandfather clauses," and "good character clauses." Poll tax laws tended to disfranchise both blacks and poor whites because annual payments, though small, accumulated over the years, reaching prohibitive totals. Moreover, they had to be paid months in advance of an election. Finally, arrangements which made Democratic primary elections a pure white process virtually removed blacks as a political force.

A striking example of this process can be seen in the voting statistics for the state of Louisiana. In 1896 some 127,000 blacks remained eligible to vote; by 1904 this number had been reduced to fewer than 2,000 registered voters. In 1896 black voters outnumbered whites in twenty-six parishes in Louisiana; by 1900 this figure had been reduced to none. Similar reductions occurred in other states. For instance, Mississippi registered only 8,600 blacks out of 147,000, and Alabama only 5,000 out of 130,000 after their disfranchisement conventions.

Segregation in public carriers, especially railroads, paralleled restrictions in voting. And, as in voting, the restrictive process did not occur immediately upon the forceful suppression of black political rights during Reconstruction. Some evidence suggests considerable mingling of the races even after the Compromise of 1877, although separation of the races increasingly became the pattern. As late as 1885, T. M. Stewart, a civil-rights-minded black, set out from Boston to travel in the South to observe race relations in the states of the Old Confederacy. Stewart went with a "chip on my shoulder," but received equal treatment. He traveled in a car filled with whites and was courteously served a meal in a Petersburg, Virginia, station restaurant.

His report praised the treatment he received in the South, even calling it superior to the way he was treated in the North. He found he could ride in first-class cars on the railroads and in the streets. "I can go into saloons and get refreshments even as in New York," he wrote. "I can stop in and drink a glass of soda and be more politely waited upon than in some parts of New England." He even observed a black policeman in Charleston, South Carolina, arrest a white man under "circumstances requiring coolness, prompt decision and courage" and noted that the crowd of whites which gathered accepted the action calmly.[25] But Stewart was an educated, middle-class black who probably received special treatment. When shortly thereafter, Ben Tillman captured the Democratic party for the racists, conditions deteriorated rapidly.

Segregation on railroads by law began with Florida's action in 1887 and spread to other states. But as late as 1898 segregationist forces had yet to establish Jim Crow laws on railroads in South Carolina. The Charleston *News and Courier* ridiculed the idea, noting that such a law had not been used since the war and did not seem needed. The editor went on to note that if such a foolish law passed there would be no stopping other practices like segregation of streetcars, boats, saloons, stations, restaurants, and jury boxes. He concluded that eventually courts would require separate Bibles for whites and blacks and termed all such moves nonsense. The editor tried in effect to undercut Jim Crow support on the railroad issue by reducing the proposal to absurdities. Ironically, the absurd became the reality. By 1907 virtually all Southern railroad, streetcar, boat, and station facilities had been segregated by law.

Once the railroads fell to the segregationists, nothing seemed immune to the craze for separation on the basis of race. An almost amusing variety of segregationist actions introduced the Jim Crow system to virtually every type of human contact. The Richmond *Times*, in 1900, insisted that "God Almighty drew the color line and it cannot be obliterated."[26] Politicians quickly accepted the challenge. Signs for "White Only" and "Colored Only" appeared over entrances, exits, fountains, theaters, boarding houses, ticket windows, and rest rooms.

Refinements crept in to perfect further the expanding system. A Louisiana law of 1914 required that the management of

---

25 Statement of T. M. Stewart in ibid., pp. 38–40.
26 Richmond *Times* in ibid., p. 96.

circuses and tent shows must not only segregate all entrances, exits, and ticket windows, but also separate them by not less than 25 feet of distance. Alabama prohibited white female nurses from attending black males no matter how ill the patients were and without regard to the wishes of the nurses. North Carolina and Virginia established that any social or fraternal order which recognized black units or divisions could not also allow the whites and blacks to address each other as "brother."

Endless laws and ordinances denied fair housing. Some towns forbade blacks the right to enter the locality's corporate limits. New Orleans established by ordinance that a person of either race who wanted to buy a home in a community had to gain the consent of a majority of the people already living there before completing the transaction. A number of towns and cities established special curfews for blacks but did not apply them to whites. Such laws usually set 10:00 P.M. as the hour for blacks to be indoors. Oklahoma passed a law in 1915 which required telephone companies to supply separate phone booths for blacks and whites.

Schools were completely segregated. But North Carolina required also that textbooks be stored between terms in separate warehouses. For a time South Carolina operated a third school system for mulatto children. New Orleans passed an ordinance which segregated black and white prostitutes in different districts of the city.

Jim Crow laws continued to be expanded with imaginative new details down through the 1930's and even beyond. As late as 1940 Atlanta approved a Jim Crow taxi law, one of a series of such ordinances passed during the 1930's across the South. The Atlanta law required that signs on taxis must clearly indicate which ethnic group was to be served; drivers had to be of the same race. Another Atlanta ordinance made it unlawful for the races to mix at any public park except "so much of Grant park as is occupied by the zoo." In 1932 a Georgia law prohibited baseball clubs of different races from playing "within two blocks of each other." Arkansas made it mandatory that all race track and gambling facilities be segregated, suggesting that even black money was inferior.

Perhaps the city fathers in Birmingham, Alabama, entered the ultimate idiocy upon the Jim Crow books when they declared it to be "unlawful for a Negro and a white person to play together or in company with each other" at dominoes or checkers.[27]

---

[27] Ibid., p. 118. Ridiculous Jim Crow actions continued far beyond the time considered here. The equal rights revolution of the 1950's and 1960's, discussed in chapter 9, resulted in many examples of white failure to see the ludicrous aspects of their actions. In 1961 in Jackson, Mississippi, city officials

The story could be detailed almost endlessly, reaching more and more incredible depths. Many examples can be cited which cast ridicule on the entire concept of Jim Crow, yet the ghastly aspects far outweigh any wry amusement which may be found in ridiculous laws like those which denied interracial checkers. The ultimate thrust of all such legislating came from violence-minded white supremacy bigots who went to any extreme to support their cause.

All such persons believed implicitly in the superior rights of the white race. John Sharp Williams of Mississippi, a U.S. congressman, said, "You could ship-wreck 10,000 illiterate white Americans on a desert island, and in three weeks they would have a fairly good government, conceived and administered upon fairly democratic lines. You could ship-wreck 10,000 negroes, every one of whom was a graduate of Harvard University and in less than three years, they would have retrograded governmentally: half of the men would have been killed and the other half would have two wives apiece." David A. DeArmond, a congressman from Missouri, said that Negroes were "almost too ignorant to eat, scarcely wise enough to breathe, mere existing human machines."[28] And an Alabama legislator, during the fight to disfranchise blacks in his state, asserted that the poorest, most low-down white man he ever met was better than any black.

The idiotic injustices of the Jim Crow system chiefly relate to the American South. Close to 90 per cent of American blacks lived in the region prior to 1900 and the greatest outrages occurred there. Yet establishment of second-class citizenship for blacks was by no means confined to the states of the Old Confederacy. Whites drew the color line all over the North in only slightly less unjust and offensive terms.

Northern segregation rested largely upon the black stereotype which magazines and newspapers presented. Blacks constantly appeared as buffoons, brutes, rapists, and watermelon eaters; they were portrayed as lazy, shiftless, slovenly, dangerous, and comical. Most Northern hotels, restaurants, and public facilities denied blacks entrance or segregated them in separate, inferior sections.

---

arrested some blacks who sat on benches in the zoo where only whites had sat before. The officials considered painting signs on the benches indicating which ones were for which race, but by 1961 the old system of segregation had ceased to be acceptable practice. After deliberation they simply removed all the benches from the zoo and patrons, white and black, tired or fresh, observed the animals from a standing position. See James Peck, *Freedom Ride* (New York: Simon and Schuster, 1962), p. 153.

28 Rayford W. Logan, *The Betrayal of the Negro* (New York: Collier Books, 1968), p. 99.

During the Republican National Convention in Philadelphia in 1900, officials quartered minority group delegates in the homes of black people because the hotels admitted no nonwhites. In the same year the General Federation of Women's Clubs had a wild time with the color line. Mrs. Josephine Ruffin, wife of a black graduate of Harvard University, caused a sensation at the Milwaukee convention when she sought to extend fraternal greetings from the Massachusetts women's club of which she was president. The majority of the delegates voted to deny her this privilege, although an active minority, led by some New York women, risked contamination while receiving Mrs. Ruffin's greetings in a small rump session. Later, on the main floor, a white delegate tried to rip Mrs. Ruffin's badge off prior to shoving her out the door; she failed, as a result of Mrs. Ruffin's agility and perseverance.

James Bryce, noted English observer of the American scene, concluded that blacks received unequal treatment almost everywhere in the nation: "Except on the Pacific coast," he wrote, "a negro man never sits down to dinner with a white man in a railway refreshment room. You never encounter him at a private party. He is not received in a hotel of the better sort, no matter how rich he may be. He will probably be refused a glass of soda water at a drug store. He is not shaved in a place frequented by white men, not even by a barber of his own colour. He worships in a church of his own. No white woman would dream of receiving his addresses. Nor does it make any difference that he is three parts or seven parts white, if the stain of colour can still be discerned. Kindly condescension is the best he can look for. . . . Social equality is utterly out of reach."[29] The editor of the *Atlantic Monthly* came to the same conclusion shortly afterward: "Remorseless as the color line is drawn in the Southern states, it is scarcely less rigid in the North. . . ."[30]

Lynching and mob violence, though not so often entered upon as in the South, nevertheless repeatedly marred the Northern scene. Between 1876 and 1910, white America, North and South, created legal and social barriers to equal citizenship. The black man suffered personal humiliation, economic deprivation, and violence. Segregation created social stagnation and economic exploitation; second-class citizenship and poverty warped the black experience. Their effects have yet to run the full course.

29 James Bryce, "The American Commonwealth," in Joel Williamson, ed., *The Origins of Segregation* (Boston: D. C. Heath, 1968), p. 30.
30 Editorial in *Atlantic Monthly*, October 1901, Vol. 88, p. 436.

# The Record of Judge Lynch

# 4

THE Jim Crow system contained so many ludicrous features that few persons seriously tried to enforce the more ridiculous restrictions. But legal enforcement of segregationist practices became less important than physical intimidation. The power of the lynch mob emerged as the most vicious aspect of the entire system. As the century waned the legal structure of Jim Crow laws received support in ever more appalling instances through the destruction of human beings, most of them black. Their violent endings discouraged those who sought to re-establish one class of citizenship for all.

The term *lynching* has been traced to various sources. Summary justice in sixteenth-century England was known as "lydford" law. Another origin may be Galway, Ireland, where, in 1674, Mayor James Lynch reportedly hanged his own son out of a window for "degrading and bilking strangers."[1]

In the United States, South Carolina back country "Regulators" put down an outbreak of crime in the summer of 1767 with flogging and house burning carried on by mobs outside the law.[2] But the American origins of "lynching" have usually been attributed to the activities of Charles Lynch, a Quaker judge born in 1736 in Lynchburg, Virginia. An influential member of a prominent family, Lynch served in the House of Burgesses prior to his appointment as a judge. Shortly before the American Revolution, Tories and Rebels contested for control of the Lynchburg area; the American Rebels sustained a slight majority. The generally unsettled state of affairs led the "patriots" to urge Lynch

---

[1] James E. Cutler, *Lynch Law: An Investigation Into the History of Lynching in the United States* (Montclair, N.J.: Patterson Smith, 1969), pp. 7 and 15.

[2] Richard M. Brown, *The South Carolina Regulators* (Cambridge: Belknap-Harvard University Press, 1963), pp. 38–39.

to take appropriate action because the colonial courts, more than a hundred miles away over the mountains, responded slowly to pressing situations. Lynch accepted the responsibility and sat with two other citizens to dispense local "justice." They adhered to generally fair procedures and provided protection for the accused. Persons acquitted went free and the community sometimes paid reparations to them. A citizen judged to be guilty received "thirty-nine lashes on the bare back, and if he did not then shout 'Liberty Forever' [he was] hung up by his thumbs until he did."[3] Few persons received the death penalty; no one was lynched by a mob.

But Lynch and his fellow judges established a precedent for extralegal justice. Vigilante groups have deep roots in frontier America. Ultimately Charles Lynch's name became identified with the most horribly indefensible blots on the American record.

Lynch mob justice in other countries, civilizations, and eras needs further study. Certainly the Bible contains many accounts of inhuman practices. The Middle Eastern custom known as stoning is an example. But whatever the record elsewhere in the world lynching has seriously marred the American scene for more than one hundred years. Laws against lynching, though frequently debated, have rarely been passed and, almost without exception, they have failed in their purpose. Despite great reduction the lynching tradition has yet to end entirely.

The post-Civil War era was especially poisoned by widespread application of extralegal "justice." In 1868 authorities counted 120 black bodies after a big "nigger hunt" in Louisiana. In 1871 in York County, South Carolina, approximately 300 persons were whipped over a period of several months. During 1870–1872, mobs lynched 107 in Alabama. Vigilantes lashed or mutilated hundreds across the entire Klan belt. The Congressional Commission that investigated the Ku Klux Klan in 1872 took more than a dozen volumes of testimony revealing inhuman oppression of blacks and their few white allies. The record of horror multiplied during the 1880's, a decade in which more than 1,200 Americans suffered the agonies of lynch mob deaths. But between 1890 and 1900 crowds lynched 1,665 persons in the United States, most of them blacks. The "high" years saw 235 lynched in 1892 and 200 in 1893, or an average of one every forty hours. No decade in American history has written a sorrier record in this regard.

---

3 Walter White, *Rope and Faggot* (New York: Arno Press, 1969), pp. 83–84. This significant work, first published in 1929, still stands as a major contribution on the subject of lynching in the United States. This chapter owes much to White's study.

Ironically, considering the generally antiblack character of American lynching, the first widely publicized incidents of the 1890's involved the lynching of whites. In March 1891, in New Orleans, mobs killed eleven Italians alleged to have entered into a conspiracy to commit murder. The lynching touched off an international furor. Italy broke diplomatic relations with the United States for a time and eventually the American government paid some $24,000 in conscience money to Italian authorities. Many citizens signed a petition to the Louisiana legislature urging the passage of an antilynching bill. Thus, perversely, the lynching of foreigners (and whites) began the agitation for legal restraints against the horror of lynch mob justice. The Louisiana legislature resisted the appeal and lynch customs continued as before.

In 1893 the Georgia legislature actually passed a weak and cryptically worded law against "illegal" lynching. However, nothing was done to enforce it. Between 1887 and 1901 citizens of the United States lynched foreigners from China, Japan, Austria-Hungary, Mexico, Great Britain, and Switzerland in addition to the Italians killed at New Orleans. These escapades cost the national government nearly a half million dollars in reparation payments.

As the decade of the 1890's "progressed," lynch mobs continued to make American blacks their main target, however. In 1890 a North Carolina mob went on a rampage. Four hundred white men, led by prominent citizens and public officials, invaded the black quarter of the city of Wilmington, killed and wounded many, chased others out, and burned most of the buildings. No public action redressed the outrage.

After blacks had been disfranchised in South Carolina, whites attacked them with increasing violence. In Lake City in 1898 the appointment of a black postmaster stirred a white mob to fury. They locked the postmaster and his family in their own home and set it on fire. As the unfortunate blacks attempted to escape, the mob shot at them as they emerged from the burning building. Some died, including the postmaster; others were only wounded.

In New Orleans in 1900, white mobs attacked any blacks who appeared on the streets. The reign of terror lasted three days; many casualties resulted. The sequence began with an attempted arrest of two blacks by three white policemen. The incident led to one of the ugliest lynch-riots in a decade of outrages. It also created one of the proudest black martyrs in American history.

Robert Charles, one of the two blacks accosted by the officers, had been distributing literature advocating black migration to Liberia. One of the policemen struck Charles with his club and then tried to shoot him. Charles drew his weapon first and, though wounded, injured the policeman and escaped. An intense hunt followed with large numbers of white mobsters joining the police. The mayor issued a notice of $250 reward for Charles, "dead or alive."

When the police again surrounded Charles, he shot and killed two of them and routed the rest. They returned with reinforcements and a mob which beat and killed several blacks in the vicinity. The final drama involved more than a thousand persons whom Charles held off for several hours. Through expert marksmanship he killed five more persons and wounded nine others. The policemen, unable to force Charles out or withstand his furious defense, finally set fire to the house. When the flames eventually compelled him to flee, Charles emerged shooting and died, Samson-like, with his fallen enemies around him.

In South Carolina a mob lynched a black named Willis Jackson. The activists cut off his fingers and distributed them for souvenirs to the crowd. Joshua W. Ashleigh, a prominent member of the South Carolina legislature, organized the mob. His son, editor of one of the local newspapers assisted his father in leading the action and gleefully recorded the story in his newspaper. Cole Blease, the governor of the state, had a case against the two Ashleighs, but he refused to take action and said that he himself would leave the governor's chair and "help in a lynching when a Negro was accused of rape."[4] The local authorities also declined to take responsibility in the affair.

The folklore of lynching postulates that most killings take place after a white woman has been brutally raped by a black man. James F. Byrnes, who was a governor and senator from South Carolina in addition to serving as a Supreme Court Justice and Secretary of State in the Truman era, once put the matter in these words: "While the press of the North and the Negro press will join the press and pulpit of the South in their condemnation of the criminality of the mob, they seldom join us in condemnation of the criminal assaults upon white women, *which is generally the cause of the lynching.*"[5] [Italics added.]

Many, if not most, whites believe the emotionally charged sequence known as rape triggers lynch mob action and in a sense, justifies the retaliation. Yet, although commonly held assump-

---

[4] Ibid., p. 172.

[5] James F. Byrnes, speech in *Congressional Record*, August 25, 1919, in I. A. Newby, ed., *The Development of Segregationist Thought* (Homewood, Ill.: Dorsey Press, 1968), pp. 120–21. Byrnes' views are typical of many that might be noted. See, for example, Robert W. Shufeldt, *The Negro: A Menace to American Civilization* (Boston: Gorham Press, 1907), p. 13.

tions connect the two items, actually less than a sixth of the blacks lynched in America were even charged with rape, and only a tiny fraction clearly guilty of the crime. But folklore is a powerful thing. The idea of queenly white woman penetrated by beastly black man dies hard. Indeed, the myth has never really died at all.

The "lynching bee," as Gilbert Osofsky has put it, "became a social institution, a community gathering spontaneously mobilized to expiate a sin; and its perpetrator was considered beyond the pale of normal judicial process. When the accused was hung, castrated, shot, tortured, or burned 'in a business-like manner,' a neighborhood returned to its normal state assured that true justice had been done. Lynching acted as a community catharsis."[6] Ida Wells had come to a similar conclusion in the 1890's when she noted that mobs acted with fury, destroying victims in the knowledge that the community condoned such actions and would not call them to account.

During the 1890's individuals, both white and black, north and south, attempted to halt the carnage. No antilynch leader deserves more credit than Ida B. Wells (later Ida W. Barnett) who, in her home town of Memphis, led a journalistic drive to outlaw the practice. She became involved after a mob lynched three young black men in 1892. Her defense of the three marked her as a fearsome presence on the Memphis scene. Few persons spoke strongly against lynching in the 1890's and even fewer blacks living in the South dared to do so. But Ida Wells possessed rare courage and she represented a threat to the established order.

In an editorial denouncing the lynching of eight blacks, she wrote, "Nobody in this section of the country believes the old threadbare lie that Negro men rape white women. If Southern white men are not careful, they will over-reach themselves and public sentiment will have a reaction; a conclusion will then be reached which will be very damaging to the moral reputation of their women."[7] Ida Wells' hint that white women might enjoy the company of black men brought a lynch mob to her home, but she was out of town when the item appeared. The mob then destroyed the newspaper office where she published *The Free Speech*.

Driven from her home, Ida Wells settled in Chicago and formed the central Anti-Lynching League which began to collect eyewitness accounts of atrocities to support the case for national

---

6 Gilbert Osofsky, *The Burden of Race: A Documentary History of Negro-White Relations in America* (New York: Harper & Row, 1967), p. 179.

7 Ida Wells Barnett, "Southern Horrors," *On Lynchings* (New York: Arno Press, 1969), p. 4.

action against vigilante justice. But her efforts availed little, although the records she collected and the pamphlets she published constitute a revealing chapter in the history of the United States. She specialized in recording eyewitness accounts by whites. Frederick Douglass paid her the strongest tribute, calling her a "brave woman" who did great "service" for blacks. "If [the] American conscience," he wrote, "were only half alive, if the American church and clergy were only half christianized, if American moral sensibility were not hardened by persistent infliction of moral outrage and crime against colored people, a scream of horror, and shame and indignation would rise to Heaven wherever your pamphlet is read."[8]

The lynching of Henry Smith in Paris, Texas, in February 1893 provided Ida Wells with some terrible testimony. Someone brutally murdered the four-year-old daughter of a local policeman named Vance. Previously Henry Smith, a local black man who did odd jobs around town, had been arrested by Vance. The officer submitted the black man to demeaning treatment while Smith was in custody. Talk among town whites tended to link Smith's name to the crime on the ground that he had been motivated by revenge. Rumor went out that Smith had assaulted the child and then killed her. A local Methodist bishop stated that Smith had "first outraged [her] with demoniacal cruelty and then [had taken the girl] by her heels and torn [her] asunder in the mad wantonness of gorilla ferocity."

The actual autopsy showed no evidence of rape and the only marks on the child had been made on her neck, where she was choked. No proof that Smith murdered her emerged from the official investigations but local gossip convicted him with certainty. The fervor against Smith seemed only to be increased by the knowledge that he was mentally retarded. Not surprisingly, Smith fled Paris when he learned he was under suspicion.

A hunt followed and authorities arrested Smith across the Arkansas border and returned him to Texas by train. Ida Wells took the main part of her report from the words of a white eyewitness: "Arriving . . . at twelve o'clock the train was met by a surging mass of humanity 10,000 strong. The Negro was placed upon a carnival float in mockery of a king upon his throne, and, followed by an immense crowd, was escorted through the city so that all might see the most inhuman monster known in current history. The line of march was up Main Street to the square, around the square down Clarksville Street to Church Street,

---

[8] Letter from Frederick Douglass to Ida Wells Barnett, October 25, 1892 in Preface to ibid., p. 3.

thence to the open prairies about 300 yards from the Texas and
Pacific depot. Here Smith was placed upon a scaffold, six feet
square and ten feet high, securely bound, within the view of all
beholders. . . . the victim was tortured for fifty minutes by red-
hot iron brands thrust against his quivering body. Commencing
at the feet the brands were placed against him inch by inch until
they were thrust against the face.

"Words to describe the awful torture inflicted upon Smith
cannot be found. . . . the child's father, her brothers, and two
uncles then gathered about the Negro as he lay fastened to the
torture platform and thrust hot irons into his quivering flesh. It
was horrible—the man dying by slow torture in the midst of
smoke from his own burning flesh. Every groan from the fiend,
every contortion of his body was cheered by the thickly packed
crowd of . . . persons. . . . the eyes were burned out and irons
were thrust down his throat. . . .

"The men of the Vance family . . . wreaked vengeance; the
crowd piled all kinds of combustible stuff around the scaffold,
poured oil on it and set it afire. The Negro rolled and tossed out
of the mass, only to be pushed back by the people nearest him.
He tossed out again, and was roped and pulled back. Hundreds
of people turned away, but the vast crowd still looked calmly on.

"Then being apparently dead, kerosene was poured on him,
cottonseed hulls placed beneath him and set on fire. In less time
than it takes to relate it, the tortured man was wafted beyond the
grave to another fire, hotter and more terrible than the one just
experienced."

The white observer's account concluded matter-of-factly, "People were here from every part of this section. They came from
Dallas, Fort Worth, Sherman, Denison, Bonham, Texarkana,
Fort Smith, Arkansas, and a party of fifteen came from Hemp-
stead County, Arkansas, where he was captured, and there were
demands at many points for special trains to bring the people
here to see the unparalleled punishment for an unparalleled
crime. When the news of the burning went over the country like
wildfire, at every country town anvils boomed forth the announce-
ment."[9]

The lynching of Luther Holbert and his wife in Doddsville,
Mississippi, in 1904 provides another illustration of the obscene
brutalities of lynch mob action. Holbert, a sharecropper,
quarreled with the white owner of the plantation where he
worked. Words went to blows. In the contest Holbert felled
James Eastland, the white man. Holbert fled with his wife when

---

9 Ibid., pp. 25-32.

he realized he had killed Eastland, but a posse quickly captured the black couple and submitted them to atrocities.

The "two Negroes . . . were tied to trees and while the funeral pyres were being prepared they were forced to suffer the most fiendish tortures. The blacks were forced to hold out their hands while one finger at a time was chopped off. The fingers were distributed as souvenirs. The ears . . . were cut off. Holbert was beaten severely, his skull was fractured and one of his eyes knocked out with a stick, hung by a shred from the socket. . . . The most excruciating form of punishment consisted in the use of a large cork-screw in the hands of some of the mob. The instrument was bored into the flesh of the man and woman, in the arms, legs, and body, and then pulled out, the spirals tearing out big pieces of raw, quivering flesh every time it was withdrawn."[10]

Then the mob burned them to death. Holbert had killed in self-defense. His wife's sole "crime" consisted of her marriage bond. According to one newspaper account, the killers forced the Holberts' son to watch the executions. He "was nearly crazed with fear, and when he saw the flames consuming his tortured parents, and heard their frightful screams, and prayers for mercy, he threw himself face downward on the ground, closing his eyes, and putting his fingers in his ears, to shut the fearful scene out from sight and hearing. After the couple were dead and only partly consumed, the mob left them and the boy took the blackened corpses of his parents, and laid them side by side in the brush, covering them over as best he could."[11]

In his classic study of lynching published in 1929, Walter White noted that although the number of persons killed yearly declined slowly the sadistic brutality of the lynch mobs seemed to increase. Thus, the intensity of individual horrors offset the reduction in the number of murders committed. Certainly the Holbert case could be cited as an example of this trend.

But the death of an obscure Southern black rarely aroused significant amounts of public support for real reform. It took a major *Northern* outbreak of white violence to accomplish this. One of the most far-reaching racial incidents in American history took place in Springfield, Illinois, in 1908. The three-day lynch-riot shocked the nation.

Again the situation involved the charge of rape of a white woman, the alleged perpetrator being black. A woman named Mabel Hallam accused George Richardson of raping her. Actually Mrs. Hallam lied about Richardson to cover up an

---

10 Account from the Vicksburg, Mississippi, *Evening Post,* in Walter White, *Rope and Faggot* (New York: Arno Press, 1969), pp. 35–36.
11 *New York Times,* February 8, 1904, p. 2.

affair with a white man. Later she admitted the lie to a grand jury, but before the truth caught up with the situation, a white mob became infuriated and lynched two blacks. One of them, a man named Scott Burton, was killed while attempting to defend his home and family from a mob.

A two-day rampage followed during which no black in the city of Springfield, inside or outside his home, remained safe. On the second day the mob committed an outrage which defies belief. William Donegan, eighty-four years old and black, was sitting on his porch in a chair. Well-to-do, respected, and owner of half a block of real estate, he had once been a friend of Abraham Lincoln. Approximately one hundred whites seized the old man, dragged him across the street and hanged him to a tree. Militiamen intervened and cut him down, but he died the next day. The mob shouted that one of Donegan's "crimes" was that "he owned too much property for a nigger."[12] The other Donegan crime? He had been peacefully married to a white woman for over thirty years.

The city's black population began to flee, leaving their life's possessions behind them. Many streamed to Chicago. The mob burned the homes of the fugitives. In the end about one half the black population, some two thousand persons, had left. The city government of Springfield increased the exodus by firing about fifty blacks, who had long served in menial functions, on the grounds that their continued public employment might inflame the white mobsmen.

A white journalist from Chicago, William E. Walling, and his wife, covered the lynch-riot for his newspaper and reported, with astonishment, that white Springfield, almost to a man, defended the mobs and insisted that the blacks deserved their treatment. Whites repeatedly told the Wallings that "the niggers came to think they were as good as we are." The antiblack outbreak took on the flavor of a righteous crusade. The mob was, in fact, led by a white woman, Kate Howard, who came to be referred to as the "Joan of Arc" of Springfield. She later committed suicide apparently from remorse for her part in the vicious rioting.

The *Illinois State Journal* of Springfield seemed to speak with general favor of the race "war" which had occurred. "While all good citizens deplore the consequences of this outburst of the mob spirit, many even of these consider the outburst was *inevitable,* at sometime, from existing conditions, needing only an overt act to bring it from latent existence into active operation.

---

[12] Account of Donegan's daughter in Arna Bontemps and Jack Conroy, *Anyplace But Here* (New York: Hill and Wang, 1968), p. 148.

The implication is clear that conditions, not the populace, were to blame and that many good citizens could find no other remedy than that applied by the mob. It was not the fact of the whites' hatred toward the negroes, but the negroes' own misconduct, general inferiority or unfitness for free institutions that were at fault."[13]

The Springfield riot evoked a substantial outcry elsewhere in the country and led to the creation of one of the most important of all movements for elimination of racial injustice, the National Association for the Advancement of Colored People.

But Springfield remained an ugly blot on the Northern record. Many white Southerners pointed to it as an example of Northern hypocrisy and the Yankee image was further marred by a vicious murder which took place on a Sunday afternoon in a small mill town in eastern Pennsylvania. Walter White presents some interesting statistics which suggest that American communities that contain a high percentage of foreign born have been especially vulnerable to violent friction between whites and blacks. Coatesville, Pennsylvania, in 1911 bears out White's generalization.

Zachariah Walker, a black laborer who had recently moved into Coatesville seeking work in the steel mills, did some drinking on a Saturday afternoon. He went out walking with his big pistol stuck in his belt. A white worker met him in a woods, rushed into town, unhurt, but with the story that Walker tried to hold him up and then shot at him as he ran away.

Edgar Rice, a company policeman at one of the steel mills, went into the woods to investigate. Several more shots rang out and Rice emerged bleeding profusely. He died without telling what happened. Walker ran, hid in a tree, and tried to commit suicide when a mob formed around the base of the tree. He fell to the ground bleeding heavily from his self-inflicted pistol wound. He was taken to the local hospital and chained to the bed; one policeman stood guard.

Rice, a well-known figure in town, was active in church work, had a son in the navy and a reputation for fairness. He proved to be a popular cause for the mob. The local police chief aided the vigilantes by not reinforcing the guard at the hospital. After Walker was pulled out of his bed, with part of the bedstead still handcuffed to his leg, the chief merely questioned the nurses at the hospital and then went home. He made no effort to recapture his prisoner. The mob took Walker to a field to lynch him. The historian of the awful happening, Eric F. Goldman, describes

---

[13] Editorial in *Illinois State Journal* in Gilbert Osofsky, *The Burden of Race: A Documentary History of Negro-White Relations in America* (New York: Harper & Row, 1967), pp. 203-4.

the climax scene, at which Walker was burned alive, in the following words: "Most of the route was uphill. Often the Negro was dumped in the road and men and boys forced him to crawl by kicks and the jabs of shotguns, pitchforks, and poles. When he collapsed, more kicks and jabs brought him to his hands and knees again. Walker resisted little now. Most of the time he moaned and begged to be shot. Occasionally, when being carried, he lay quietly, his lips moving in what seemed to be a prayer.

"With every passing minute the mob increased in size. Men, women, and children—the total crowd was almost half female— came running from the hesitant group at the hospital, from Coatesville, and from surrounding areas. As the number mounted close to five thousand, the noise tore through the mists in great snarling waves. 'Burn the nigger.' 'Lynch the beast.' 'Burn him. Burn him. Burn him.' Along the way somebody gave the mob its favorite. A voice rang out: 'Last night you were in Coatesville and you murdered a policeman. Tonight you will be in a fiery furnace and tomorrow you will be in hell.' Over and over again the crowd chanted: 'Tonight you'll be in a fiery furnace, tomorrow you'll be in hell.' "

When he was finally on the pile for burning and someone touched a match to the straw, Walker cried out: "For God's sake, give a man a chance. I killed Rice in self-defense. . . . Don't give me a crooked death because I'm not white."

But the lynching went on without pause. "As the flames crackled seven and ten feet high, the mood relaxed. The dance around the fire turned into a laughing caper, joined in by small boys and girls. There were cheers, pleasant cheers, like the cheering at a baseball game people remembered. 'Very much of a social affair,' resembling a big 'carnival,' others said. On the outer fringes of the crowd, where farm roads cut in automobiles pulled up with trimly dressed men and women, most of the women demurely holding motor veils over the lower part of their faces. The thousands just stood, chatting, pointing out this or that happening around the flaming mound, reaching across to shake hands with a friend.

"There was camaraderie and thoughtfulness, and chivalry too. Near the fire, the reporter of the Coatesville *Record* observed, 'there was no loud talking, no profanity,' and the 'utmost deference' was shown to women. The leaders would stop stoking the flames to doff their hats to some female friend they recognized. In the crowd men stepped aside to provide women a better position or led them to a place of vantage. Fathers and mothers hoisted children to their shoulders."

Near the end, "with a desperate heave, Zachariah Walker

burst up through the wood and started to drag himself off the pile. Charred flesh hung from his body; the foot of the bedstead had somehow come loose but the iron chain glowing red, clung to his right leg. Pitchforks, poles, and shotguns jabbed him back. The crowd cheered.

"Again Walker tried. This time the leaders let him get completely off the logs, work himself to the lane, and start fumbling to get over a broken part of the fence. Then, with hoots of derision, they looped a rope around his neck, half pulled and half threw him back on the flames. The cheers were louder than ever.

"With a superhuman heave and a terrible scream, the Negro hurled himself to the edge of the pyre. Fence rails and gun butts went into action. Men bashed him in the face and across the body, and he fell back into the center of the fire. The cheers were thunderous.

"Zachariah Walker was barely visible now. He lay a flaming crumple, shrieking. Soon the shrieks softened to moans. Then the moans stopped. Some twenty minutes after the first straw was lit, about 10:30 this summer Sunday evening, all was quiet on the pyre except the softening crackle of the flames."[14]

Walker's death paralleled that of many unfortunate blacks who incurred the hatred of a lynch mob. Samuel Petty of Leland, Mississippi, was the third of three blacks to die by violence during the same week in February 1914. Petty allegedly killed a Deputy Sheriff named Charles W. Kirkland.

An eyewitness described the lynch scene in these words: "The news spread like wildfire and in twenty minutes the entire white population was armed and heading for the cabin [where Petty lived]. I looked in every direction and could see men and mere boys, some not over twelve years old, carrying rifles, shotguns, pistols and, in fact, every imaginable thing that would shoot. They were acting as though there was an Army of Negroes to be taken.

"[Petty] . . . submitted to arrest by the mob, which by this time numbered about 400. Placing a rope around his neck he was led to the center of the town and in the presence of women and children they proceeded to hold a conference as to the kind of death that should be meted out to him. Some yelled to hang him; some to burn him alive. It was decided in a few minutes.

"Willing hands brought a large dry-goods box, placed it in the center of the street; in it was straw on which was poured a tub of oil; then the man was lifted with a rope around his neck and

---

[14] Condensed from "Summer Sunday," by Eric F. Goldman. ©Copyright 1964 by American Heritage Publishing Co., Inc. Reprinted by permission from *American Heritage*, June 1964.

placed in this box head down, and then another tub of oil was poured over him. A man from the crowd deliberately lit a match and set fire to the living man. While in this position the flames shot up at great height.

"The crowd began to yell as the flames shot upward. In an instant the poor creature managed to lift himself out of the box, a mass of flames. He was fighting the flames with his hands in an effort to shield his face and eyes, and in this condition attempted to run. The crowd allowed him to run to the length of the rope, which was held by willing hands, until he reached a distance of about twenty feet; then a yell went up from the crowd to shoot. In an instant there were several hundred shots and the creature fell in his tracks.

"The crowd deliberately walked up to the prostrate form and . . . [emptied] their guns into his lifeless body. With the flames still leaping into the air, he was pulled back into the fire that was now roaring with boxes and oil brought out of the different stores by men and boys. Every time they would throw on more oil and boxes the crowd would yell as though they were at a bull fight. Standing about . . . seventy-five feet from the scene I could actually smell the flesh of the poor man as it was being burned. Not a voice was raised in defense of the man. No one attempted to hide their identity. . . . The faces of men whom I knew to be officers of the town lending a willing hand in the burning of this man. No wonder the coroner who held the inquest returned a verdict that the Negro came to his death at the hands of an enraged mob unknown to the jury, because to get a jury in that town they had to get some who participated in the burning. . . .

"After burning the body into ashes the burned bones and ashes were buried in the edge of the street in front of a colored barber shop.

"May God forbid that any other living man will ever see a sight as I witnessed. . . . "[15]

Individual horror stories could be detailed at almost any length. Although the total number of persons lynched in the period 1920–1960 continued to decline each decade, atrocities have blotted the American scene down to the present time. For example, on February 3, 1921, in Camilia, Georgia, a mob lynched James Roland, a well-to-do black farmer, after he refused to dance at gun point for Jason Harvel, a white man.

On April 20, 1923, a crowd in Missouri, including some University of Missouri students, lynched a black janitor accused of

---

[15] Account from Cleveland *Gazette*, July 22, 1905, in Leslie H. Fishel, Jr., and Benjamin Quarles, eds., *The Black American: A Documentary History* (Glenview, Ill.: Scott, Foresman and Co., 1970), pp. 374–75.

assaulting the daughter of the chairman of the German department. James Scott pleaded his innocence while the mob put a
rope around his neck, which was then tied to the undergirding of
a bridge. His pleas evoked sympathy and the crowd began to
have second thoughts. Suddenly a strong student lifted Scott
and pitched him over the rail. He died instantly of a broken
neck. Later investigations established his innocence.

On October 19, 1933, 3,000 white persons in Princess Anne,
Maryland, overpowered fifty state troopers and lynched George
Armwood, a black accused of attacking a white woman. They
dragged his body through the streets and burned it in the town
square.

On March 26, 1944, a mob murdered a sixty-six-year-old black
minister in Amite County, Mississippi. His "crime" was in hiring
a lawyer to protest against losing his farm. The farm, although
debt free, had a title issue involving an oil lease sought by some
aggressive whites.

On July 26, 1946, in Monroe, Georgia, two black couples
rode in a car toward the farm of Loy Henderson who had just
hired them. One of the blacks, George Dorsey, had recently been
honorably discharged after serving five years in the army during
World War II.

A mob of whites stopped the car and charged one of the men
with the stabbing of his former employer, another white farmer.
The vigilantes forced both men from the car and when the wives
began to scream, a leader ordered the mob to "Get those damned
women too." The mob led the four a short distance down a side
road and killed them. According to the news accounts "at least
60 bullets were pumped into the bodies. . . . "[16]

During 1953 and 1954 no lynchings were reported and the
Tuskegee Statistics Center issued a statement of commendation.
*The Washington Post* judged there was "good reason to believe
that having wiped out this offense to American civilization, the
states will continue to maintain their new record."[17]

But the next year Emmitt Till, a fourteen-year-old Chicago
boy was lynched for "wolf whistling" at a white woman in a
store in Greenwood, Mississippi. His body eventually rose to the
surface of the Tallahatchie River.

The horror of any one murder renders the national statistics on
lynching even more shocking. Since 1880 more than 4,700 Americans have been lynched by mobs of various sizes. Of this total
some 3,400 have been black and approximately 1,300 white. Inas-

---

16 *New York Times* account, July 27, 1946, pp. 1, 32.
17 Editorial in *Washington Post* ,January 2, 1954, in Ralph Ginzburg, ed.,
*100 Years of Lynching* (New York: Lancer Books, 1969), p. 240.

much as blacks have, during this period, totaled approximately 10 per cent of the nation's population the ugly reality of white racism in America becomes clear. If white supremacist views had not distorted the issue, the black percentage would have been only 130 lynchings. Moreover, brutal, illegal acts tend to breed brutal illegal acts. Many of the 1,300 whites lost their lives through the pattern of violence established by the lynching of blacks; many whites suffered the accusation "nigger lover."

Not surprisingly, the states of the deep South have led in the lynching of humans. The record shows the following states at the top of the list: Mississippi (574), Georgia (530), Texas (493), Louisiana (491), and Alabama (347). The five states at the bottom of the statistics list are: Delaware (1), New York (2), New Jersey (3), Wisconsin (6), and Nevada (6). Arizona, Nevada, Idaho, South Dakota, and Wisconsin have lynched whites but not blacks.

The really *honor* states, in which no lynching of a white or a black has been recorded, are the six New England states—Maine, New Hampshire, Vermont, Massachusetts, Connecticut, Rhode Island—and the new state of Hawaii.

The 1950's and 1960's have been relatively quiet with few lynchings taking place anywhere in the country. However, bigot groups have intimidated, whipped, and mutilated many persons and a few really dramatic lynchings have taken place. The events of the summer of 1964 in Philadelphia, Mississippi, alone attest that lynching has not ended in America. The deaths of three young civil rights workers, Michael Schwerner, Andrew Goodman, and James Chaney demonstrate the continued strength of racist thought.

William Bradford Huie, a courageous white Alabaman, has written a powerful, detailed account of the Philadelphia lynchings in his *Three Lives for Mississippi;* Don Whitehead, in his *Attack on Terror: The FBI Against the KKK in Mississippi,* has published a study of the FBI's successful exposure of the part played by the Ku Klux Klan in the killings. The events suggest among other things the extent to which some "peace officials" and "officers of justice" sustain white racism in America.

Huie begins his book by illustrating the white supremacy terrorist mentality which could plan and carry out a brutal lynching like the action in Neshoba County in the summer of 1964. The castration of Edward Aaron, a "quiet, slender, peaceable citizen" from Barbour County in Alabama, demonstrates bigotry in practice. Aaron, who was thirty-four years old in 1957, had served honorably with the Quartermaster Corps at the end of World War II, had never been in jail, had never led a civil rights movement, and had never offended anyone in his life.

Unfortunately for Aaron, Bart Floyd was in the process of proving his right to a proper position in the local KKK unit which included Jesse Mabry, who in 1957 received publicity for attacking Nat "King" Cole during the latter's singing appearance in Birmingham. Floyd said he was willing to "get nigger blood on his hands."

Six KKK leaders saw Aaron walking along a country road. They chased away his girl, jumped him and threw him into the back of a car for a ride to their clubhouse some six miles away. They brought Aaron in, never asked his name, addressed him only as "nigger" or "black son-of-a-bitch." They beat him to his knees and refused to permit him to stand erect. In this position they kicked, slugged, and verbally abused him for about half an hour.

Repeatedly they asked questions like "You think any nigger is as good as a white man?" "You think you're as good as I am?" "You ever hear of a nigger-loving communist named Earl Warren?" "You think nigger kids should go to school with white kids?" "You got a right to vote?" "Use a white man's toilet?"[18]

Finally they decided that Floyd would either kill or castrate him. Aaron pleaded that neither be done but Floyd castrated him while the others held him down, Floyd then doused the mutilated areas with turpentine before the gang took the victim to a road-side, dumped him out bleeding profusely, and drove off. Aaron had a further agonizing moment when they returned to pick up the paper cup that contained the souvenirs of Floyd's proof of manhood, left on the roadside by mistake while they were throwing Aaron out of the trunk of the car.

The police found Aaron staggering along the road more dead than alive. They took him to a Veterans Hospital and eventually he lived, although merely a shell of a real human being. The case got to the courts and four of the men were imprisoned after two of the Klansmen turned state's evidence and received suspended sentences. Their early release from twenty-year terms followed George Wallace's election to the governorship of Alabama in 1963.

Almost any action to maintain racial supremacy can be justified by this type of approach to human relations and this mentality lies behind the lynching of Schwerner, Goodman, and Chaney. They were killed in Mississippi, then governed by a man known as a racial "moderate" who nevertheless insisted in many of his campaign speeches that NAACP stood for "Niggers, Apes, Alligators,

18 William Bradford Huie, *Three Lives for Mississippi* (New York: Signet, 1968), pp. 12–17. (First published by New American Library, New York, 1965.)

Coons, and Possums." He received a large vote but most white Mississippians found him "soft" on civil rights after Governor Ross Barnett, the hero of the effort to block James Meredith from entering Ole Miss in 1962. Mississippi voters returned the governor's office to a more traditional leader with the selection of John Bell Williams in 1968.

Schwerner, Goodman, and Chaney offended white racism by engaging in a variety of small-scale efforts to get black citizens in Mississippi to register and vote. After the three civil rights workers disappeared, the FBI spent forty-four days trying to find the bodies. During this time virtually no Mississippi "peace officer" did anything but make fun of the federal "invasion." At one point two FBI agents were dragging a creek in the blazing sun. Three Mississippi "peace" officers sat in the shade on the bank and chuckled. Finally one of them shouted, "If you want to find that goddam nigger, why don't you just float a relief check out on top of the water? That black sonofabitch 'll reach up and grab it."[19]

Deputy Sheriff Cecil Price and Sheriff Lawrence Rainey of Neshoba County, Mississippi, are Christian men who felt that they were doing right. So did the several dozen other whites who participated in the lynching and so did the thousands of whites across the South and the nation who secretly felt good about the lynching. ("It serves them right. I'm against violence, but those who come in from outside to stir up trouble will find it.")

Schwerner, the leader from New York, had been marked for death by local Klansmen in two counties. Goodman and Chaney happened to be with him when he went to investigate the burning of a Negro church. The day was Sunday, June 21, 1964.

The three were arrested by Deputy Sheriff Price and two state troopers and jailed on the charge they had broken the speed limit. But the jailing merely supplied the necessary time for the exterminators to lay final plans. Sam Bowers, leader of the lynch effort, later told friends that he was pleased about the killing of Schwerner because "it was the first time the Christians had planned and carried out the execution of a Jew."[20]

Schwerner, a social worker, went to Mississippi because he felt that it was the front line of the real civil-rights war. His zeal may have been misplaced, but what American can be properly termed an outsider anywhere in the country? His actions involved peaceful citizen contacts. He ran a Community Center which held biracial classes in such nonrevolutionary activities as cooking and

19 Ibid., p. 25. This summary account of the Philadelphia murders owes much to Huie's treatment.
20 Ibid., p. 29.

sewing; he also taught unlettered blacks how to register and vote.

The white citizens in Meridian, Mississippi, harassed the Community Center, but about fifty young people, white and black, struggled to improve racial relations. White women mainly used the tactic of tying up the Center telephone lines with threatening, abusive, and obscene calls. But the men planned more decisive moves. Among other actions they burned more than two dozen churches owned by congregations of blacks.

Most Klan meetings are opened with a prayer. Klansmen and other bigots believe they are patriotic Americans. Whitehead concluded that "perhaps the most frightening aspects of the Klan's resurgence in the early 1960's were the elements of religious fanaticism and super-patriotism that were part of the movement. [They] . . . justified the terrorism with the appalling argument that Klansmen were merely carrying out 'God's will' and that no guilt attached to attacks on Negroes and Jews and those they chose to call communists."[21] Deputy Sheriff Price doubtless felt he did right to hold Schwerner, Goodman, and Chaney until after dark, only releasing them when the lynch trap had been set.

One of the forty vigilantes boasted during the early part of the evening: "When the night's over they'll know how Mississippi stands. They're not gonna cram niggers into our schools or restaurants and no more niggers are gonna vote in Mississippi. Martin Luther King may run the rest of the country, but he ain't gonna run Mississippi. And every Communist-atheist-nigger-loving-bearded Jew sonofabitch who comes down here looking for trouble is gonna find it."[22]

About 10:15 the three were released from jail and then caught again by the lynch mob after a wild chase. Chaney, who drove the station wagon in the getaway attempt, knew the area well. He turned on a side road and would have escaped had he not seen that one of the trailing vehicles was a police car with the dome light flashing. The three civil rights workers pulled over only to provide Deputy Sheriff Price with his opportunity to lead the lynch sequence which followed. The mob pulled them from the car chanting "Ashes to ashes, Dust to dust, If you'd stayed where you belonged, You wouldn't be here with us." One said, "So you wanted to come to Mississippi? Well, now we're gonna let you stay here with us." Before shooting Schwerner a man with a pistol shouted, "You still think a nigger's as good as I am?"[23]

---

21 Don Whitehead, *Attack on Terror: The FBI Against the KKK in Mississippi* (New York: Funk & Wagnalls, 1970), p. 313.
22 William Bradford Huie, *Three Lives for Mississippi* (New York: Signet, 1968), p. 106.
23 Ibid., p. 118.

They killed Goodman without a word. Chaney fought and tried to break away. His assassin shouted, "Save one for me!" He pumped three shots into Chaney and then remarked, "At least I killed me a nigger."[24] The murderers used a bulldozer to bury the bodies in an earth dam. All forty participants swore themselves to secrecy; they agreed that anyone who talked would be killed by the rest.

The Federal Bureau of Investigation began an intensive search for the killers which pitted the strength and prestige of the FBI against the undercover apparatus of terror constructed by the KKK. The power struggle revealed the continuing brutality against black people committed by white citizens of the area. After a month of effort the FBI arrested a number of persons for violations of the civil rights of blacks over an extended period of time. Some of the Klansmen were also police officers. After they had been indicted and released on bail, one bystander scoffed at the federal action with the words, "All that fuss over a few niggers."[25]

Eventually several Klansmen began to talk to the federal officers about the Philadelphia murders. After the forty-four-day search, one informer directed federal officials to the earth dam and they dug up the bodies. Deputy Sheriff Price was, at the last, very attentive. A photographer snapped his picture as he helped to lift the partly decomposed corpses into a station wagon for the trip to the morgue.

Schwerner's wife, Rita, wanted her husband buried next to Chaney in a Mississippi cemetery but she could not arrange it. Although the three civil rights workers were buried side by side for forty-four days in an unmarked earth dam they had to be segregated after "proper" burial.

Mississippi could find no cause to indict anyone for the crime of murder, though clear evidence had been advanced by informers. More than three years later, the federal government tried eighteen men for "conspiring to violate the civil rights" of the victims. The maximum penalty is ten years in jail and a fine of $5,000.

The trial included testimony from many persons variously involved in events leading to the conspiracy but no witness supplied a more moving account than an elderly black woman who had been caught up in a Klan attack during a church burning. The assault occurred when some Klansmen thought an innocent meet-

---

24 Ibid., p. 157.
25 Don Whitehead, *Attack on Terror: The FBI Against the KKK in Mississippi* (New York: Funk & Wagnalls, 1970), p. 174.

ing on church business included plans to aid the civil rights workers. The court room exchange went as follows:

Q. "And then what happened?"

A. "Well . . . he flashed his flashlight in [my husband's] face. He says, 'What kind of meeting is this you having out here?' "

Q. "Who said that?"

A. "This man with the flashlight. . . . He told him to cut his lights off. He said, 'What kind of a meeting . . . you having here?' He said, 'Official leaders and stewards meeting.' He said, 'Where are your guards?' He says, 'We don't have guards in our church meeting.' He said, 'You are a damn lie . . . get out of this car.' And, well, he snatched him out of the car."

Q. "Is that your husband?"

A. "My husband."

Q. "Then what happened?"

A. "Well, after he cut his lights off, and [this man] snatched him out of the car, he says, 'Where your guards?' He says, 'We don't have any guards.' And then they began to slug him. He says, 'You better say something, say where your guards are. If you don't, we will kill you.' And they began slugging him and he didn't say anything."

Q. "Were there other men present?"

A. "They was."

Q. "Were they white or Negro?"

A. "They were white."

Q. "Then what happened?"

A. "Well, he walked up to me, this man did. He says, 'Old woman, what is this you got in this purse?' He says, 'Get out of this car.' And he snatched me out and snatched my purse and searched my purse."

Q. "And then what happened?"

A. "Well, it was a man standing over there, he says, 'What do you find?' He says, '. . . nothing but Sunday School literature! . . .' He threw my purse back in the car."

Q. "Then what happened?"

A. "Well, then they begin to search my husband."

Q. "Who is they?"

A. "Just a bunch of people. They . . . made him get up to the car and stretch his hands up over the car and searched him."

Q. "After you were taken out of the car what happened?"

A. "Well . . . he walked me a little piece down the road, and I was standing there."

Q. "And what happened?"

A. "I was looking kindly east, and he says, 'Turn back this way.' That was in the direction of where my husband was."

Q. "All right."

A. "They were still beating my husband and I was praying."

Q. "Go ahead."

A. "I was praying very hard. I was just praying, saying, 'Lord have mercy! Lord have mercy! Don't let them kill my husband!' "

Q. "Just tell the Court and jury what happened."

A. "And then after that I heard a voice. Sound like a woman scream down the road just a little piece below me. Then a man walked up with a club, and I was continue saying, 'Lord have mercy!' He drew back to hit me, and I asked would he allow me to pray. This one was on the right, and one was on the left. The one on the right says, 'If you think it will do you any good, you had better pray.' The one on the left says, 'It's too late to pray.' . . . and so . . . I fell on my knees and I begin to pray. And as I prayed, I just said, 'Father, I stretch my hands to Thee. I stretch my hands to Thee. No other help I know.' "

Q. "And then what happened?"

A. "He said, 'Leave him living.' . . . Well, then I went to my husband. He was laying on the ground. I lifted him up a second time to his knees, and he just flopped back to the ground."

Q. "And then what did you do?"

A. "Well, I pulled my husband up, best I could, and he staggered to the car."

Q. "Were these men still there?"

A. "They were."

Q. "And what did you do then?"

A. "Well, he lent up against the car for a while trying to study hisself. Then he tried to drive home."

Q. "And did he drive home?"

A. "Yes, sir. Some way he did."[26]

Schwerner, Goodman, and Chaney had been investigating this incident when Deputy Sheriff Price arrested them. The jury in a compromise verdict, found seven of the conspirators guilty, including Price and Sam Bowers, the Klan leader who masterminded the affair but was not present at the execution scene. Appeal after appeal followed. Not until February, 1970, after final review by the United States Supreme Court, did the murderers actually begin serving time on terms which ranged from three to ten years in length.

Walter White, writing forty years ago, saw the future in America's lynch-blotted past. "Lynching," he wrote, "rule by rope and faggot and tar-bucket instead of by orderly and civilized

---

26 From *Attack on Terror* by Don Whitehead, pp. 271–73. Copyright © 1970 by Don Whitehead. Reprinted with permission of Funk & Wagnalls, publishers.

processes—has far too long been a curse to America and an affront to decency and humanity. Against it is needed a larger, more active, more valiant and more articulate public opinion to restore sanity, truth and the reign of law. If that organized opinion and action are not forthcoming, sad and terrible days, not only for the lynching states, but for all of America, seem inevitable."[27]

No fair assessment of the white response to black emancipation in America can overlook the intimidating power of the violently repressive force which the white majority has applied to the black minority. The color line in America has indeed been, in Lerone Bennett's words, a "long red line of violence."[28]

---

[27] Walter White, *Rope and Faggot* (New York: Arno Press, 1969), p. 226.
[28] Lerone Bennett, Jr., *Black Power U.S.A.* (Chicago: Johnson Publishing Co., 1967), p. 336.

# Early Equal-Rights Movements

# 5

AMERICAN whites generally exhibit considerable confusion regarding the nature of the black experience in this country. Stereotypes and false assumptions cloud the vision of members of both races, of course. But blacks, moving constantly within a white majority, have more opportunities to sort out the contrasting details of first- and second-class citizenship. One of the many hangups which confuse whites in their analysis of the race problem in America involves the matter of black efforts to break out of the mold of second-class citizenship.

Most whites assume that the country is made up entirely of minority group persons, all of whom have risen, mostly by their own drive. "Why not the blacks? If they had sufficient ambition they could gain whatever they sought! Look at the Irish, for example." This line of criticism insists, moreover, that black leadership has been weak and cites evidence which suggests that black organizations have failed in their purpose.

The first perspective overlooks the special nature of the black situation in America; the second speaks too little knowledge of the actual facts of black organization, leadership, and pressure for change. White Americans ignore or do not know that a great many *ad hoc* and long-range attempts to end racially based second-class citizenship have been made, sometimes by whites and blacks together but frequently by blacks working alone. None of these attempts has succeeded fully. All have helped a bit.

The first major effort to form a black organization which would effectively combat lynching and Jim Crowism, was called the Afro-American League. T. Thomas Fortune, militant editor of the *New York Age* and author of several basic books on blacks in labor and in politics, led the first national convention which met in Chicago in 1889. More than a hundred delegates, all black, formed the League into a working group dedicated to the cause of equal rights. The League later became known as the Afro-American Council.

The Afro-American League, its membership made up almost entirely of blacks, attempted to reduce the pressures of second-class citizenship during an era when no public authority, federal or state, consistently favored equal opportunity. But the League faced great internal problems as well as external opposition. Booker T. Washington exercised control, always pushing the League in the direction of "moderation," as he defined it. Militants like Du Bois, William Monroe Trotter, George Forbes, and others fought the "Tuskegee machine," but for the most part lost out. Washington's approach appealed to whites because it avoided confrontation.

Externally, the League in the 1890's faced insuperable odds. White America monolithically opposed moves toward equality, whether advanced by blacks or whites. The Afro-American League gradually drowned in the bloody record of the most lynch-marred decade in our national history. Although it lived past the turn of the century the organization was rendered ineffective by its internal and external conflicts.

A different organization rose to take its place. Black women began to play a leading part in the struggle for equal rights for a particular and painful reason. The most suppressed segments of a culture tend to produce a disproportionate percentage of the prostitutes used by that society. Leading black women, in 1895, formed the National Association of Colored Women under the motto, "Lifting As We Climb." The society attempted to assist wayward girls and to perform other charitable functions. Leaders like Mary Church Terrell and Josephine St. Pierre Ruffin exerted increasingly militant influence through the NAACW. As the decade ran its dreadful course Ida Wells Barnett added her tireless antilynch efforts to the work of her black compatriots. A small woman with tremendous drive and an uncompromising outlook, she personally launched the Anti-Lynching League and supplied it with much of its thrust. Her verbal assaults on man's inhumanity to man carried modern overtones. Any Black Panther would be proud to take her advice on self-defense. "A Winchester rifle," she wrote, "should have a place of honor in every black home, and it should be used for that protection which the law refuses to give. When the white man who is always the aggressor knows he runs as great a risk of biting the dust every time his Afro-American victim does, he will have greater respect for Afro-American life. The more the Afro-American yields and cringes and begs," she concluded, "the more he is insulted, out-raged and lynched."[1]

Beyond the women's organizations, accommodationists and militants fought to determine the course of black resistance to white oppression. The continuing contest between the moderates led by Washington, and the radicals led by Du Bois increasingly paralyzed the black minority. Du Bois long tried to avoid an open break, but other militants felt no such constraint. William Monroe Trotter emerged as an uncompromising fighter for true equality. Repeatedly he clashed with Washington and anyone else who took a cautious stance. In 1903 Trotter, his sister, and two others, Bernard Charles and Martin Granville, heckled Washington so vigorously at a Boston meeting that the police were called. Authorities fined Granville and jailed Trotter. Du Bois, writing in his influential *The Souls of Black Folk*, published in 1903, said, "Easily the most striking thing in the history of the American Negro since 1876 is the ascendancy of Mr. Booker T. Washington."[2] Trotter, and eventually Du Bois, sought to combat the Washington influence through the Niagara Movement.

The Movement took its name from Niagara, Canada, the city to which the leaders of a 1905 meeting adjourned from Buffalo, New York, after failure to get equal treatment in American hotels. Niagara also had symbolic value as one of the major terminal points of the underground railroad before the Civil War. In comparatively mild language the leaders issued a first Declaration of Principles opposing second-class citizenship in all its aspects. In earnest words the Declaration states, "The Negro race in America, stolen, ravished and degraded, struggling up through difficulties and oppression, needs sympathy and receives criticism, needs help and is given hindrance, needs protection and is given mob-violence, needs justice and is given charity, needs leadership and is given cowardice and apology, needs bread and is given a stone. This nation will never stand justified before God until these things are changed."[3]

The following year the Niagara group met at Harpers Ferry, West Virginia, and adopted a more militant line. They de-

---

1 Ida Wells Barnett, "Southern Horrors," *On Lynching* (New York: Arno Press, 1969), p. 23.
2 W. E. B. Du Bois, *The Souls of Black Folk* (Greenwich, Conn.: Fawcett Publications, 1967), p. 42. (Originally published by A. C. McClurg, Chicago, 1903.)
3 Declaration of Principles of the Niagara Movement in Gilbert Osofsky, *The Burden of Race: A Documentary History of Negro-White Relations in America* (New York: Harper & Row, 1967), pp. 217–18.

nounced second-class citizenship and made a dramatic, barefooted march to the firehouse where John Brown's raiders staged their final defense in 1859. Du Bois wrote, "We will not be satisfied to take one jot or tittle less than our full manhood rights. We claim for ourselves every single right that belongs to a freeborn American, political, civil, and social; and until we get these rights we will never cease to protest and assail the ears of America. The battle we wage is not for ourselves alone, but for all true Americans. It is a fight for ideals, lest this, our common fatherland, false to its founding, become in truth the land of the Thief and the home of the Slave—a by-word and a hissing among the nations for its sounding pretensions and pitiful accomplishment."[4]

They then made five demands:
1. Full manhood suffrage.
2. Freedom from all "un-American, undemocratic and silly discriminations in public facilities."
3. Complete freedom of association.
4. Enforcement of laws equally on rich and poor, black and white.
5. Full education for all on an equal basis with the federal government playing a major role.

They denounced the spread of Jim Crow laws with the powerful statement: "Never before in the modern age has a great and civilized folk threatened to adopt so cowardly a creed in the treatment of its fellow-citizens, born and bred on its soil. Stripped of verbiage and subterfuge and in its naked nastiness, the new American creed says: fear to let black men even try to rise lest they become the equals of the white. And this is the land that professes to follow Jesus Christ. The blasphemy of such a course is only matched by its cowardice."

They closed the second declaration with insistence that "We do not believe in violence, neither in the despised violence of the raid nor the lauded violence of the soldier, nor the barbarous violence of the mob; but we do believe in John Brown, in that incarnate spirit of justice, that hatred of a lie, that willingness to sacrifice money, reputation, and life itself on the altar of right. And here on the scene of John Brown's martyrdom, we reconsecrate ourselves, our honor, our property to the final emancipation of the race. . . ."[5]

In 1907 the Niagara Movement met in Boston and in 1908 at Oberlin, Ohio. All of the meeting places thus had symbolic identification with the original abolitionist movement. The sub-

4 Ibid., p. 219.
5 Ibid., pp. 220–21.

jects discussed and the declarations issued tended to overlap those of the previous year. In a sense the Niagara Movement made little forward motion. Furthermore, William Monroe Trotter kept injecting his fiercely individualistic views in a manner which gave the opposing "moderates" many opportunities to isolate the Niagara people. Despite difficulties the spirit of common endeavor in a desperate cause infused the participants with a deep desire to right past wrongs. The single most important equal rights organization—the National Association for the Advancement of Colored People—grew from their efforts.

All of these early equal-rights initiatives occurred during an era of social change. The Progressive Movement, which began to gain momentum with the rise of the Populist party in 1892 and which was strengthened by the nomination of William Jennings Bryan for the presidency by the Democratic party in 1896 and 1900, gained its greatest single leader in 1901 when a pistol ball took the life of President William McKinley and brought Theodore Roosevelt to power. Roosevelt, assisted by Robert Marion LaFollette, William Jennings Bryan, the muckraking journalists, and others, did much to restructure society and permit the common man to escape from poverty and exploitation. The average American had lost control of his destiny to the great power concentrations of the industrial process. A counterpower had to be found and the progressives effectively used federal authority for this purpose.

How much of their efforts aided blacks? Preliminary evaluation indicates that some small, forward steps may have been taken, but that in the main, the black man was the forgotten figure of the Progressive era. The white racist viewpoint caused the nation to miss another great opportunity to eliminate second-class citizenship. In this missed opportunity, Theodore Roosevelt emerges as a disappointing failure. Perhaps early twentieth-century white America could not have withstood the process of genuine racial change. Yet Roosevelt promised so much and performed so little that the absence of his leadership in this vital area seems tragic indeed.

When entering the White House Roosevelt made the usual "black appointments" but added some additional selections and in general during his first term spoke out for equal rights. He named William D. Crum as Collector of the Port in Charleston, South Carolina, and for a time kept the post office at Indianola, Mississippi, closed because the Negro postmistress had been forced to resign by adverse local reaction. Racism has so many ludicrous aspects. For example, at one point farmers in a small area in Kansas ripped down their mailboxes and announced they would go to the post office for the mail. The reason? A black man had been appointed to serve as rural route mail deliverer. Black Americans took some hope in the Roosevelt leadership and some even referred to him as "our President—the first since Lincoln set us free."[6]

His most celebrated action resulted in a heated controversy from which he emerged a more cautious actor. Shortly after becoming president, Roosevelt invited Booker T. Washington to lunch at the White House. The press reflected widely varied views, but the general tone opposed this innovation in American social custom. One editor "deplored" the president's taste and "distrusted" his wisdom.[7] Another called the luncheon "the most damnable outrage which has ever been perpetrated by any citizen of the United States" and a third argued that the president sought to have "white women . . . receive attentions from Negro men." A prominent politician insisted that the "action of President Roosevelt in entertaining that nigger will necessitate our killing a thousand niggers in the South before they will learn their place again."[8] An anonymous poet wrote, "The Statue of Liberty hung her head;/Columbia dropped in a swoon;/The American eagle drooped and died,/when Teddy dined with a coon."[9] Roosevelt did not again open himself to this type of criticism.

Actually, for all his reformist flair, Roosevelt held to the white supremacist viewpoint. In one public speech he stated that "laziness," "shiftlessness," "vice," and "criminality of every kind" among Negroes were far greater sources of evil to the black race than "all acts of oppression of white men put together."[10] His

---

6 John Hope Franklin, *From Slavery to Freedom* (New York: Alfred A. Knopf, 1969), p. 435.

7 Editorial in the Richmond *Dispatch* in ibid., p. 434.

8 Comments from the Memphis *Scimitar* and the Richmond *Times* in John D. Weaver, *The Brownsville Raid* (New York: Norton, 1970), p. 99.

9 Arna Bontemps and Jack Conroy, *Anyplace But Here* (New York: Hill and Wang, 1968), p. 156.

10 TR speech at Lincoln dinner, Republican Club of New York City, February 13, 1905 in John Hope Franklin and Isidore Starr, *The Negro in 20th Century America: A Reader* (New York: Vintage books, Random House, 1967), p. 82. The tendency of American whites to shift the blame for the entire race problem to blacks can be found in a wide variety of materials. For example, R. W. Shufeldt, in his *The Negro: A Menace to American Civilization* (Boston: Gorham Press, 1907), puts the idea this way: "It is the presence of the negro among us that is responsible for lynching, and not the tastes of our people for such brutal horrors. Among a progressive race, such as the Indo-European in the United States is, it is the effect of their own higher and elevating civilization that as time goes on eliminates crime, bestiality, brutality and all else that is ethically and morally undesirable in man's composition; but when a cultured, advancing, highly plastic and superior race of this kind has introduced among it another race in large numbers characterized by its lack of truthfulness, its bestial sensuality, its morbid criminal characteristics, its mental density and its religious and other superstitions, and its physical repulsiveness, the influence of such an introduc-

view obviously placed additional burdens on the black for self-advancement while ignoring the possible causative relationship between white oppression and alleged nonwhite backwardness. In his Sixth Annual Message to Congress of December 3, 1905, he came close to blaming lynching on Negroes themselves. On still another occasion Roosevelt revealed his basic misconception of the white problem when he said: "I have not been able to think . . . of any solution . . . for the terrible problem offered by the presence of the Negro on this continent."[11] Perfect and full equality did not, apparently, seem to be the answer he sought.

In the Progressive party convention of 1912, Roosevelt denied seats to black delegates from Southern states. Roosevelt rationalized his action with the argument that the exclusion policy would serve to gain Progressive support from Southern whites and reduce the number of controversies that already swirled around the new party. His exclusionist view became a major issue at the party convention. At one point during a discussion caucus, a black spokesman interrupted the colonel to ask where he really stood on the race question. Roosevelt went into some detail in defending his policy on the ground that too often black delegates to national conventions exhibited distinct tendencies to bribery and corruption. The ex-president said that he wanted to see "intelligent and educated negroes, men of the type who are elected in the north, come to the front" to lead their race rather than the "ignorant and debased kind of people that have so often misrepresented them at national gatherings."[12]

Blacks reacted sharply to the Roosevelt sellout; a leading Georgia politician stated, "Ninety-nine percent of the colored people of the South regard the denial of admission into the Progressive Party by Mr. Roosevelt as a greater crime against human liberty than was ever perpetuated by any southern disenfranchising law."[13]

But undoubtedly the most damaging and revealing evidence of

tion is bound to be felt. The case is precisely the same as though we were to introduce into a large boarding-school composed of refined moral, educated, progressive and mentally and physically healthy boys and girls, a lot of new pupils largely given to lying, to thieving, to masturbating and other varieties of sexual looseness, to criminal propensities of various kinds, and other human frailties." (p. 177)

[11] Letter from Roosevelt to Albion W. Tourgee, November 8, 1901 in ibid., pp. 83–84.

[12] *New York Times,* August 7, 1912, p. 2. See also August 6, 1912, p. 2. The letter in which TR spelled out his views in detail was to Julian La Rose Harris, August 1st, 1912, in Elting G. Morison, ed., *The Letters of Theodore Roosevelt,* Vol. 7 (Cambridge, Mass.: Harvard University Press, 1954), pp. 584–90.

[13] Statement of William F. Penn, *New York Times,* September 1, 1912, p. 1.

TR's white-supremacist bias can be found in his handling of the Brownsville, Texas, "riot" of 1906. In a routine move the army stationed three companies of experienced black soldiers at Fort Brown and the townspeople immediately began to show hostility. Incidents multiplied during the month of August. One night someone fired approximately a hundred rounds of ammunition in the town's business district. The shots slightly damaged several buildings, wounded a police lieutenant, and killed a young bartender. Citizens quickly blamed the black soldiers for shooting up the town square.                                                      ,

The commanding officer had in fact been keeping his troops on the base because of tensions in the town. Yet shots had been fired; town leaders presented shells as evidence. Eight and later fourteen residents swore that black soldiers had done the shooting. Contrary evidence indicated the soldiers had been mustered and placed on guard duty shortly after the incident. A dawn inspection of all soldiers' rifles showed that not one appeared to have been fired recently. Petty officers reported that a box of empty shells, used on the rifle range, had disappeared from the porch of one of the barracks. The soldiers could thus have easily been framed by townspeople who wanted to rid themselves of the black troops.

President Roosevelt became involved in the investigation that followed. The white officer in charge could never explain satisfactorily what had actually happened, but agreed that his men must have done the shooting. Roosevelt then discharged the soldiers "without honor," not on the grounds that all had been involved, but on the premise that those who did not take part were covering up for those who had.

The dismissed men included some who had been in the army for fifteen years with distinguished records, including combat service in the Spanish-American War. Six had won Congressional Medals of Honor and thirteen held Certificates of Merit for bravery. One sergeant had served for more than a quarter century and needed only two and a half years to retire on three quarters pay. He had an excellent reputation, including combat time in Cuba and the Philippines. He pleaded for an opportunity to finish his career. "I am now passed half a century," Sanders said to the military court of inquiry, "and I am . . . pleading to this court for mercy . . . because when a man gets to my age there is nobody wants him, and I wish that this court would consider my case to the bottom of their heart. . . ."[14] But the sergeant failed to convince the officers. The discharge removed all pension rights

14 Testimony of Sergeant Sanders in John D. Weaver, *The Brownsville Raid* (New York: Norton, 1970), pp. 95, 244.

as well as military honors and denied the men the right to serve in either the military or the civilian branches of the government.

Senator Joseph B. Foraker of Ohio became convinced that Roosevelt had erred and forced a congressional investigation into the incident. In a highly unusual move for a senator in the president's own party, Foraker introduced a resolution demanding that the president inform the Senate of all details of the situation. Roosevelt became angry and defensive and declared that if Congress passed a law "restoring the discharged men . . . to duty he would seek by other . . . [administrative] means to defeat the law, and failing in that would endeavor to get the Supreme Court to sustain his order of dismissal."[15]

The Roosevelt-Foraker dispute became a major topic in Washington. It erupted during a banquet for public officials sponsored by the Washington press corps. Roosevelt spoke before Foraker and made an emotional defense of his actions against the black soldiers. Foraker responded with a factual talk that brought the newspapermen to their feet cheering. Roosevelt, furious, demanded the floor again and further offended the audience. He received only scattered applause and left after making several highly offensive remarks to those seated around him. One diner heard the president say, "There may have been but two companies of that regiment engaged in that unwholesome business . . . but 'all coons look alike to me.' "[16]

Roosevelt eventually allowed fourteen of the men to return to service, but never admitted fault in his handling of the case. The remaining 153 soldiers suffered as suspects at large, their careers shattered and many occupations closed to them. None of them had been given the normal rights of civilian courts, to confront accusers in public and defend themselves against criminal charges. The commanding officer of the regiment, who carried ultimate responsibility for the men, resumed his career in the army, but he was white.

Roosevelt's leadership failed this crucial test but how many white Americans honestly differed with his actions? The president's move received wide support in a variety of quarters. One congressman went so far as to introduce a bill to bar all blacks from service in the armed forces. The sponsor felt that Roosevelt's dismissal of the black soldiers would be suitably supported by passage of this bill which would rid the army of "dangerous elements."[17]

15 *New York Times,* December 24, 1906, p. 1.

16 Comment by James Watson in John D. Weaver, *The Brownsville Raid* (New York: Norton, 1970), pp. 140–42.

17 *New York Times,* December 5, 1906, p. 3.

William Howard Taft, Roosevelt's Secretary of War and presidential successor, did nothing to correct the injustice to the soldiers. John D. Weaver, the historian of the Brownsville incident, concluded: "The soldiers were never exonerated, and by the time a handful were reinstated in 1910, Brownsville was of so little interest to white newspaper readers that most editors wasted no space on the story. Since then, two generations of youngsters, black and white, have been reared in ignorance of this massive assault by two presidents on the civil rights of one hundred and sixty seven black Americans. They lived and died in the black man's limbo. Alive, they were denied the equity of the white man's justice and, dead, the vindication of his Jim Crow history."[18]

The Springfield, Illinois, lynch-riot of 1908, coming at the end of the Roosevelt era, caused the nation's white and black intellectuals to express deep concern for the "colored problem." To have Lincoln's home town bloodied by such an incident demanded action. Black organizations already in existence became involved in a major new effort to force the nation to eliminate racist practices. A number of white intellectuals, descendants of the abolitionist spirit of the nineteenth century, joined these initiatives. One was William E. Walling, who wrote articles on the Springfield riot. Another was Mary White Ovington, a wealthy New Yorker with humanitarian views. "Either the spirit of the abolitionists, of Lincoln and of Lovejoy, must be revived," Walling wrote, "and we must come to treat the Negro on a plane of absolute political and social equality or Vardaman and Tillman will soon have transferred the Race War to the North. . . . Yet who realizes the seriousness of the situation and what large and powerful body of citizens is ready to come to their aid?"[19] Oswald Garrison Villard, a grandson of William Lloyd Garrison, helped to bring together a powerful nucleus which included Jane Addams, William Dean Howells, and John Dewey.

The new grouping included a majority of the young black radicals of the Niagara Movement, although some, like William Monroe Trotter, opposed involvement on the grounds that too many whites hurt the effort and could not be trusted. Ida Wells Barnett also voiced strong reservations. But the National Association for the Advancement of Colored People took form in 1909 and officers set to work in 1910. Moorefield Storey became the

---

18 John D. Weaver, *The Brownsville Raid* (New York: Norton, 1970), p. 278.
19 William E. Walling, "Race War in the North," in Gilbert Osofsky, *The Burden of Race: A Documentary History of Negro-White Relations in America* (New York: Harper & Row, 1967), p. 244.

white president; W. E. B. Du Bois, the only black officer, served as Executive Secretary. The pattern of an honorary, white president and black executive secretary, has continued to be the policy of the NAACP. Du Bois, a powerful radical, quickly became the moving force of the new organization.

He served as editor and chief writer for *The Crisis*, a magazine which fought to expose America's most shameful social wrongs— lynching and mob violence. Du Bois also influenced the NAACP to initiate court actions of all sorts to undermine legal support of second-class citizenship. The new group flourished; soon chapters had been formed in more than fifty cities. By the start of World War I *The Crisis* reached more than 30,000 persons per month and the legal staff participated in its first case in 1915 when the Supreme Court ruled against "grandfather clause" voting restrictions (*Guinn* v. *United States*). Du Bois left his position at Atlanta University and worked full time to promote the Association. Eventually, with his resignation in 1934, Du Bois became a firm critic of the NAACP accusing it on the one hand of being too moderate on questions of discrimination and on the other too little interested in black separatism. But by then the organization had outgrown its early dependence on Du Bois' powerful personality.

In 1916 the NAACP received a strong boost when the brilliant author James Weldon Johnson became national organizer. Johnson had attended the important NAACP conference at Amenia, New York, earlier in the year and accepted the newly created position of Field Secretary. He proved to be an extremely able spokesman for the new program of racial equality which the NAACP advocated. He also demonstrated keen talent for administration, which resulted in accelerated expansion of the Association structure. Within three years Johnson had increased the number of chapters to more than three hundred, operating in virtually every area of the country, including all parts of the deep South. Later, Walter White supplied strong leadership, particularly with his antilynching efforts. Although the Association has its limitations and was increasingly out of the mainstream of change in the 1960's the NAACP has made great contributions toward elimination of the system of second-class citizenship in the United States. More radical organizations have played an important role from time to time, but establishment of a completely just, color-blind society requires communication between concerned blacks and whites. The NAACP continues to serve in the capacity of a major bridge between the races as well as an effective agent for social change.

In 1911 several small organizations merged to form the National Urban League, which filled a further need for equal-rights leadership. While the NAACP attacked discrimination, largely with legal actions on a broad front, the NUL sought to improve job opportunities and assist blacks to adjust to city living. In addition, the League trained many blacks to serve other blacks through social work. George Edmund Haynes, the first black to receive a degree from the New York School of Social Work, was one of the central figures during the early years of the NUL. And the League attracted significant financial support through the interest of Julius Rosenwald and John D. Rockefeller, Jr. The movement of Southern, rural blacks to Northern cities provided the Urban League with compelling opportunities for usefulness. Its activities expanded rapidly and by World War I it had matured into a major social force among the black minority. E. Franklin Frazier has asserted that within the first decade of its existence the League became the "most important agency in the country in dealing with the mass migration of Negroes to northern cities."[20]

Like the NAACP, the NUL has been too conservative to suit the young militants of the decade of the 1960's. Together, however, these two organizations have assisted endless numbers of deserving blacks. Although their efforts have not destroyed the myth of white supremacy, they have materially reduced the chances of its indefinite continuance.

The list of early equal-rights organizations should include brief mention of William Monroe Trotter's National Equal Rights League and the National Independent Political League. Although the groups accomplished little, they supply a model of the equal-rights organizations of the 1960's—militant, aggressive, all black, and insistent upon freedom now! Trotter was almost incapable of compromise of any sort and could not go the NAACP, NUL, or any conservative, route. Possessed of a brilliant mind, holder of the first Phi Beta Kappa key voted to a black at Harvard, Trotter grew up in a family that refused to accept second-class status. His father inspired, but also embittered him. Trotter's zealousness made him almost impossible to work with in any situation which required a practical compromise.

He dedicated his life to equal rights at once. Under Trotter's influence Boston became the leading center of militant racial thought. Trotter later received credit for shifting W. E. B. Du Bois away from Booker T. Washington and into the radical camp. As Lerone Bennett, Jr., has well put it, "When he couldn't get a

---

20 E. Franklin Frazier, *The Negro in the United States* (New York: Macmillan, 1949), p. 527.

whole loaf, he unhesitatingly turned down a half a loaf. It was typical of the man that he consistently opposed Negro YMCA's and Negro social settlements. In a sense, his life was a long arc of failures; yet, in some respects, it was a splendid triumph. Alone, forgotten by friends, ridiculed by foes, he held fast to one obsessive idea; the complete integration of Negroes into every facet of American life. On his sixty-second birthday, on a night in April, 1934, he jumped or fell to his death from the roof of his boardinghouse in Boston."[21] He deserves more scholarly attention than he has yet received.

Many Americans fail to see the need for aggressive, separatist organizations like Trotter's National Equal Rights League. Politically conscious blacks, however, insist their role is vital, because less aggressive organizations tend to dialogue on questions which admit of no delay. For example, most whites, and some blacks, accept the validity of discussing the *rate* at which first-class citizenship can be "earned" by "deserving" minority group persons. Yet the Declaration of Independence, the Constitution, numerous laws, many court decisions, and large numbers of executive judgments clearly establish that the nation permits only one class of citizenship. Questions regarding the rate, style, militancy, and degree of violence by means of which blacks become accepted fully into first-class citizenship seem important even to more tolerant whites. Yet to socially conscious blacks such questions have no relevancy whatsoever. Anything which has been defined out of the national code, like second-class citizenship, cannot be assessed; no grounds for discussion exist.

Of the early equal-rights organizations probably only the NAACP has received sufficient study. The record, when it has been adequately researched, will doubtless show that shortly after 1900, a tiny fraction of the nation's population determined to take action which would alter the country's future. Conscientious citizens can effect genuine social change even when their number is small and their beginning efforts feeble. The equal-rights revolution of the present decade has roots which reach back to the early years of the century and which stem from the dedication of a high-minded few representative of both races.

---

[21] Lerone Bennett, Jr., *Before the Mayflower* (Baltimore: Penguin Books, 1966), p. 285. (First published in 1962 by Johnson Publishing Co., Chicago.)

# Internal Migration and the
# Making of the Northern Ghetto

# 6

Previous comments on the post-Civil War period, the Jim Crow era, the record of Judge Lynch and early equal-rights movements have stressed racial events in the Southern portion of the country. But no moral judgments should be drawn from this preponderance of evidence from a single geographic area. Prior to World War I the race problem was largely confined to a single region because the majority of American blacks—approximately 90 per cent—lived in the South. From the turn of the century to the present, the white problem in America has increased with the spread of blacks to Northern and Western urban centers. This movement of American blacks toward better opportunities has been called the greatest internal migration in the history of peoples. All such movements involve social pressure and are often accompanied by substantial amounts of friction between groups. The movement of poor white farmers from the dust bowl to California during the 1930's serves as one illustration of an internal migration which had painful but not tragic outcomes. The internal migration of American blacks also brought social pain to the American people but beyond this discomfort lay genuine tragedy. The tragedy came not in the migration itself but in the failure of geography to solve the white problem. Inasmuch as the source of the strife exists in the *minds* of whites, perhaps the failure of real estate to ease racial antagonism should not be surprising.

America has always been a nation on the move. Representatives of all ethnic groups have, from the beginning of the settlement of this continent, pushed restlessly for a better opportunity elsewhere. Throughout the nineteenth century the general pattern involved westward migration to frontier farming states. During the twentieth century the movement has been from rural areas into the cities. In the 1970's approximately 25 per cent of the nation's population moves every year.

But the dimensions of the black migration to the North and West go well beyond the general propensity of Americans to shift their locale. Successive waves of black migration had by the time of World War II brought nearly 2 million blacks from the rural South to the cities of the North and West. From the early nineteenth century onward many white racist spokesmen advocated forcible removal of blacks from the nation as the final solution to the race problem. Outspoken racial bigots openly admitted they desired to make the United States a white man's country but less biased whites with genuine humanitarian concerns, also failed to consider the wishes of black people in advocating forced emigration. Blacks entered the nation prior to virtually all other ethnic groups—before the Irish, the Germans, the Jews, the Italians—yet white American resistance to assimilation of blacks kept alive the separation idea. The American Colonization Society founded Liberia as one expression of the separation idea. President Lincoln still favored this approach during the Civil War, once requesting judgments from the army regarding the logistics involved in removal of all blacks to Africa or the Caribbean.

After the Civil War, as conditions for blacks in the rural South grew worse through sharecropping and peonage, if not actual slavery, many began thinking in terms of an exodus to more hospitable areas. Because racism flourished in Northern states, blacks thought first of moving to the undeveloped lands of the West. Trans-Mississippi land, as yet unpopulated, was being rapidly taken up by Norwegians, Swedes, and Poles. Other eastern Europeans streamed in to farm the prairie, often induced to come through promotional advertising. The federal government at least indirectly supported this trend with the subsidy program for western railroads.

In January 1879, as the idea of black movement to the West drew attention, Senator William Windom from Minnesota introduced a resolution to study the possibility of a federal subsidy for internal migration of blacks. The resolution precipitated a considerable debate in Congress. Southern senators generally opposed the idea as an insult to their region. A few Northern senators favored the idea of black migration not to their own states, but rather to territories of the trans-Mississippi West not near their own borders. Windom felt that Southern rural blacks must enter upon an "exodus" or face "extinction" but he suggested

Arizona, New Mexico, and Indian Territory (Oklahoma) and not his home state of Minnesota.[1] Although the Windom resolution never passed, the migration idea gained strength in the black communities of the South.

Henry Adams of Louisiana and Benjamin Singleton of Tennessee, two ex-slaves, founded a movement in the spring of 1879, which involved a migration sufficiently massive to be called the Year of the Exodus. Adams claimed that nearly 100,000 blacks had been organized to move but only 40,000 blacks left Mississippi, Alabama, Louisiana, and Georgia, for the Midwest, most of them going to Kansas. In some areas black communities grew up almost overnight. Baxter Springs, Nicodemus, Morton City, and Singleton flourished for a time. At first the Kansans welcomed the blacks, but as their numbers increased, the hostility of the whites grew. The destitute migrants had little more than their hands with which to start a new life. Although the black families worked hard their lack of capital placed them at a disadvantage to the whites, who looked upon the newcomers as paupers who might be criminally inclined. Singleton became disgusted and tried to shift his movement toward Canada or Liberia, but with little success.

Efforts to promote internal migration continued, including a subsidy proposition by President Harrison in his annual message of 1889. The Senate debated the subject from time to time, with the majority, mainly Southern senators, opposing migration, because the loss of blacks threatened their region with the economic loss of its laboring class. Senator Henry W. Blair, a militant equal-rights thinker from New Hampshire entered the debates with caustic comments on the treatment blacks received in both the South and West. As noted above, on one memorable occasion, after the Senate had been debating an exodus of blacks to Africa as the solution to the white problem in America, Blair acidly suggested that 10,000 carefully selected white men be sent to Africa and kept there and America's problem would then be solved.

Edwin P. McCabe led another significant exodus in the 1880's. He hoped to make the Oklahoma Territory into an all-black state. The Indians, to whom this territory had been given in perpetuity, treated blacks equally at first but soon resisted immigration. Whites eventually "opened" the territory in 1890 and the "Sooners" ultimately overran the Indians.

The 1890's brought increasingly unjust and violent treatment

---

[1] *Congressional Record*, 45th Congress, 3rd Session, January 16, 1879, p. 483, and February 7, 1879, p. 1077.

to blacks remaining in the South. Leaders began to look at territories outside the United States as possible places of refuge. The Central and South American Immigration Association and Equal Rights League, formed in Kansas in 1893, tried to get support for moves to Latin America. The League failed in its main objective, but W. H. Ellis succeeded in organizing several thousand blacks who moved to the Mexican state of Durango. The black migrants suffered in the severe winter of 1895 and most of them returned to the United States in economic distress. President Cleveland arranged for the federal government to reimburse the railroads which had transported the blacks back to their home area, but no federal aid went to the penniless migrants themselves.

In 1879 some citizens advanced Hawaii as a possible place to establish a black state and in 1903 similar arguments supported the idea of a move to the Philippines. Small numbers of disillusioned American blacks emigrated to Liberia in 1877, 1894, and 1895 aided by the American Colonization Society which continued to struggle toward this solution of the race problem. Its efforts received increased impetus during the 1880's and 1890's through the ardent advocacy of Bishop Henry M. Turner of the African Methodist-Episcopal church. Bishop Turner participated in the Black Reconstruction movement in Georgia but became totally disillusioned with American racial practices and repeatedly urged blacks to migrate to Africa.

During these trying decades only a handful of persons seriously considered the real solution—firm federal action to assist internal black migration and at the same time, insure equal rights in all areas of the nation. The London *Times* once put it correctly, "What is most to be desired is the quiet but firm interposition of the central government to insure the Negro protection and equal justice."[2] This has always been and remains a fundamental ingredient to the solution of the white problem in America.

Exodus to the urban North gained momentum when in 1892 a tiny insect from Mexico provided a factor for change. The boll weevil began to destroy cotton all across the South and rendered the position of the Southern rural black even more untenable. Dependent still upon a single cash crop, the black tenant farmers, ruined in increasing numbers, received no state or national aid.

In 1915 and 1916 the boll weevil and World War I joined together to thrust blacks into the stream of Northern migration. The weevil devastated crops and the war cut off labor supplies from Europe, thus enabling blacks to enter many new jobs in

---

[2] London *Times,* in Arna Bontemps and Jack Conroy, *Anyplace But Here* (New York: Hill and Wang, 1968), p. 64.

Northern war industries. Between 1910 and 1920 the largest cities in the North increased their black population by more than 50 per cent. Some cities made far larger gains; Chicago increased by nearly 150 per cent, Cleveland by more than 300 per cent, and Detroit, which started the decade with a low base, by more than 600 per cent.

Generally the black press advocated a "Great Northern Drive," sincerely believing that only through migration could the black better himself. Robert Abbott's influential *Chicago Defender* spoke for this point of view. Abbott, himself an immigrant from rural Georgia, published William Crosse's "The Land of Hope" in the *Defender,* and other black newspapers reprinted the message.

> *I've watched the trains as they disappeared*
> *Behind the clouds of smoke,*
> *Carrying the crowds of working men*
> *to the land of hope,*
> *Working hard on southern soil,*
> *Someone softly spoke;*
> *Toil and toil and toil and toil,*
> *And yet I'm always broke.*
>
> *On the farms I've labored hard,*
> *And never missed a day;*
> *With wife and children by my side*
> *We journeyed on our way.*
> *But now the year is passed and gone,*
> *and every penny spent,*
> *And all my little food supplies*
> *Were taken 'way for rent.*
>
> *Yes, we are going to the north;*
> *I don't care to what state,*
> *Just so I cross the Dixon Line,*
> *From this southern land of hate,*
> *Lynched and burned and shot and hung,*
> *And not a word is said.*
> *No law whatever to protect—*
> *It's just a "nigger" dead.*
> *Go on, dear brother; you'll ne'er regret;*
> *Just trust in God; pray for the best,*
> *And at the end you're sure to find*
> *Happiness will be thine.*[3]

---

[3] Poem in ibid., p. 163. The discussion of the "Exodus" movement which follows owes much to Bontemps and Conroy. See especially Chapter XI, "The Exodus Train."

All over the South signs like "Farewell—We're Good and Gone," "Bound for the Promised Land," and "Bound for the Land of Hope" expressed black desire for change. The migrants, called "exodusters," sometimes left together by the hundreds. Industrial agents from the North and from the railroads encouraged the migration. Southern business and farm groups opposed it; violence sometimes flared between the conflicting economic interests. On occasion entire black work crews walked off jobs leaving their tools and even their final paychecks behind.

As the exodus continued, the black press issued many instructions to the inexperienced migrants who were entering city environments for the first time. They urged them to stand up and clean up and to be respectable and pleasant, but not subservient. On one occasion the *Defender* advised: "Quit calling the foreman boss. Leave that word dropped in the Ohio River. Also captain, general, and major. We call people up here Mister This and Mister That. When your pay day comes, take it home. Depend on your work to keep you in a job and not the dollar or two you have been used to slipping the foreman. Cut that out. If you are working for $18 keep it.

"Your employer pays the foreman much more than you, and if he has got to graft let him go to the employer. If you can't stay because you don't pay, quit and go somewhere else, or go in person to your employer and complain.

"When you get among white workmen, treat them as you want them to treat you—AS A MAN—not as his inferior. Keep your hand off your hat when you pass men in and around the shop or plant. There is no law that requires you to tip your hat to a man because he is white."[4]

Although conditions up north were by no means ideal, few blacks seriously thought of returning south, except for brief visits. The *Defender* published Sparrell Scott's poem:

### When I Return to the Southland It Will Be

> When lions eat grass like oxen
> And an angleworm swallows a whale,
> And a terrapin knits a woolen sock,
> And a hare is outrun by a snail.
>
> When serpents walk like man,
> And doodle-bugs leap like frogs,
> When grasshoppers feed on hens,
> And feathers grow on hogs

---

4 Ibid., pp. 169–70.

*When Tom cats swim in the air,*
*And elephants roost in the trees,*
*When insects in summer are rare,*
*And snuff can't make you sneeze.*

*When fish live on dry land,*
*When mules on velocipedes ride,*
*And foxes lay eggs in the sand,*
*And women in dress take no pride.*

*When a German drinks no beer,*
*And girls deck in plumes for a dime,*
*When billy goats butt from the rear,*
*And treason is no longer a crime.*

*When the mockingbird brays like an ass,*
*And limburger smells like cologne,*
*When plowshares are made of glass,*
*And the hearts of true lovers are stone.*

*When ideas grow on trees,*
*And wool on cast-iron rams,*
*I then may return to the South,*
*But I'll travel then in a box.*[5]

As the black population in Northern and Western cities increased, the white problem began to emerge in various forms. Resistance to equal employment opportunities surfaced as a major white concern. So did white opposition to patterns of racial concentration in residential settlement. At first some cities like Detroit tried to maintain open housing and a general air of welcome for blacks, but the white majority quickly resorted to stopping the newcomers from living where they wished. Social change involves pain. Nowhere has this truism been more precisely demonstrated over longer periods of time than in the matter of white opposition to living next to blacks. As recently as 1964 the nation's most populous state, California, defeated an open housing law two to one in a public referendum. Defense of "property values" characterizes the white problem in America.

*"They shall not pass."* These heroic words attributed to Marshal Pétain of France held up the German advance during the battle of Verdun. One day in 1916, enthusiastic citizens strung a huge banner with the same words across Grand Boulevard (later South Parkway) at 43rd Street in Chicago. However, in this case the sign had nothing to do with the war in Europe. Paul Laurence Dunbar, a sensitive artist and one of the great poets

---

[5] Ibid., pp. 171–72.

of American literature, chose to ignore the sign and moved five blocks into white territory to a home he had purchased. Dunbar had had many experiences with racial discrimination. Not long before the Chicago situation, Dunbar walked into the lobby of a major hotel in Albany, New York, and went to the desk to register. The clerk, impolitely, asked him what he thought he was doing. The poet replied: "There's a room reserved here for me. I'm Paul Laurence Dunbar."

"Oh no, there ain't! Not for you!" the clerk said insolently.

Dunbar refused to leave and the clerk called the manager who exploded: "Call the police and tell them to come down here and get a crazy nigger."[6] Eventually, Dunbar got the room through the help of a prominent local white.

The first night that Dunbar occupied his new home in Chicago, racists bombed it. The dramatic happening seemed to touch off a pattern of such incidents. Between July 1917 and March 1921 fifty-eight black homes in white districts in Chicago suffered similar attacks. Other Northern cities with large numbers of black migrants, including New York, Philadelphia, Detroit, and Cleveland, also experienced bombings.

One Chicago group, the Property Owners' Association, published a *Journal* which typified the philosophy of hate thy neighbor. During one "invasion" of a white neighborhood by blacks the *Journal* editor wrote, "There is nothing in the make-up of a Negro, physically or mentally, which should induce anyone to welcome him as a neighbor. The best of them are insanitary . . . ruin alone follows in their path. They are as proud as peacocks, but have nothing of the peacock's beauty. . . . Niggers are undesirable neighbors and entirely irresponsible and vicious."[7]

More squeamish whites who opposed violence found other ways to deny housing opportunities to their fellow black citizens. The restrictive covenant emerged as the chief weapon against the "black invasion." Whites relied upon civic associations designed to maintain residential patterns. The purchase of an apartment or home in white areas increasingly carried with it a signed agreement stating that no resale to a black would be undertaken for the indefinite future. Although the Supreme Court ruled city ordinances against open housing to be unconstitutional in 1917 (*Buchanan* v. *Warley*), private housing restrictions were signed by the thousands all across the North and West. The courts con-

---

6 Ibid., pp. 95–96.

7 Included in the Report of the Chicago Commission on Race Relations, 1922, in Allan H. Spear, *Black Chicago* (Chicago: University of Chicago Press, 1967), p. 220. The Commission Report, a powerful document, was titled *The Negro in Chicago*. The Kerner Commission Report of 1968 is similar in both tone and detail.

sistently upheld them as legitimate expressions of the "rights of private property." Not until *Shelley* v. *Kraemer* in 1948 did the Supreme Court undermine private housing covenants. And as recently as the presidential election of 1952, two of the major candidates, Sparkman of the Democrats and Nixon of the Republicans, were embarrassed by revelations that they had lived in Washington homes which they purchased after signing restrictive housing covenants.

What are the rights of property? What are the rights of sale? What are the rights of purchase? In sorting questions of this nature one should avoid the James Buchanan stance. He favored the Union and believed the Constitution writers had established a permanent fusion. Yet he saw no way in which he, as president, could properly use federal power to defend the Union against the divisive actions of individual states.

But not all rights are equal. Rights sometimes conflict. Decisions regarding primary and secondary rights must be made. Only thus may society properly resolve the problems inherent in social change. The right of sale to whomever one pleases cannot be prior to the right of purchase. Acquisition takes precedence, for without possession considerations concerning release have no basis whatsoever.

The Sweet case in Detroit in 1925 can be taken as a typical example of the white problem in America as it relates to housing. Detroit's large black population had been seething for some time. Six incidents involving a mob attack on a black owner in a white residential district had taken place in recent months. In one of these attacks, a black doctor had been driven from his home on a street not far from the Sweet home. Furthermore, the white police department had killed more than fifty blacks in various shootouts during the twenty-two months before the Sweet incident. The police department had been heavily infiltrated by a Ku Klux Klan dominated in-group which called itself the Black Legion. They had succeeded in making the department a center of civic resistance to black advance in the Detroit area.

Ossian Sweet, a well-educated black physician, and his wife, Gladys, purchased their home in a white neighborhood on Charlevoix Avenue. The night they moved in a mob gathered, incited to violent action by the leaders of The Water Works Improvement Association, a local "civic" group using this innocuous name as a cover for its racist sentiments. The city maintained a water works and park whose facilities were to be expanded near the Sweet home. Citizens banded together ostensibly to guard against decline in property values through adverse city action at the water works.

Other members of the Sweet family joined Ossian and Gladys during their first evening in the new neighborhood. The group in the house included two of Ossian's brothers who courageously entered to help defend the family as the crowd milled outside. When the mob began stoning the building the people inside became frightened. They had armed themselves previously and when the whites started to move on the house the occupants opened fire. One bullet struck and killed a member of the mob. Later, at his trial, Ossian Sweet described the scene in these words:

"We were playing cards. It was about eight o'clock when something hit the roof of the house.

"Somebody went to the window and I heard them remark, 'People, the people.'

"I ran to the kitchen where my wife was. There were several lights burning. I turned them out and opened the door. I heard someone yell, 'Go and raise hell in front; I am going back.' Frightened and after getting a gun, I ran upstairs; stones were hitting the house intermittently. I threw myself on the bed and lay there a short while—perhaps fifteen or twenty minutes, when a stone came through the window. Part of the glass hit me.

"Pandemonium broke loose. Everyone was running from room to room. There was a general uproar. Somebody yelled, 'There's someone coming.' They said, 'That's your brother.' A car pulled up to the curb. My brother and Mr. Davis got out. The mob yelled, 'Here's niggers, get them! Get them!'

"As they rushed in, a mob surged forward, fifteen or twenty feet. It looked like a human sea. Stones kept coming faster; I was downstairs. Another window was smashed. Then one shot, then eight or ten from upstairs. Then it was all over.

"When I opened the door and saw the mob, I realized I was facing the same mob that had hounded my people through its entire history. In my mind I was pretty confident of what I was up against. I had my back against the wall. I was filled with a peculiar fear, the fear of one who knows the history of my race. I knew what mobs had done to my people before."[8]

When the police arrived at the riot scene they arrested, not the members of the mob, but most of the Sweet family. The case gained national publicity; the NAACP took up the defense and hired Clarence Darrow, one of the great trial lawyers in American history, to defend the Sweet family against the charge of murder.

Some jurists feared to become involved, but Frank Murphy saw great opportunities in the situation and accepted the respon-

8 Thomas J. Fleming, "Take the Hatred Away and You Have Nothing Left," *American Heritage*, Vol. XX, No. 1, December 1968, p. 79.

sibility of presiding judge. Later he became Governor of Michigan and a U.S. Supreme Court Justice, partly on the liberal reputation he built in handling this case.

Darrow's famous courtroom presence dominated the proceedings. He used the history of white racism in the United States as the chief defense against the charge of murder. At one climax point he read from the black poet Countee Cullen:

> *Once riding in old Baltimore,*
> *Heart full, head full of glee,*
> *I saw a Baltimorean*
> *Stand gazing there at me.*
>
> *Now, I was eight and very small,*
> *And he was no whit bigger,*
> *And so I smiled, but he stuck out*
> *His tongue and called me 'Nigger.'*
>
> *I saw the whole of Baltimore*
> *From April till December,*
> *Of all the things I saw there*
> *That's all I remember.*[9]

Darrow made good use of the case of the *People* v. *Augustus Pond*, 1860, which occurred in Michigan and in which the decision specified that "a man assaulted in his dwelling is not obliged to retreat, but may use such means as are absolutely necessary to repel the assailant from his house . . . [and] if the assault or breaking is felonious, the homicide becomes, at common law, justifiable. . . ."

He pointed out that the Sweets "spent their first night in their first home afraid to go to bed. The next night they spent in jail. Now the State wants them to spend the rest of their lives in the penitentiary. . . .

"There are persons in the North and in the South," Darrow continued, "who say a black man is inferior to the white and should be controlled by the whites. There are also those who recognize his rights and say he should enjoy them. To me this case is a cross section of human history. It involves the future, and the hope of some of us that the future shall be better than the past." But despite Darrow's eloquence the first trial ended in a hung jury.

In the second trial Darrow took more than eight hours to present his summation for the defense. He said in part: "the life of the Negro race has been a life of tragedy, of injustice, of

---

9 "Incident" from *On These I Stand* by Countee Cullen. Copyright 1925 by Harper & Row, Publishers, Inc. Renewed 1953 by Ida M. Cullen. By permission of the publishers.

oppression. The law has made him equal, but man has not. And, after all, the last analysis is, what has man done? And not, what has the law done . . . ?

"There isn't a man in Detroit who doesn't know that the defendant did his duty, and that this case is an attempt to send him and his companions to prison because they defended their constitutional rights. Now that is the case, gentlemen, and that is all there is to this case. Take the hatred away, and you have nothing left."[10]

The same can be said for the white problem in America.

This time the jury accepted Darrow's analysis and rendered a verdict of not guilty. Twice since the Sweet case, in 1943 and in 1967, Detroit has been the scene of particularly vicious race warfare. Doubtless white attitudes have changed somewhat over the years and it would be questionable to conclude that these examples of America's race problem all evolved from identical conditions. Yet something most revealing of white assumptions in general can be seen in the remarks of Detroit's white mayor following the Sweet case. The mayor criticized the role of the Ku Klux Klan but he also exhibited little sympathy for blacks who sought to escape from the restrictions of ghetto existence: "I must say," the mayor wrote, "that I deprecate most strongly the moving of Negroes or other persons into districts in which they knew their presence may cause riot or bloodshed. I believe that any colored person who endangers life and property, simply to gratify his personal pride, is an enemy of his race as well as an incitant of riot and murder. These men who have permitted themselves to be tools of the Ku Klux Klan in its effort to fan the flames of racial hatred into murderous fire, have hurt the cause of their race in a degree that cannot be measured."[11] The mayor's honest views reveal a basic white inability to distinguish between justice and injustice when the issue involves integrated housing.

The Sweet case offers a dramatic example of the friction which occurs in America when blacks attempt to alter existing residential patterns. Defense of white neighborhoods lies at the sensitive center of racial bigotry in practice. The great northward migration of American blacks threatened thousands of communities. Although most whites theoretically concede the right of blacks to live in a decent home, the majority resists the idea when applied to its own locale. Conroy and Bontemps titled their

---

10 Ibid., pp. 80, 104–5.

11 Interview with John W. Smith, Mayor of Detroit, *Detroit News*, September 13, 1925, in Kenneth T. Jackson, *The Ku Klux Klan in the City, 1915–1930* (New York: Oxford University Press, 1967), p. 141.

valuable study of black migration *Anyplace But Here,* an apt description of white resistance to open housing all over the nation.

Today, when most of the major Northern and Western cities have large black ghettos, it may be difficult to recall that this is a relatively recent trend. At the turn of the century, few Northern cities had large black populations. Philadelphia, Chicago, and New York first experienced a major influx of blacks. Of the three, New York's Harlem stands out as a classic case of the formation of a Northern black ghetto. Its story has been well told by several writers. Kenneth Clark's *Dark Ghetto* and Gilbert Osofsky's *Harlem: The Making of a Ghetto* present historical analysis and Claude Brown's *Manchild in the Promised Land* and James Baldwin's *The Fire Next Time* describe personal experience with powerful insight.

The black population in New York City stayed approximately the same during the nineteenth century; at the close of the Civil War slightly fewer than 10,000 blacks lived in Manhattan as compared to some 10,400 in 1820. Their number gradually increased after the war and began to expand rapidly during the 1890's. The blacks lived in different spots in the city, nearly always in the worst and oldest dwellings. As early as 1842 Charles Dickens, on his tour of the United States, visited homes of poor blacks in New York City and described them as places where "dogs would howl to lie . . . [and] women and men . . . slink off to sleep, forcing the dislodged rats to move away."[12]

Prior to the 1890's few blacks lived in Harlem. Instead a number of smaller ghettos, a block or two in length, were scattered between 20th and 63rd Streets. The "Tenderloin" in the 42nd Street area and "San Juan Hill" (so named because of the many interracial battles there), between 60th and 64th Streets, contained the two largest concentrations. Here blacks suffered overcrowding in inferior housing at high rents. The average family income for blacks in New York City at the turn of the century totaled $12 to $15 per week or $600 to $800 per year.

Beginning about 1890 blacks flowed into the city from the South. By 1910 the black population had grown to more than 90,000 and intense racial fear began to spread over Manhattan. The influx brought special strain to the black community as well as the white. The Southern rural black, less educated than the blacks in the North and usually more poverty-stricken, often came to New York by ship, berthed separately, given inferior food in

---

[12] Charles Dickens, "American Notes," in Gilbert Osofsky, *Harlem: The Making of a Ghetto* (New York: Harper & Row, 1968), p. 10. The analysis of black Harlem which follows has been drawn largely from Osofsky's treatment.

quarters reserved for the dogs and pets of white passengers. When they arrived in New York City they were as penniless and under-privileged a group as any brought by immigrant ships from Europe. In August of 1900 the increasing racial tensions erupted into a severe riot, the worst in New York since the antidraft chaos of 1863. Gilbert Osofsky vividly describes the start of the 1900 riot in the following words:

"In August of 1900 New York City was in the midst of a heat wave. The weather bureau recorded stifling temperatures throughout the month: 'The warmest August since the Local Bureau kept track of it.' At noon on August 12, the temperature reached 91 degrees. New Yorkers spilled out of their tenements seeking relief. Stoops in the Tenderloin were crowded through-out the night. Local saloons were packed to capacity.

"Arthur J. Harris left his house at 241 West Forty-first Street on the evening of August 12 to buy . . . cigars and pass some time at McBride's Saloon. Harris, twenty-two, was typical of many young Negroes who came to New York City at that time. Born in Richmond, Virginia, of an unstable family (his mother lived in Washington, D.C., . . . and his father in Cranford, New Jersey), he had left home at fourteen and lived in Washington for seven years. In 1899 he came north to visit his father and find work. The Washington police never had any trouble with him; his record showed 'No Prior Convictions.' When asked about his previous education, he responded, 'Yes, he could read and write.' . . .

"In Jersey City, in 1899, he had picked up money working at odd jobs—as a cook, baker, carpenter, and poolroom attendant—and lived with 20-year-old May Enoch, who had left the husband she had married at sixteen. Harris and 'his woman' or, as he often referred to her, 'my wife,' came to Forty-first Street, at the beginning of August 1900, rented a room at Annie Johnson's, and said they were looking for work. At 2 A.M. on August 13, May came down to McBride's: 'I said to Harris, "Kid come on up home." ' While she waited for him at the corner of Forty-first Street and Eighth Avenue, Robert J. Thorpe, a plainclothes police-man, approached her and charged her with 'soliciting.' To Harris he looked like a white man who was mishandling his woman. 'The policeman grabbed my girl. I didn't know who he was and thought he was a citizen like myself,' he maintained later at his trial. Harris was clubbed in a struggle with the policeman. He said the policeman pummeled him with his club and shouted, 'Get up, you black son-of-a-bitch.' I thought the man was trying to kill me, and I believed that he would kill me if I didn't pro-tect myself." Harris pulled out a knife and 'cut him twice.' May ran home where she was later picked up and arrested; Harris took a train to his mother's home in Washington; Thorpe died in Roosevelt Hospital the next day."[13]

Harris was sent to prison for life and died in Sing Sing in 1908. A similar account might be written numbers of times to describe the start of racial riots in various cities with only the names and the situations changing slightly. Police repression has long been a reality for dwellers of black ghettos. Fear and hatred poisons the mind of any majority which indulges in racial assumptions. Policemen are subject to the same human limitations as exist in the general public because they too grew up in the community which employs them. Few individual policemen can be properly defined as brutal and inhuman, although an occasional disturbing example may be cited. But an equally small number can be said to be free of the influences of their background. A policeman raised in a family which had little contact with blacks and considerable fear or hatred of them cannot be expected to escape the dangerous personal assumptions which will be present in whatever social situations he may meet in the line of duty.

Rioting began after policeman Thorpe's funeral; white mobs raged throughout the city attacking every black they could find. The police did little to stop the assaults. In some cases, the police led the mobs; a number of eyewitness accounts by whites described policemen, in uniform, assisting mobs to drag blacks off streetcars and beat them.

In one instance the police arrested William J. Elliott, a black waiter, for carrying a pistol. Several reporters saw Elliott escorted unhurt into the 37th Street police station. When they released him the next morning he had been beaten into a bloody state. In the investigation that followed, Elliott reported that when he entered the station the lights went out and he was beaten from all sides. Because of the dark, he could identify no assailant. The Board of Inquiry ruled that because the evidence "was contradictory . . . no conviction of a violation of the Rules of the Department could be sustained."[14]

After a dozen deaths and hundreds of beatings, the rioting tapered off. The official police report summarized, "In the month of August the west side of the city was threatened with a race war between the white and colored citizens. . . Prompt and vigorous action on the part of the Police . . . kept the situation under control and . . . quiet was restored in districts . . . which were affected."[15]

---

[13] Ibid., pp. 46–47.
[14] Police Report in ibid., p. 49.
[15] Police Department "Annual Report" in ibid., p. 52.

Not until 1911 did the first black policeman receive appointment to "New York's finest." His name was Samuel J. Battle. His beat became a regular tourist stop. White children (and sometimes black ones) followed Battle shouting, "There goes the nigger cop, there goes the nigger cop!"[16]

Prior to 1870, Harlem was a poor, rural village, almost all white. Isolated from New York City by several miles of open farm land, it became increasingly popular as a white upper-middle-class residential district. It was Manhattan's first suburb. The city annexed it in 1873.

By 1881, with the coming of the elevated railroad, Harlem became incorporated into the life of the city. But racially it remained mostly white. Harlem real estate men advertised the area to encourage further influx of affluent whites. On the edges of the Harlem River, in the lowest land and the worst buildings, lived a few Italian immigrant families and some poor blacks.

In 1893, a young but influential black educator spoke to a large group in the Lenox Avenue Unitarian Church. He asked for contributions for his school in Alabama and took up a sizable collection. His name was Booker T. Washington and he was one of the few blacks the white residents of Harlem had ever seen.

Because of its many attractions, Harlem enjoyed a lively building boom around the turn of the century. But overbuilding coupled with high rents made it difficult for landlords to fill the space. The panic of 1907 further deflated the Harlem real estate market. In this circumstance, the loosely scattered black population of Manhattan served as a natural group to be enticed into the empty Harlem blocks. The riot of 1900 helped to make Harlem the most famous black ghetto in the world because blacks, fearful of further violence, sought a community concentration. The construction of Penn Station with the accompanying destruction of part of the black Tenderloin served to accelerate the influx which both black and white real estate interests promoted vigorously.

Philip A. Payton, Jr., formed the Afro-American Realty Co. and devised a successful plan for filling up the empty Harlem apartment houses which white speculators had built. He leased entire buildings, guaranteed an annual return, and then charged blacks a 10 per cent rental surcharge to live there. Many blacks found the offer attractive. They were charged outsize rents wherever they lived in the city and so the money made little difference. The excellent new quarters were most attractive and blacks began to move into Harlem in large numbers. All-black

---

16 Ibid., p. 166.

blocks soon emerged. Payton's Afro-American Realty Company sold stock to the public and expanded its operations rapidly to include ownership, as well as leasing of buildings. Eventually, Payton overextended the company and it failed, but prior to its failure black Harlem was born. The area contained 50,000 black residents by the start of World War I.

The inevitable white reaction to the black influx formed around the Harlem Property Owners Improvement Corporation which John G. Taylor led. He put the question bluntly: Will the white man or the black man rule Harlem? The HPOIC used restrictive housing covenants in an attempt to keep the blacks out. Typically the covenants read: "Each of the parties does hereby covenant and agree [not] to . . . hereafter . . . cause to be suffered, either directly or indirectly, the said premises to be used or occupied in whole or in part by any negro, quadroon, or octoroon of either sex whatsoever. . . ."[17] Some of the covenants went on to limit the number of black janitors, bellboys, laundresses, and other servants who could be employed in the building.

Taylor and others recorded the covenants in the city records office and thus gave them official status. But they proved to be no real bar to the now strongly black residential trend. A variety of subterfuges broke the covenant blocks and, once the first black family entered, the whites moved out, usually completing the turnover within two to three years. More recently Whitney Young defined integrated housing in America as that period of time between the in moving of the first black family and the out moving of the last white.

Taylor of HPOIC, an angry and fear-ridden man, typical of many whites in similar circumstances, fought to keep Harlem Caucasian. At one meeting he shouted his solution to the race contest: "Drive them out and send them to the slums where they belong."[18] In cases where this could not be accomplished, Taylor suggested that whites, living next to black blocks build 24-foot-high fences to keep the races apart. Although the Supreme Court, as noted, ruled in 1917 (*Buchanan* v. *Warley*) that city-blessed restrictive housing covenants were unconstitutional, private agreements remained legal until 1948 (*Shelley* v. *Kraemer*).

Harlem, though it had turned largely black, was not yet a slum during the first fifteen years of the twentieth century. It was a comfortable and attractive place to live. Very importantly, no overcrowding occurred. Affluent blacks as well as the many who

---

17 Ibid., pp. 106–7.
18 Ibid., p. 107.

were poor lived, for the first and last time, in New York City in spacious, decent housing. Churches began to change hands and large black congregations took over formerly white-owned buildings. Adam Clayton Powell, Sr., often preached on "A Model Church" and urged his Abyssinian Baptist congregation to move to Harlem, which it eventually did. Many black churches purchased not only church buildings, but land and apartments, and this increased the black influx into Harlem.

The atmosphere was pleasant and relaxed in comparison to the smaller ghetto areas from which blacks had moved. In 1919 the Equitable Life Assurance Society finally began selling to blacks and within eight months practically all the beautiful Harlem brownstones designed by Stanford White had been purchased by well-to-do blacks.

By 1920, 70,000 blacks lived in Harlem, approximately two thirds of the entire black population of Manhattan. The area had become the "Mecca of the colored people of New York City." As one prominent black leader said, "If my race can make Harlem, good lord, what can't it do?"[19] His comment reflected the general belief that only whites who had sold at scare prices really lost out in the residential change-over. The district seemed to be almost a black paradise.

Within ten years Harlem became a terrible slum. Why?

Two factors dictated the change. The tremendous internal migration of blacks from the rural South caused Harlem's population to swell far more rapidly than the absorption abilities of the district. Neither the city authorities nor private enterprise supplied a significant amount of special investment to offset the deleterious aspects of rising population pressures. The minority group background of most of the new residents further reduced the chances of meaningful public concern. Harlem's black population grew more than 100 per cent in the decade of the 1920's, to some 160,000 persons; they were joined by more than 40,000 Puerto Ricans. Crowding, with all its problems, followed inevitably.

The adverse effects of the Depression then drove blacks increasingly below the poverty line and led to taking in boarders and further overpopulation. White prejudice made it dangerous for blacks to reside in other parts of the city. Even those who could afford it hesitated to buy property isolated from Harlem. The Depression further reduced black mobility. The conflicting currents began to make Harlem an unsafe place. By 1925 Manhattan's population density had reached 223 persons per acre, but

---

19 Ibid., p. 123.

in black districts, mostly in Harlem, 336 persons crowded into each acre. Philadelphia, the second-ranking black city, with only 111 per acre in black districts, and Chicago, with a mere sixty-seven, stood far below the Harlem congestion rate. Several blocks in Harlem probably became the most impacted living districts in the world.

By 1927 Harlem blacks paid $8 more per month than the average New Yorker for a three-room apartment, $10 more for four rooms, and $7 more for five rooms. On the average, whites paid $6.67 per room per month while Harlem blacks paid $9.50. At the same time the average black family earned only $1,300 per year, substantially below the income of the average white family. In sum, New York whites spent about 20 per cent of their income for rent, whereas blacks spent about 33 per cent. A great many spent more than 40 per cent for rent and a 1928 study showed that Harlem residents in a large number of tenements paid 48 per cent of their income for rent. During the same general period the Urban League conducted a survey of black Chicago and discovered that nonwhites suffered heavy discrimination in housing costs. Third-rate apartments which had rented for less than $20 per month to whites cost up to $45 when blacks moved in. Another study of rents in Philadelphia in 1923 showed that although all rents had tended to rise, only about 35 per cent of white tenants had to absorb significant increases, whereas during the same period, more than 60 per cent of blacks suffered rent hikes.

Lodgers provided the only practical relief from high rents and the overcrowding and family dislocation added to the slum conditions. Where approximately one white family in nine found it advisable to take in boarders, one black family in four found it necessary to do so.

Many of Harlem's newcomers, including those from the West Indies and Puerto Rico, as well as the South, caused community disruption even as they themselves suffered the most. E. Franklin Frazier, the great sociologist, judged that many Harlemites were "ignorant and unsophisticated peasant people without experience in urban living. . . ."[20] The rural black seemed at first to be an oddity. As his number increased the more sophisticated urban dweller tended to ridicule him. "Ultimately," as Robert Weaver has noted, "he was feared" for the pressures he created, especially in the competition for decent housing.[21] The steady influx of down-country blacks kept pushing rents and prices upward even

20 Ibid., p. 139.
21 Robert C. Weaver, *The Negro Ghetto* (New York: Russell and Russell, 1948), p. 29.

as the increasing population density caused the buildings to deteriorate more rapidly.

Crime increased. Health conditions worsened. Harlem's death rate during the 1923–1927 period was 42 per cent in excess of the death rate in the rest of the city. Twice as many Harlem mothers died in childbirth and nearly twice as many children died in infancy. Infant mortality in the city totaled 64.5 per thousand live births, whereas in Harlem the figure reached 110 per thousand.

Schools became predominantly black and terribly overcrowded; some ran on three shifts. The unstable and diverse population created schools with such a wide disparity between learning levels that no real progress could be made even by keeping classroom registration down to twenty-five or thirty. Classes ran to sixty and seventy students per room. School populations shifted constantly, with some schools having 100 per cent turnovers in a single year. Most whites correctly think of the public school as the mechanism by which opportunity has been extended to generations of young Americans. This assumption includes the belief that the public schools have served as the central feature of the national melting pot. But for blacks the system has never worked well. Schools in black districts have been allowed to offer substandard education. Perhaps at no time in our history did the American public school system fail more completely than in Harlem during the period of the district's decline.

When the Depression struck the nation in 1929, the immediate effects were actually less harsh in black Harlem, where residents had been in terrible depression increasingly from 1920 onward. Elimination of the overcrowding trends and increased job opportunities required far more sophisticated social engineering programs than anything the nation had ever tried. The conditions which caused Harlem to become a black slum similarly infected many urban centers. With apparently no chance for genuine betterment, Harlem and other black communities seethed.

The conditions for the creation of urban black ghettos still exist. A 1969 study of health conditions in Harlem indicated that little relative progress has been realized. The people of the area have a tuberculosis rate approximately three and a half times the level in the rest of the city and an infant mortality rate nearly twice that of the white population. In addition, Harlem suffers from the highest levels of alcoholism, narcotics addiction, and venereal disease in New York. Similar figures could be advanced for black ghettos in other places.

Although discrimination in housing has been illegal since 1948, the practice continues tacitly in one form or another. In lower-class white neighborhoods, resistance to black influx often takes forms as violent as in the past, and whites sometimes receive similar treatment in black districts. In higher-class white suburbs, the practice of racial exclusion is usually carried out by real estate agents, civic associations, the leading business forces of the community, and public zoning ordinances which exclude build-ings with lower costs and rents. State open-housing laws do not seem to have much effect.

Statistics reveal the central features of the problem. Blacks, who number approximately 11 per cent of the nation's popula-tion, occupy less than 5 per cent of the nation's housing. Part of this discrepancy arises from segregationist practices and part from the restriction of limited purchasing power. Although black family incomes have improved since World War II, the American caste system has kept a large percentage of blacks at the poverty line. At the start of the 1960's nearly two thirds of American blacks still lived on family incomes which placed them in the bottom sector of the national economy. Almost endless examples of continued white hostility to black neighbors could be cited.

The record of the 1960's in Chicago might serve as an illustra-tion of this nationwide phenomenon. Repeatedly during the decade, Martin Luther King and allied leaders organized marches and other efforts to break blacks out of the housing noose; their endeavors merely triggered violent, white racist reaction. The first such sequence occurred in Marquette Park twenty blocks beyond the invisible wall which separates the white from the black district at Ashland Avenue and 63rd Street. A group of blacks led by King marched to the "white" park where they planned to eat a picnic lunch before picketing a real estate office nearby. They failed to realize their objectives when a mob of whites set upon them, drove them from the public park with rocks, and stoned them back to the black sector. Only the police lines separating the groups prevented a genuine slaughter.

The white suburb of Cicero, Illinois, proved to be an even more dangerous target for the civil rights marchers. Scene of a terrible lynch-riot in 1951, Cicero residents maintained total opposition to attempts at social change. During the summer of 1965, according to one account, two black youths "naively job-hunting in Cicero, were set upon by a group of whites with base-ball bats. One got away to the safety of the police station; the other was beaten about the legs until both knees were broken and he couldn't run, and then systematically pounded to death."[22]

---

22 Account given by Gene Marine, "I've Got Nothing Against the Colored, Understand," in Barry N. Schwartz and Robert Disch, eds., *White Racism: Its History, Pathology and Practice* (New York: Dell Publishing Co., 1970), p. 224.

King himself had to end the confrontation marches because of the dangers. He termed the Chicago area reaction the most "hostile" and "hateful" he had ever seen.[23] Another observer concluded that "without exaggeration" a black citizen is still "literally risking his life" to move into many sections of almost any American city, north or south.[24] William H. Moyer, the white executive director of HOME, a Chicago effort to open housing to blacks, stated, "The suburbs are just as much a closed society as the South. Chicago's system of separation of the races differs from Mississippi's only in degree. In Mississippi, the Ku Klux Klan burns churches . . . [but] in Chicago . . . houses are burned to the ground because they are purchased by Negro citizens."[25]

Dick Gregory, Martin Luther King, and Al Raby led a major campaign in Chicago in 1965. Raby declared, "Bridgeport [Mayor Daley's white neighborhood] is involved in what amounts to a major conspiracy that prevents the Negro from achieving first-class citizenship and human dignity. A web is woven by real estate interests, city officials, the school board, employers, some unions, and citizen organizations that entraps the Negro in his ghetto. A city-wide pattern is dramatically illustrated. . . ."[26]

Daley maintains a mixed image on the race question. His statements and some of his actions favored open housing, yet his home district remained all white. In 1965 an idealistic teacher took Daley at his word regarding equal rights. He purchased a home in the mayor's neighborhood and promptly rented it to a black student. A white mob gathered, stoned the house, and tried to set it on fire. The black student decided to move out. A Chicago *Daily News* reporter visited the scene after the student had left and found a large number of whites celebrating their victory. A worried-looking elderly white man with a strong European accent which suggested that he might once have fled from Hitler's oppression came along and asked what had happened. One of the celebrators assured him that the black student had moved out and would not be back. The old man answered, "Dat's goot. Ve don't vant outsiders" causing trouble.[27]

23 Interview with Martin Luther King, Jr., *New York Times*, August 6, 1966, in Gilbert Osofsky, *The Burden of Race: A Documentary History of Negro-White Relations in America* (New York: Harper & Row, 1967), p. 628.

24 Hamilton J. Bims, "Housing—The Hottest Issue in the North," in *The White Problem in America* (New York: Lancer Books, 1966), p. 93. (First published as a special issue of *Ebony* magazine, August 1965.)

25 Statement of Moyer in Arna Bontemps and Jack Conroy, *Anyplace But Here* (New York: Hill and Wang, 1968), p. 328.

26 Statement of Raby in ibid., p. 337.

27 Statement of Michael Royko in ibid., p. 337.

Another Chicago confrontation followed the death of Dessie Mae Williams, who was killed by a Chicago fire department truck in 1965. She had been standing on a street corner when she was struck by the careening vehicle. A riot broke out led by black youths. Sherman Kennedy, an eighteen-year-old participant who later helped to sponsor a Dessie Mae Williams Community Center regretted his part in the violence but said in explanation of his behavior, "We're sorry about the bricks and bottles, but when you get pushed, you shove back. Man, you don't like to stand on a corner and be told to get off it when you got nowhere else to go. And we want somewhere else to go."[28]

Allan H. Spear, a cogent observer of the ghetto scene in Chicago, has concluded that "remarkably little" has changed in black Chicago since 1920. The same factors which circumscribed black lives after World War I still operate in the present decade. "Four civil rights bills, dozens of court decisions and thousands of brave words" have "barely touched" the lives of black citizens who remain crowded into the worst districts, remote from the sources of jobs and lacking in meaningful political power to effect necessary changes. The King-led housing marches of the mid 1960's accomplished little more than demonstrate that "thousands of white Chicagoans were still determined to preserve the status quo. . . ."

"The persistence of the Chicago Negro ghetto," Spear notes, "has been not merely the result of continued immigration from the South, but the product of a special historical experience. From its inception, the Negro ghetto was unique among the city's ethnic enclaves. It grew in response to an implacable white hostility that has not basically changed. In this sense it has been Chicago's only true ghetto, less the product of voluntary development within than of external pressures from without. Like the Jewries of medieval Europe, Black Chicago has offered no escape. Irishmen, Poles, Jews, or Italians, as they acquired the means, had an alternative: they could move their enclaves to more comfortable environs, or, as individuals, leave the enclaves and become members of the community at large. Negroes—forever marked by their color—could only hope for success within a rigidly delineated and severely restricted ghetto society. No physical wall has encircled the black belt. But an almost equally impervious wall of hostility and discrimination has isolated Negroes from the mainstream. . . . Under such conditions, Negroes have tried, often against impossible odds, to make the best of their circumstances by creating a meaningful life of their

---

28 Statement of Kennedy in ibid., p. 342.

own. But they have done so, not out of choice, but because white society has left them no alternative."[29]

Black Americans suffered greatly as slaves and rural tenants in the South. Escape to the North long offered hope of upward social mobility. Yet internal migration, under the restrictions of prejudice, merely created the Northern city ghettos which have become the most unseemly features of the white problem in America. No citizen, white or black, can escape their blight.

[29] Allan H. Spear, *Black Chicago* (Chicago: University of Chicago Press, 1967), pp. 224 and 229.

# World War I and Its Aftermath

# 7

Large numbers of blacks made contributions to the American effort during World War I. In the United States they came north to take advantage of job openings in war plants and on the battlefield, they carried on the tradition established in America's earlier wars, even those fought during the slavery period. They volunteered in significant numbers to fight and do whatever else was asked of soldiers.

During the Civil War, American blacks fought for the Union in segregated units under white officers, and only after an extended national debate over whether they should be accepted at all. Nearly 200,000 volunteered, although the Enlistment Act of 1862 paid them only $10 per month instead of the $16.50 paid to whites. Some black regiments refused to accept wages under the discriminatory pay scale, but stayed in the service and fought; in 1864 after two years of protest, Congress equalized pay scales.

Authorities assigned black troops to menial jobs instead of combat missions. Frequent protests brought modest change. At Southern whites gave them no quarter. Thirty-eight thousand South Carolina, and the battle of the crater at Petersburg, Virginia, in 1864, black units formed the key assault force. The few black regiments which saw combat suffered heavy casualties, partly because of the desire to prove themselves but also because Southern whites gave them no quarter. Thirty-eight thousand died, giving black troops in the Civil War a 40 per cent higher death rate than whites!

After the war, many blacks served the U.S. government in the Indian "wars" in the western states and also made a significant combat contribution to the American cause in the Spanish-American War of 1898. Blacks seem, in general, no more immune than whites to support of national ventures of whatever sort, even the more questionable engagements like the Spanish-American War and the Vietnam conflict. Twenty-two blacks died when the battleship Maine blew up in Havana harbor. Later four black units saw action in Cuba. The 9th and 10th cavalry supported Teddy Roosevelt's Rough Riders in several actions including the battles at San Juan and Kettle Hills. At Las Guasimas a black regiment saved the Rough Riders from annihilation after the Spanish had mauled the Roosevelt unit.

Following the action, one white Rough Rider termed the blacks to be "all right. They can drink out of our canteens." Roosevelt himself remarked, "The Spaniards called them 'Smoked Yankees' but we found them to be an excellent breed of Yankees." Major General Nelson A. Miles, U.S. Army commander, said of the victory over the Spaniards, "The white race was accompanied by the gallantry of the black as they swept over entrenched lines and later volunteered to succor the sick, nurse the dying and bury the dead in the hospitals and the Cuban camps."[1]

When America entered World War I blacks and whites flocked to enlist. Under the draft laws, 31 per cent of the registered blacks received call-up notice as against only 26 per cent of the whites. John Hope Franklin points out that this discrepancy had nothing to do with better health among blacks, but resulted merely from the fact that many Southern draft boards reversed the usual practice of discrimination and called blacks first.

Some 350,000 blacks served in segregated units commanded largely by whites, although eventually nearly 1,000 blacks received commissions. Assignments, as in the Civil War and the Spanish American War, emphasized menial functions instead of combat roles.

Again, blacks who did get into combat did extremely well. The same, of course, can be said for the white Americans who fought in World War I. Americans proved their fighting mettle beyond question and U.S. units suffered casualties, with reference to the number of men in combat, higher than any nation in the war.

Some black units particularly distinguished themselves. Harlem's Hell Fighters received the French Croix de Guerre as did two other black regiments. Fighting as the New York 15th (U.S. 369th), the Hell Fighters spent more days in combat (191) than any other American unit. Following one great victory by the 369th, Marshal Foch, Commander in Chief of the Allied Armies,

---

[1] Various quotes in John Hope Franklin, *From Slavery to Freedom* (New York: Alfred A. Knopf, 1969), pp. 422–23.

wrote, "After having boldly stopped the enemy, you have attacked them for months with indefatigable faith and energy, giving them no rest.

"You have . . . saved the most sacred cause, the liberty of the world.

"Be proud of it.

"With immortal glory you have adorned your flag.

"Posterity will be indebted to you with gratitude."[2]

The Germans gave the 370th black infantry from Illinois the nickname "Black Devils." Led almost entirely by blacks, the 370th fought the final battle of World War I.

There were brilliant black "Sergeant York" incidents too. In May 1918, during what John Hope Franklin has called "The Battle of Henry Johnson," two black privates, Henry Johnson of Albany, New York, and Needham Roberts of Trenton, New Jersey, defended a post against twenty raiding Germans. Though both men were wounded they stood the ground until their position was overrun. After the Germans had made Roberts a prisoner, Johnson counterattacked with his bolo knife, killed four of the enemy and freed his buddy.

General John Pershing said of the all-black 92nd Division, "I want you officers and soldiers . . . to know that the . . . division stands second to none in the record you have made since your arrival in France. I am proud of the part you have played in the great conflict. . . . You have . . . done what the American people expected . . . and . . . have measured up to every expectation of the Commander in Chief."[3]

The record clearly demonstrates that black servicemen nobly sustained the patriotic image during the "war to end wars" as they had in previous conflicts. Yet many white Americans either never learned or quickly forgot the gallant role of black Americans in the nation's wars. Whites commonly disparaged black morale and bravery and blatant discrimination marred black participation in World War I at home and abroad. For example, at Camp Greene, North Carolina, the YMCA established five facilities for white troops but none for blacks, although 10,000 black soldiers were stationed on the base. A large sign over the door of one of the recreational headquarters stated, "This building is for white men only."[4] The white secretary in charge of the facility placed

2 John D. Silvera, *The Negro in World War II* (New York: Arno Press, 1969), Appendix I, no page number. Foch's order is reproduced in facsimile.
3 General John Pershing in John Hope Franklin, *From Slavery to Freedom* (New York: Alfred A. Knopf, 1969), p. 467.
4 Ibid., p. 459.

a small table outside the front door so that black soldiers could at least sit down to write letters home.

Black units from the North stationed in the South often faced extreme hostility. At Houston, Texas, authorities disarmed the 24th Infantry after a number of interracial incidents. Thirteen black soldiers were hanged and forty sent to jail for life as a result of the investigation which followed.

The 15th New York Infantry was stationed in Spartanburg, South Carolina, for a time. When Noble Sissle, the drum major of the band, went into a hotel to buy a newspaper, white employees cursed and kicked him out. His fellow black soldiers almost raided the hotel in retaliation but a black officer stopped them. The War Department, upon receiving a report on the incident, immediately ordered the unit overseas; as noted above it proceeded to establish one of the best American combat records of the war.

In general, the French people treated black soldiers as equals but many whites in the American Expeditionary Force tried to discourage friendship toward black troops. White American officers urged issuance of the notorious directive "Secret Information Concerning the Black American Troops," officially released by the French high command but really the creation of white American bigotry. The document contains such key quotes as the following: "American opinion is unanimous on the 'color question,' and does not admit of any discussion."

"The increasing number of Negroes in the United States . . . would create for the white race in the Republic a menace of degeneracy were it not that an impassable gulf has been made between them."

"Americans . . . are afraid that contact with the French will inspire in black Americans aspirations which to . . . whites appear intolerable."

"Although a citizen of the U.S., the black man is regarded by the white American as an inferior being with whom relations of business or service only are possible. . . . The vices of the Negro are a constant menace to the American who has to repress them sternly."

"We must prevent the rise of any pronounced degree of intimacy between French officers and black officers."

"We must not commend too highly the black American troops, particularly in the presence of white Americans."

"Make a point of keeping the . . . population from 'spoiling' the Negroes. White Americans become greatly incensed at any public expression of intimacy between white women with black men."[5]

This secret order to French officers shortly became public and infuriated black Americans at home and abroad.

Black soldiers returned convinced they had done well for their country under adverse circumstances. W. E. B. Du Bois, who supported the war, called for full equality at home: "Make way for Democracy!" he wrote in the *Crisis* (in 1919) "We saved it in France and by the great Jehovah, we will save it in the United States of America, or know the reason why."[6]

The myth of black inferiority dies hard, however. A segregated social system which fostered second-class citizenship for blacks convinced most white Americans that nonwhites deserved what they got. During World War I the White Response to Black Emancipation flowed strongly; blacks, regardless of individual merit, suffered humiliation.

The Wilson administration did little to lessen the burden. In keeping with previous presidential leadership since the Civil War the Princeton professor resisted meaningful change in the racial equation. Indeed, in many ways he increased the size and scope of black disadvantage.

Thomas Woodrow Wilson was a powerful leader. A student of American government and history, he promoted major reform measures like the Federal Reserve System and the Clayton Anti-Trust Act. A courageous president in war, Wilson emerged as a visionary advocate of a system which might have avoided World War II and moved mankind significantly toward genuine peace in the world.

But in the matter of equal rights for blacks Wilson's deficiencies stand out. He had been born in Virginia and lived in Georgia. This background, reinforced by the bias of his Southern-born first wife, did great damage at a crucial point in American history.

Some blacks supported Wilson's election in 1912. At this time Roosevelt had shown open prejudice and Taft offered small attraction. Although Booker T. Washington held to the regular Republican line, W. E. B. Du Bois broke with the tradition of supporting the "party of Lincoln" and spoke out in Wilson's favor. In fact he helped write some Wilson statements on the race question. In one letter the then New Jersey governor said he wished "justice done to the colored people in every matter; and

---

[5] Albert P. Blaustein and Robert L. Zangrando, eds., *Civil Rights and the American Negro: A Documentary History* (New York: Washington Square Press, 1968), pp. 335–36.

[6] Ibid., p. 335. Quote taken from *The Crisis,* May 1919.

not mere grudging justice, but justice executed with liberality and cordial good feeling. . . . I want to assure . . . [American blacks] that should I become President of the United States they may count upon me for absolute fair dealing, for everything by which I could assist in advancing the interests of their race in the United States."[7]

Despite Du Bois' leadership black support for Wilson was reserved and cautious. The *New York Age,* an influential black newspaper, warned that "Both by inheritance and absorption . . . Wilson has most of the prejudices of the narrowest type of Southern white people against the Negro."[8] A check of Wilson's earlier statements suggest this to be a well-founded caution. In a 1901 article, for example, Wilson described the black freedmen as "insolent and aggressive; sick of work, covetous of pleasure, a host of dusky children untimely put out of school."[9] Princeton University during the period of Wilson's leadership from 1902 to 1910 was the only significant Northern university that positively refused admission to blacks. Wilson's single term as reform governor of New Jersey had accomplished much by way of corporation control, but nothing for the state's black citizens.

During Wilson's first administration two events pushed American race relations toward a nadir. Booker T. Washington died in 1915 and his influence, though not a militant one, was thus removed. A vacuum of black leadership followed. In that same year a powerful film, "The Birth of a Nation," became a tremendous success. It was based on the racist writings of Thomas Ryan Dixon, Jr., a friend of Woodrow Wilson from his college days. The first really effective movie, it unfortunately projected a viciously negative stereotype of American blacks. President Wilson, upon hearing of the film's success, arranged a special showing at the White House and observed that the film "wrote history with lightning."[10] Although adverse reaction from civil rights groups later caused Wilson to mute his initial support, millions of white Americans went to see the lionization of the Ku Klux Klan and the further degradation of the friendless blacks depicted as brutes in the technically innovative movie.

But even before 1915 blacks had reason to fear the Wilson

7 Letter from Woodrow Wilson to Alexander Walters, October 1912, in Ray Stannard Baker, *Woodrow Wilson: Life and Letters* (New York: Doubleday, Doran, 1931), pp. 387–88.

8 Editorial from *New York Age,* July 11, 1912, in Rayford W. Logan, *The Betrayal of the Negro* (New York: Collier Books, 1968), p. 360.

9 Woodrow Wilson, "Reconstruction in the Southern States," *Atlantic Monthly,* Vol. LXXXVI, January 1901, p. 6.

10 Richard Griffith and Arthur Mayer, *The Movies* (New York: Simon and Schuster, 1957), p. 37.

administration. Trouble began after members of Wilson's official family visited government bureaus and saw blacks and whites working at equal jobs, a practice which the Pendleton Civil Service Reform Act of 1883 had pointed toward. They influenced the president to alter the situation and, starting in 1913, blacks and whites began to be segregated in the federal service. Many blacks received no active consideration for jobs after the administration began requiring photographs with all applications. Those who did have work increasingly found themselves assigned to menial jobs in separate, unequal facilities.

Much of the segregation resulted from executive orders issued by department secretaries appointed by Wilson. William G. McAdoo, Secretary of the Treasury, took an active part in this process. He and Postmaster General Albert Burleson earned reputations as the most ardent white supremacists in the administration's official family. Both enjoyed ready access to Wilson's policy making through friendship with Mrs. Wilson. She supported McAdoo's and Burleson's white-collar bigotry but the president needed little encouragement, believing as he did in the concept of white superiority. Work, lounge, and cafeteria facilities became increasingly segregated, as were public services all over the Capitol city. Authorities also segregated public restrooms. In the Department of the Interior, blacks had to go down to a small janitor's restroom in the basement.

William Monroe Trotter became so incensed upon finding black employees segregated in the Post Office sorting letters behind a row of lockers in the back of a room, that he insisted upon an audience with the president. He took other leaders of similar mind to the White House with him. Trotter spoke his views so forcefully that Wilson ordered him from the presidential office and reported that he had never been spoken to "in such an insulting fashion before."[11] The presidential secretary, Joseph Tumulty, later reported that Trotter's speech was extremely eloquent. However, no modification of discriminatory practices resulted from Trotter's bold objections.

Oswald Garrison Villard, grandson of William Lloyd Garrison, and a strong white voice for justice, repeatedly tried to persuade Wilson to restrain the segregationists in his administration. Villard urged Wilson to appoint a National Race Commission to look into all aspects of the race problem, but Wilson refused on the grounds that the effort would create a "feeling of irritation" in the South. In fact Wilson actually defended segregationist prac-

---

11 *New York Times*, November 13, 1914, p. 1. See also Rayford W. Logan, *The Betrayal of the Negro* (New York: Collier Books, 1968), p. 362.

tices on the grounds that they protected *blacks* from embarrassing friction within the departments and asserted that "a number of colored men with whom we have consulted have agreed with us in this judgment."[12]

Wilson had given up on the problem and told Villard that he had thought about the matter for twenty years and saw "no way out. It will take a very big man to solve this thing," he added. Villard eventually broke with Wilson on the race question and gave spirited public talks exposing the ugly realities in Washington. He concluded finally: "The colored people were left much worse off than when Wilson took office, for the precedent had been set; for the first time the American democracy had officially told the world that there were two classes of citizens under its flag. The supreme wrong," Villard added, "came in 1917 when the Negroes . . . were drafted to go to France to make the world safe for democracy! What hypocrisy! What injustice! They were forced to die for the country which was still for them what Wendell Phillips had called it in Abolition days, "a magnificent conspiracy against justice."[13]

In Congress no black citizen held a seat. Encouraged by the administration's passive stance, racist legislators introduced a flood of white supremacy bills and, while few of them passed either House, they reveal the sentiment of the day. A highly publicized incident heightened congressional concern for legal props with which to maintain two classes of citizenship. The marriage of the flamboyant black heavyweight champion Jack Johnson to a white girl precipitated the introduction of several congressional bills to outlaw racial intermarriage through federal statute. When Congressman Roddenbery of Georgia introduced his bill he asserted, "No brutality, no infamy, no degradation in all the years of southern slavery possessed such villainous character and such atrocious qualities as the provisions of . . . [state] laws which allow the marriage of the negro Jack Johnson to a woman of the caucasian strain."[14]

The Wilson administration's plainly racist policies served to frustrate black hopes for increased democracy at home. Federal officialdom encouraged local bigotry. Excesses followed almost inevitably and the closing years of the World War I period probably record the meanest phase of the white response to black emancipation. Shortly before his death Booker T. Washington,

---

[12] Oswald Garrison Villard, *Fighting Years* (New York: Harcourt, Brace, 1939), p. 238.
[13] Ibid., pp. 236–41.
[14] Congressional Record, 62nd Congress, 3rd Session, December 11, 1912, p. 502.

traditionally an optimist on race relations, reported that he had "never seen the colored people so discouraged and embittered" at the racial trends of the national administration.[15]

Prior to the end of the war, a lynch-riot erupted in East St. Louis, Illinois. It turned into the most one-sided racial confrontation in the history of the nation. Shockingly, the East St. Louis riot culminated a series of increasingly hostile clashes across the country. During 1917 Chester and Philadelphia, Pennsylvania, and Houston, Texas, also saw bloody racial outbreaks, and between 1915 and 1919 no less than eighteen race riots occurred in cities of all types, north and south.

East St. Louis, "The Pittsburgh of the West," experienced a series of minor incidents suggestive of increasing racial hostility. Blacks who had recently migrated in search of war jobs appeared to threaten employment patterns; white business leaders had long used blacks as a source of cheap labor.

In early May of 1917, Alexander Flannigan, a lawyer and aspiring politician, gave an inflammatory speech to a group of white aluminum workers in which he cried, "There is no law against mob violence."[16] That afternoon whites assaulted a number of black workers as they left various plants around the city. On May 29 John Lee, father of four, who had lived in East St. Louis for several years, was beaten outside the Swift plant. Fearing for his family and his life, he agreed to leave the city, although he had always maintained a good work record and a completely clean civic reputation. His only crime? Blackness!

On June 17 a sixty-year-old black refused to surrender his seat on a trolley to a white woman; a group of riders beat him brutally.

On July 1 a hysterical black woman in a torn dress rushed into a black neighborhood and reported that white men had beaten her for no apparent reason. Later that evening a Ford car cruised through the neighborhood with two whites riding in it. They fired a number of shots into black homes from the fast-moving car. Negroes began to arm. Still later the same evening a similar-appearing Ford car carrying four white policemen cruised down the same street. Blacks mistook the car for the earlier intruder and fired several shots; two of the policemen were killed. Police now began to take a one-sided part in the disturbances. They searched and disarmed blacks but left whites

---

15 Oswald Garrison Villard, *Fighting Years* (New York: Harcourt, Brace, 1939), p. 237.
16 Elliott M. Rudwick, *Race Riot at East St. Louis* (Carbondale, Ill.: Southern Illinois University Press, 1964), p. 28. The account of the riot which follows owes much to Rudwick's study.

unmolested. In a few cases white policemen actually led anti-black mobs.

During the late afternoon of the next day rioting surfaced everywhere and the situation was almost completely out of control. White mobs attacked blacks wherever they found them. They set a number of homes on fire, sometimes boarding up the owners inside. In cases when the occupants could flee the fire the mobsmen shot them as they emerged. The St. Louis *Republic* reported, "A crazed negro would dash from his burning home, sometimes with a revolver in his hand. Immediately revolvers by the score would be fired. He would zig-zag through the spaces between buildings. Then a well directed shot would strike him. He would leap into the air. There were deep shouts, intermingled with shrill feminine ones. The flames would creep to the body. The negro would writhe, attempt to get up, more shots would be fired. The flames would eat their way to him, past him and further east along Railroad Avenue."[17]

Whites, filled with fear and hatred, burned one entire square block of black homes; most of the residents, male and female, young and old, who were in the buildings suffered unspeakable deaths.

White rioters seized many blacks and hanged them from telephone poles or trees; they left them dangling for hours. One reporter for the St. Louis *Post Dispatch* saw six blacks killed by gunfire. He observed that each one had his hands above his head, pleading for mercy as the crowd opened fire. The white congressman for the district said that "civil government in East St. Louis completely collapsed at the time of the riot. The conditions there at the time beggar description. It is impossible for any human being to describe the ferocity and brutality of that mob. In one case . . . a little ten-year-old boy, whose mother had been shot down, was running around sobbing and looking for his mother, and some members of the mob shot the boy, and before life had passed from his body they picked the little fellow up and threw him in the flames. . . . The horror of that tragedy in East St. Louis can never be described. It weighted me down with a feeling of depression that I did not recover from for weeks."[18]

The Illinois National Guard came to the city to restore order. Outnumbered, they did little to stop white assaults on individual blacks. Thousands of blacks fled across the river to St. Louis, Missouri, which, surprisingly, was otherwise untouched by the

[17] St. Louis *Republic* account in ibid., p. 46.
[18] Speech of Congressman Rodenberg in James Weldon Johnson, *Along This Way* (New York: Viking Press, 1943), p. 320.

riot. The strong antiriot stand of the *Post Dispatch* may have been a factor.

When the riot began to cool down, authorities withdrew some of the troops. A local postman announced to a newspaper reporter: "The only trouble with the mob was that it didn't get niggers enough. You wait and see what we do to the rest when the soldiers go. We'll get every last one of them."[19] His prediction proved correct; the riot kept breaking out in isolated places around the city. One black woman later told a typical story. She, her son, and her husband were riding on a streetcar. The crowd stopped the car by pulling the overhead wire down. A "man reached through the window and grabbed my dress and tore it partly off. . . . He said, 'Come on out you black bitch, because we want to kill you. . . .' Then he . . . came into the car and said, 'All you white people get out. We're going to kill these niggers.' The white people got off. I told them that we . . . didn't live in East St. Louis and hadn't hurt anybody there. . . . That man . . . took my husband by the collar and pulled him to the back platform and threw him off and shot him. . . . [Then he] took my boy and started to drag him out. I took hold of him. 'You've killed my husband,' I said, 'Don't kill my boy.' He jerked him away, beating him over the head with his revolver, and that was the last time I saw my son alive. . . . Then . . . [he] came back and dragged me out of the car, and men beat me, and kicked me, and pulled my hair out. A white man got in front of me and called out, 'Don't kill the women folks.' The men started beating him, and I crawled on my hands and knees into a store. . . . I fell over in this doorway and at that time some tall white fellow came running there and said, 'don't beat her any more. I am not going to let them kill you,' he said, 'stay back there.' And so he threw his arm across the door like that and I was behind him and he says, 'in the name of the Lord don't kill the woman,' and then some way or other they got me into the ambulance, and there was another fellow lying there, a colored fellow on the side of the ambulance, and I saw he had a big handkerchief and I took it and wiped the blood out of my eyes, and when I looked down I saw my husband lying there and my boy right under me; they had their eyes open and they were dead."[20]

Altogether nine whites and at least thirty-nine blacks died. The exact number of black deaths was never determined because many burned up in the building fires. The 1917 East St. Louis

19 Elliott M. Rudwick, *Race Riot at East St. Louis* (Carbondale, Ill.: Southern Illinois University Press, 1964), p. 69.

20 Ibid., p. 104.

riot is generally considered to have been the most bloody race riot in the history of the United States.

The country registered shock at this fresh evidence of white racism in America. Ex-President Theodore Roosevelt issued a vigorous statement calling for a full investigation. Editorials across the nation condemned the violent destruction by the white mobs. President Wilson, however, refused to accept any federal responsibility for preserving local order even after investigation clearly showed the city police and state National Guard troops to have been unjust and one sided. Wilson refused to agree to the use of federal troops, although he had used soldiers to protect property during a coal strike in Colorado.

The NAACP sponsored a "silent parade" of protest in New York and other cities. Thousands of blacks and a few white supporters marched quietly up Fifth Avenue to the beat of muffled drums. They carried banners with such words as:

Mother, Do Lynchers Go to Heaven?

Treat Us So That We May Love
Our Country

Mr. President, Why Not Make
America Safe for Democracy?

Several marchers stretched a banner across the street and walked slowly ahead of a man carrying an American flag. The banner read, "Your Hands Are Full of Blood."[21] The marchers, who wore black armbands, sent a delegation to the White House to plead for a national law against lynching and mob violence. Wilson refused to see them, although his secretary assured them the president supported the idea. Nothing was done.

Some black youths spoke openly in favor of refusing to be drafted unless the president expressed a willingness to use federal troops to protect black citizens. The Negro press printed many outraged comments. One black journalist wrote after the East St. Louis riot, "We are perfectly well aware that the outlook for us is not encouraging. . . . We, the American Negroes, are the acid test for occidental civilization. If we perish, we perish. But when we fall, we shall fall like Samson, dragging inevitably with us the pillars of a nation's democracy."[22]

Study of race relations history in America leads to the conclu-

---

21 James Weldon Johnson, *Along This Way* (New York: Viking Press, 1943), p. 321.
22 Comment of Jessie Fauset in Elliott M. Rudwick, *Race Riot at East St. Louis* (Carbondale, Ill.: Southern Illinois University Press, 1964), p. 65.

sion that the majority of whites in any era learn little from mere awareness of racial conflict in the country. An incident, humiliating to blacks, in one town has no apparent carry-over effect in other places. A lynching in one county does not seem to discourage similar outrage in another. A violent riot in one city has little power to dissuade mobs from atrocities in the population centers of other states.

No better illustration could be advanced to support these generalizations than that supplied by events close following the 1917 lynch riot in East St. Louis. Outbreaks during 1919 suggest that the events of East St. Louis accomplished little by way of sobering effect. More than twenty small-scale lynch-riots erupted around the country.

In Washington, D.C., three days of fighting and widespread killing ended finally after federal troops "occupied" major portions of the city. The riot began when about two hundred white servicemen in uniform attacked several black civilians in the downtown area. The soldiers and marines, acting on a rumor of the rape of a white woman, asserted that the city's blacks needed to be taught a lesson. The firm resistance of many Washington blacks, some of them heavily armed, slowed the rampaging whites. For the first time in American history black citizens armed themselves in sizable numbers and beat off attempted white incursions into black residential areas.

The worst riot during 1919 took place in Chicago, only half a state away from East St. Louis. Chicago, the tough "city of the big shoulders," experienced increasing racial friction during the spring of 1919. Many blacks had come into the city in search of jobs. As tension mounted, warning signs of a bad riot appeared. Racial incidents increased, and attacks involved greater boldness with sharper violence. During 1917–1919 bombings destroyed an average of one black home in Chicago each month.

In the early spring whites murdered two blacks on the streets of downtown Chicago. The police made no arrests. Repeatedly newspapers carried accounts of white attacks on isolated blacks. On June 21 white youth gangs killed two blacks to underscore their reported interest in "getting a nigger." Again police arrested no one. Signs appeared in many areas of the city stating "All Niggers" would be gotten on July 4th. But the day passed without major disturbance.[23]

And then, on July 27, 1919, Eugene Williams, a black youth, went swimming in Lake Michigan off a beach traditionally "re-

---

[23] Allan H. Spear, *Black Chicago* (Chicago: University of Chicago Press, 1967), p. 213.

served" for blacks. When he drifted toward a nearby white beach some boys on the shore stoned him and he drowned. Rioting broke out at the beach after the outraged blacks failed to persuade the single white policeman on duty to arrest those who had done the stoning.

That night Chicago was hell. Whites and blacks assaulted each other wherever the occasion could be forced. In white areas isolated blacks suffered death and beating. In black areas, isolated whites received the same treatment.

Many innocent victims became involved in the rioting as they tried to return home after work. Accounts sprinkled through the newspapers suggest a genuine reign of terror during which few persons in central Chicago felt safe. After three days of horror 15 whites and 23 blacks lay dead; 178 whites and 342 blacks suffered serious injury.

The Chicago riot emerged as a more even contest than the fight in East St. Louis two years before. But the mostly white grand jury which investigated the riot decided that the white state attorney tried to load the case against blacks and also that "the colored people suffered more at the hands of the white hoodlums than the white people suffered at the hands of the black hoodlums."[24] Despite the preponderance of black deaths and injuries over those among whites, the courts tried and punished twice as many blacks as whites for participation in the riot.

One of the great pieces of historic reporting on the white problem in America emerged from the Chicago riot of 1919. In 1922, after three years, a mostly white investigating commission issued a powerful report. The account of the Chicago Commission on Race Relations left little doubt that the elimination of racial conflict in America required white acceptance of black equality. White attitudes toward blacks created the problem; whites, therefore, controlled the solution. Had the majority of American whites in 1922 seen this reality and demanded action by their peers, they could have altered the course of our national history.

In essence, the Kerner Commission Report of 1968 is identical to the record issued in 1922 by the Chicago Commission. Dr. Kenneth B. Clark, outstanding black intellectual, appeared as a witness before the Kerner Commission. Among other things he observed, "I read the report . . . of the 1919 race riot in Chicago, and it is as if I were reading the report of the investigating committee on the Harlem riot of '35, the report of the investigating committee on the Harlem riot of '43, the report of the McCone Com-

---

24 Chicago Commission on Race Relations, *The Negro in Chicago* (Chicago: University of Chicago Press, 1922), p. 35.

mission on the Watts riot. I must again in candor say to you members of this Commission it is a kind of Alice in Wonderland—with the same moving picture re-shown over and over again, the same analysis, the same recommendations, and the same inaction."[25]

The two riots in Illinois in 1917 and 1919 demonstrate traditional white fear and hatred of those born black. Periodically white fear brings surging hate punctuated by violent friction between the races. Housing and jobs stand out as the most common grounds of challenge; struggle over the fundamental necessities of daily existence precipitates contest. In both cases, the convenient assumption—"Black Skin Means Something Challenging and Bad"—triggers action deemed necessary to sustain white advantage.

The preceding chapter analyzes trends in the continuing racial friction over housing. The question of jobs calls for a brief look at the record of business and the labor unions. American business and labor have abused the black worker; to the business leader, black migrants from the rural South consistently supplied cheap, nonunion labor. The unionists increasingly viewed the black man as a scab. Neither business nor labor assumed any significant measure of responsibility for bringing blacks into the main economic stream of the nation. Yet they could easily have done so at almost any point.

The common failure of business and unions in the matter of racial equality redounds particularly to the discredit of organized labor. Unions have initiated a wide variety of social reforms. Fair wages, job protection, disability insurance, social security, reduced hours, the five-day work week, special protection for women and children—these and more can be traced directly to union insistence upon a decent life for the average citizen. But in the matter of racial equality, few social institutions in American history have less to show for numerous opportunities to effect genuine improvement.

The rise of "free" trade unionism in the North generally discouraged blacks from seeking equality of opportunity, although exceptional unions favored full and equal alliance between the white and black worker. The first significant American labor organization, the National Labor Union, emerged in 1866. On sensible economic grounds the NLU welcomed black labor and urged full participation for members of all races.

---

[25] Statement of Kenneth B. Clark to Kerner Commission, *Report of the National Advisory Commission on Civil Disorders* (New York: Bantam Books, 1968), p. 483. (First published by E. P. Dutton, New York, 1968.)

The National Convention of Negro Labor formed at about the same time faced the knotty question of amalgamation. Would submergence in the NLU bring true job equality or merely serve to subordinate minority interests to those of the majority? Would amalgamation bring advance? Or would black workers merely be buried in the larger context? For some three years whites and blacks thrashed out the amalgamation issue. The sides differed on immediate needs and priorities. Politically, black union leadership held overwhelmingly pro-Republican party views, whereas white labor chiefs opposed the GOP. Other splits occurred over majority control, particularly in the building trades, where whites, in spite of the generally friendly sentiment toward biracial participation in the National Labor Union, refused to admit black apprentices. Finally, the Negro Labor Congress, meeting in New Orleans in 1872, voted against affiliation with the NLU. The long split between black workers and the American labor movement had opened.

The NLU died as a result of the Panic of 1873. Its replacement, the Noble Order of Knights of Labor, also took a stance friendly to full black participation in all aspects of the unionization process. Many black workers entered the new organization, and by the middle of the 1880's some 60,000 blacks held membership in the Knights. The color line broke in many places, but again, not in the building trades, where white workers turned back all moves to open training on an equal basis to blacks. Yet the Knights of Labor established a better record than the NLU and a much superior one to the AFL which followed.

Indeed, the strong civil-rights stance of the Knights of Labor accelerated the antiblack thinking of trades-oriented whites who wished to preserve the racial "purity" of the basic industries. In 1886, when the AFL emerged with its strong trades emphasis, the promising equal-rights start of the Knights of Labor faded before traditional white desires to avoid black competition.

In 1900 Booker T. Washington, who opposed all unions black or white, formed the National Negro Business League in an effort to get members up the economic ladder by means of black capitalism. However, the NNBL never flourished.

W. E. B. Du Bois, as in other racial matters, opposed Washington's approach. He insisted that only full participation in the union movement could bring equal opportunity. In one ringing indictment he said, "I hold these truths to be self-evident, that a disfranchised working class in modern industrial civilization is worse than helpless. It is a menace not simply to itself but to every other group in the community. It will be diseased, it will be criminal, it will be ignorant, it will be the plaything of mobs, and it will be insulted by caste restrictions."[26] As was so often the case, Du Bois saw the future clearly.

During the great years of the American Federation of Labor, from about 1890 to 1950, virtually all of its affiliated unions maintained rigid practices which effectively barred blacks from equal opportunity in the competition for jobs. Explanations to justify these exclusions were endlessly varied. For example, the Glass Workers Union excluded blacks "universally on the ground that the pipe on which the glass is blown passes from mouth to mouth and no one would use it after a Negro."[27] The International Brotherhood of Electrical Workers long excluded all blacks yet insisted that the union did not discriminate because it favored black locals holding independent affiliations with the parent AFL. Such minority group locals, isolated from the main union power, almost never received equal treatment. Impotent and impoverished, they served little economic or social purpose.

The Plumbers and Steamfitters Union never had an exclusion clause in its constitution. However, the union dominated city boards of licensing. These boards, which always included representatives from the union, nearly always excluded black applicants for apprentice programs. The Plumbers Union controlled the trade so successfully that they also excluded many qualified whites. The plumbers have moved wages up and held competition down by restrictive practices which would have graced the planning of the tightest guild of medieval Europe.[28]

White supremacist views lie at the root of union opposition to black equality in the labor movement, just as they lie at the root of the white problem in America. One delegate to an early national convention of the AFL put it this way: "I do not think there is a member in this room that believes in taking the Negro in with him on social equality. I believe that God in his infinite mercy made the Negro but he never made him to be a . . . [union] worker. I do not believe the time will ever come when he should

---

26 Statement from unpublished paper by W. E. B. Du Bois, in Sterling D. Spero and Abram L. Harris, *The Black Worker* (New York: Atheneum, 1968), p. 52. The analysis of the unions and black workers here presented owes much to Spero and Harris' study.

27 Charles S. Johnson, *Abstracts of the Report of the Research Committee to the National Interracial Conference,* Part IV, 1928, in ibid., p. 58.

28 One New York City plumber in the 1950's had long since mastered his trade, yet he had to work under his father's name. Although he had been plumbing for years and his father was no longer active, the only way he could practice plumbing was to continue operating under his father's license. Specifically he had been waiting fourteen years for his own license to practice; he did not know when he would be fully accepted as a master plumber. Meanwhile his father delayed departing for a Florida retirement.

come into a union. . . . I was born with an abolitionist father; but when the time does come that I must sit down in social equality with the Negro . . . I want to be carried to the nearest insane asylum."[29]

Faced with this general attitude blacks sought solutions. They pressed for equal treatment and increasingly the national leadership of the AFL worked against written exclusion clauses. However, unwritten practices of discrimination served white-supremacist purposes equally well, and compelled black reactions which took various forms. Affiliated, all-black locals sometimes worked well, but in general they were second-class organizations with little real power. All-black unions with their own exclusion policies occasionally succeeded. For example, beginning in 1925, the Brotherhood of Sleeping Car Porters and Maids, under the leadership of A. Philip Randolph, became one of the truly significant forces for equality in American life, while maintaining an all-black policy in its own ranks. However, portering and maid work hardly constituted a major breakthrough into white-collar status.

Blacks sometimes received genuine equality within the main union movement. The beginnings of real change came through the efforts of radical unions, especially the International Workers of the World. In 1910 the IWW began a vigorous recruitment drive to attract black workers and eventually approximately 10 per cent of the 1 million membership cards issued by the union went to blacks. During World War I the Wobblies made some remarkable racial breakthroughs in the lumbering regions of the South and a few port cities in the Northeast. Never had any union succeeded so well in following policies which submerged racial issues to more vital economic considerations. Union literature reminded the workers that leaving blacks outside the organization would make them scabs "dangerous to the organized worker. . . . Race prejudice on the job could only have one result —keeping the workers fighting each other, while the boss gets the benefits." Such a stand earned the union the admiration of black militants like Du Bois, who praised the organization as "one of the social and political movements in modern times that draws no color line."[30]

But Wobbly radicalism brought repression, and the promising beginnings of racial justice in the union movement failed to survive the defeat of the IWW in the early 1920's. Later, John L.

[29] International Car Workers, Proceedings, Special Session, September 1905, in Sterling D. Spero and Abram L. Harris, *The Black Worker* (New York: Atheneum, 1968), p. 66.
[30] Philip S. Foner, "The IWW and the Black Worker," *Journal of Negro History*, Vol. LV, No. 1, January 1970, pp. 47, 58.

Lewis led the United Mine Workers to further racial progress and the Reuther brothers purged the United Auto Workers of prejudiced practices. The industrial union movement during the 1930's generally established a better racial record than that of the older AFL. A. Philip Randolph's American Negro Labor Congress, which began meeting in 1925, assisted the slow process of upgrading the racial record of the unions.

Yet the current (1970) struggle for equal jobs in the building trades demonstrates the continued bias of much of the union movement. In the fall of 1969 a coalition of blacks and whites began a series of protest marches in Pittsburgh designed to force the building trades to open their ranks through fair hiring practices. Although the Laborers Union lists about a quarter of its membership as black, the skilled building trades remain virtually all white. Less than 1 per cent of the Plumbers Union and of the Sheet Metal Workers Union is black and trades like carpentry, bricklaying, glazing, and electrical contracting have only slightly higher percentages of nonwhites. The Pittsburgh protesters concentrated on trying to shut down work on multistory buildings. Although they gained some national publicity, local response took the form of abusive language and brickbats thrown down from scaffolds above the streets onto the heads of the marchers. The Pittsburgh experience follows the classic union pattern, and was duplicated in Chicago, Illinois, and Buffalo, New York, during the same year.

Historically, more or less violent friction has characterized union resistance to equality for blacks. As one report put it: "Through many experiences Negroes came to believe that the only way they could get into a unionized industry was through strikebreaking."[31] The East St. Louis riot of 1917 was precipitated when the Aluminum Ore Co. imported about 10,000 blacks to break a strike.

Blackness of skin has tended to touch off extremes of passion on the part of white workers even when the strikebreaking force has been predominantly white. For example, in a teamsters' strike in Chicago in 1905, the company imported approximately 5,800 strikebreakers, of which 5,000 were white. Yet the blacks received most of the abuse and were the targets of widespread acts of violence. Labor newspapers consistently presented strikebreakers as being almost entirely black. The Chicago riot of 1919

---

31 Commission of Inquiry, Report on the Steel Strike of 1919 in Sterling D. Spero and Abram L. Harris, *The Black Worker* (New York: Atheneum, 1968), p. 261.

stemmed from the general infusion of blacks into many job areas, particularly in the stockyards.

In 1927 and 1928 many coal companies in Pennsylvania brought black strikebreakers in; much violence and bloodshed followed. To the credit of the UMW it fought successfully to integrate the black workers fully into the union movement and largely succeeded during the 1930's under the Lewis leadership. But the great majority of labor unions have consistently failed to put ideals of justice into full practice. Their failures, after apparent black advances during the fluid, labor-scarce era which accompanied the war, increased black disillusionment.

The social ferment created by World War I brought little advantage to the average American black. Because of this the considerable impact of a militant separatist immigrant from the West Indies, named Marcus Garvey, should have occasioned no particular surprise. Yet white insensitivity to the socially imposed plight of their black fellow citizens caused Garvey to be both feared and hated.

Garvey, typical of many West Indian blacks, had strong racial pride and began his movement, The Universal Negro Improvement Association, in his native Jamaica in 1914. He came to the U.S. in 1916 and the UNIA rapidly gained strength among lower-class blacks who felt the full disadvantage of second-class citizenship. Garvey drew support from many; he claimed five to six million members by the mid-1920's. The official figure was probably closer to a half million active members with several millions more who agreed with Garvey's indictment of American white racism and who sympathized with his goals. Whatever the exact numbers, the Garvey organization clearly became the first mass movement of blacks in American history.

Pure black in ancestry—not a mulatto like many upper-caste Jamaicans—Garvey not only refused to accept any implications of minority group inferiority, he went to great lengths to assert black superiority. To build pride he formed counterparts to everything white, a Black Eagle Flying Corps, a Black Cross Nursing Corps, a Black Star Steamship Line, and even a Black House to match the White House. He ardently believed there was no solution to white antagonism to blacks in America. White racism could never allow equality; therefore, blacks should return to Africa. His Black Star Steamship Line served this purpose. Thus was reborn an often white-supported solution to the race question dating back to the American Colonization Society of the 1830's. Such distinguished white leaders as Abraham Lincoln and Theodore Roosevelt at times advocated this "solution."

Garvey might have attracted an even more impressive following had he been able to appeal to black intellectuals as well as to the laboring class. Many black leaders found Garvey unacceptable. Du Bois became an outspoken critic as did most of the NAACP intellectuals and other middle-class types. Du Bois called Garvey bombastic and his UNIA impractical. A. Philip Randolph and Chandler Owen, editors of a radical black newspaper, the *Messenger,* were even more contemptuous. A 1923 issue of the *Messenger* called Garvey "Squat, stocky, fat, and sleek with protruding jaws and heavy jowls; small, bright, piglike eyes, and rather full dog-like face. Boastful, egotistic, tyrannical, intolerant . . . gifted at self-advertisement . . . promising ever, but never fulfilling . . . a lover of pomp, tawdry finery, and garish display . . . a sheer opportunist and demagogic charlatan."[32]

Garvey fought back eloquently. On one occasion he wrote of Du Bois and the NAACP leadership: "The NAACP wants us all to become white by amalgamation, but they are not honest enough to come out with the truth. To be a Negro is no disgrace, but an honor, and we of the Universal Negro Improvement Association do not want to become white. . . . We are proud and honorable. We love our race and respect and adore our mothers."[33]

On another occasion Garvey sued Robert Abbott, editor of the influential Chicago *Defender,* for implying there was fraud in the collections process by which Garvey's Black Star Steamship line gained support in the black community. The all-black quarrel became a farce in the courts when Garvey won the case, but instead of getting the million dollars he had sued for he was awarded damages of only 1 cent.

In 1922 federal authorities indicted Garvey for using the mails to defraud; eventually convicted he received a sentence of five years in the federal penitentiary at Atlanta, Georgia. When he entered jail he spoke to the spirit of his many followers through an editorial in the UNIA organ, *Negro World:* "Look for me in the whirlwind or the storm, look for me all around you, for with God's grace I shall come and bring with me countless millions of black slaves who have died in America and the West Indies and the millions in Africa to aid you in the fight for Liberty, Freedom and Life."[34] President Coolidge commuted Garvey's sentence in

---

32 Comment by Robert W. Bagnall in "The Messenger," in Arna Bontemps and Jack Conroy, *Anyplace But Here* (New York: Hill and Wang, 1968), p. 200.

33 Amy Jacques Garvey, *Philosophy and Opinions of Marcus Garvey* (New York: Atheneum, 1969), Vol. II, pp. 325–326. (First published by Universal Publishing House, New York, 1923.)

34 Ibid., p. 239.

1927 but the government immediately deported him as an undesirable alien and he never returned to the U.S. Yet his movement survived him in various forms. His separatist approach led
in the direction of the Black Muslim religion through such
splinter organizations as the Abyssinian Movement, the Moorish-
American Science Temple, and the Ethiopian Peace Movement.

The passage of time has favored Marcus Garvey. His reputation
as an unyielding advocate of the sacredness of black humanity has
grown through the years while the tawdry aspects of the UNIA
have gradually been forgotten. Amy Jacques Garvey, divorced
first wife of the leader of the UNIA, though critical of her ex-
husband in some of his personal foibles, defended his movement.
She contended that his "Back to Africa" effort which had been
ridiculed in both the white and the black press during his lifetime really sought an awakening of the soul of the black race on
all continents. The "Back to Africa" idea was more symbolic than
real.

In November 1956, Jamaica unveiled a proud statue to Marcus
Garvey and the main speaker, William L. Sherrill of the United
States, said, "Because Garvey lived, Jamaica is different; because
Garvey lived Negro America is different; because Garvey lived,
Africa is different. His work and teachings gave birth to a new
Negro, a New Africa. . . . He did more to crystallize National
sentiment in so-called backward countries than any single indi-
vidual in our times. Measured by the standard of change, Garvey
rises to the heights of greatness."[35]

Du Bois, Garvey's strongest critic, on hearing of the UNIA
leader's death in 1940, spoke gently of Garvey's sincerity and
though he re-emphasized the impractical nature of the Back to
Africa idea he added, "Within a few years, news of his movement,
of his promises and plans, reached Europe and Asia, and penetrated every corner of Africa."[36] Kwame Nkrumah, who often
praised Garvey, invited Du Bois to live in Ghana and serve as editor in chief of the *Encyclopaedia Africana*. Du Bois accepted.
Whereas Garvey never set foot on African soil, Du Bois died there,
a citizen of Ghana, in 1963. Malcolm X, whose father had been a
Garveyite, made many Garvey-like comments. He too visited the
black Republics of Africa; his final life endeavor, the Organization
of Afro-American Unity, also sought to awaken the "soul of the
black race on all continents."

A persistent theme of the Garvey movement and of all black
nationalist efforts in the United States has been the assertion that

---

35 Dedication speech by William L. Sherrill in Arna Bontemps and Jack
Conroy, *Anyplace But Here* (New York: Hill and Wang, 1968), p. 215.
36 Comment of W. E. B. Du Bois, in ibid., p. 215.

no black citizen can hope for justice under a social structure filled with institutionalized prejudice. The ultimate test of this assertion involves assessment of the judicial system under which the nation operates. Most whites have long believed that American courts supply valid approximations of "Equal Justice Under Law." Many blacks reject this belief; a variety of major decisions can be cited to support black contentions that American courts dispense "justice" which takes different forms depending on the color of the person charged with the crime.

A number of the celebrated court cases in American history have centered upon the white problem. In general blacks have fared poorly. In the Dred Scott case, just prior to the Civil War, the black plaintiff not only lost his individual plea for freedom, but black citizenship as a whole received a setback when the Supreme Court ruled that blacks were property without any civil rights whatsoever. A crucial clause asserted: "No word can be found in the Constitution . . . which entitles property . . . [in slaves] to less protection than property of any other description."[37]

The case of *Plessy* v. *Ferguson* (1896), already discussed, arrived at a slightly less harsh decision, but gave little ground for black confidence in the judicial process. The most celebrated racial decision of the twentieth century, the Scottsboro case, contributed even less to black hopes.

The issues involving establishment of a single class of citizenship have been termed the "acid test" of American civilization.[38] If this be true, the crucial judgment of this "acid test" lies in proper analysis of the records of the courts. Such analysis points inevitably to events in northern Alabama during the spring of 1931.

The original incident, the trial, the appeals, and the outcome all raise and answer many questions regarding the reality of second-class citizenship for blacks. On March 25, 1931, a white youth who had been in a fight with some blacks aboard a freight train in northern Alabama reported to a station master that he had been forced off the train. The station master wired ahead and officials stopped the train near Scottsboro, Alabama; detectives searched the train and found nine black youths aged twelve to nineteen, one white youth and two white girls, aged seventeen and twenty-one. The white youth had also been involved in the

---

[37] Supreme Court of the United States, 19 How. (60 U.S.) 393, 1857, in Albert P. Blaustein and Robert L. Zangrando, eds., *Civil Rights and the American Negro: A Documentary History* (New York: Washington Square Press, 1968), p. 168.
[38] See footnote 22.

fight but by the time he was to be thrown off, the train had gathered so much speed that some of the blacks took pity on him and let him stay. The fight had started when two of the white hobos had almost shoved one of the blacks off the train.

As the sheriff rounded up the group to charge them with vagrancy, Victoria Price, one of the girls, whispered to town officials that both she and Ruby Bates had been raped by the blacks. Two local doctors examined the girls and found evidence of recent sexual intercourse but no particular signs of bruising or struggle. The girls remained calm and chatty. One of them admitted that they both were generally promiscuous. However, this crucial piece of evidence did not become public until much later. The white man's red flag, "rape" of Caucasian woman by black man, aroused the town. A mob gathered and only the calling of the Alabama National Guard averted a mass lynching that night.

Traditionally, American justice moves deliberately but a short two weeks later the case of the nine "Scottsboro boys" went to trial. They were defended halfheartedly by two white court-appointed lawyers who failed even to force a change of venue, although the boys had already been tried and found guilty in the press and gossip of the entire area. One prominent Alabama newspaper wrote: "All Negroes Positively Identified by Girls and One White Boy Who Was Held Prisoner with Pistol and Knives While Nine Black Fiends Committed Revolting Crime. . . . some of the negroes held the two white girls [while] others of the fiends raped them, holding knives at their throats and beating them when they struggled. . . . [They were] found in the [freight] car in terrible condition mentally and physically after their unspeakable experience at the hands of the black brutes."[39]

The jury quickly found the first eight defendants guilty and condemned them to death, chiefly on the statements of Victoria Price, who made an appealing and dramatic witness. The ninth boy, only twelve years of age, Leroy Wright, received no sentence because of a hung jury. Despite the fact that the *prosecution* appealed for clemency on account of his youth, six of the all-white jurors insisted upon the death penalty for Wright also.

Within a month the Scottsboro case became known all over the nation, partly owing to the participation of the American Communist party, through their legal agency, the International Labor

---

[39] Accounts in Scottsboro *Progressive Age,* March 26, 1931, and Scottsboro *Jackson County Sentinel,* March 26, 1931, in Dan T. Carter, *Scottsboro: A Tragedy of the American South* (Baton Rouge: Louisiana State University Press, 1969), p. 13. The account of the Scottsboro case here presented owes much to Carter's study.

Defense committee. The NAACP also belatedly involved itself but later withdrew after various disputes with the publicity-hungry Communists.

The Supreme Court overturned the first trial convictions on the grounds that the boys had not received proper legal defense. They were tried again in 1933 with the Communists as their major defenders, working in support of a brilliant non-Communist New York white lawyer named Samuel S. Leibowitz. A black lawyer in such a case was worse than useless. Granting a victory to a representative of the inferior black race over the superior white race was unthinkable to the minds of all-white juries. The merits of the case would have been completely submerged in the larger question of a black lawyer's success in defeating his white opposition.

Authorities moved the new trial to Decatur in the next county and, again, the National Guard kept order around the courthouse. Thousands of angry whites milled about threateningly at both trials.

In the second trial Leibowitz tried to impugn the entire system of law in Alabama on the grounds that jury calls included no blacks. He raised considerable doubts on this point, but failed to win his main contention. One Scottsboro civic leader involved in the jury selection insisted the nonpresence of black jurors implied no racial prejudice. He stated that blacks had not been "trained" for jury duty in the county and he did not think their judgment could be depended upon altogether. "They will nearly all steal," he added. The white spectators chuckled at this.[40]

Again, as in the first trial, Victoria Price served as the star witness, but this time, Ruby Bates was not around. She had disappeared in the interim and supplied no corroborating testimony regarding the alleged multiple rape. Leibowitz brilliantly weakened Victoria Price's credibility as a witness. He showed that she was a well-known prostitute in Huntsville, where she was commonly known as "Big Leg Price."[41] She had been arrested for soliciting and also for adultery with a prominent Huntsville man.

The medical doctor called by the prosecution actually assisted the defense. And the other examining doctor stated his belief that the girls had never been raped at all: "Judge, I looked at both the women and told them they were lying, that they knew they had not been raped, and they just laughed at me."[42]

40 Dan T. Carter, "A Reasonable Doubt," *American Heritage*, Vol. XIX, No. 6, October 1968, p. 42.

41 Dan T. Carter, *Scottsboro: A Tragedy of the American South* (Baton Rouge: Louisiana State University Press, 1969), p. 84.

42 Letter from Judge James E. Horton to Dan T. Carter, September 28, 1967, in ibid., p. 215.

The most dramatic testimony of the trial came when Ruby Bates suddenly appeared to speak, not for the prosecution, but for the defense. She denied the story of the rape, after stating that she and Victoria had both had repeated sexual intercourse with two whites in a hobo park the night before.

But majority passions in the town and area, aroused against the black boys, threatened mob violence if the blacks escaped conviction. Judge James E. Horton, a lifetime resident of Alabama who conducted the first two trials, became troubled at the threats to both the black prisoners and the "New York Jew lawyers" for the defense. On one occasion he had the jury retire. . . . Then he lectured the audience in emotional tones: "the man who would engage in anything that would cause the death of any of these prisoners is a murderer; he is not only a murderer, but a cowardly murderer. . . ." The judge insisted that anyone who attempted to take the lives of the prisoners could expect that his own life would be forfeited because he would make no compromise with mob violence.[43]

Leibowitz later called Horton one of the finest judges he had ever met because the Alabamian ran an eminently fair trial. Unfortunately the jury did not view the evidence carefully. They deliberated for some twenty-three hours, which suggests careful thought, but later it was learned that they only discussed the death penalty vs. life in prison. They found Haywood Patterson, the first of the nine to be tried, guilty on the initial ballot, 12 to 0, five minutes after they got the case. They never even discussed the testimony of Ruby Bates. On the next vote eleven favored sending Patternson to the chair while one held out for life imprisonment. Finally, the following morning, the twelfth juror gave in and thus "justice" spoke.

Judge Horton granted a defense motion and overturned Patterson's conviction, ending his own public career in the process. Horton could be put among those American public officials who have placed truth above personal advantage. Patterson, eventually tried four different times, finally received a sentence of seventy-five years in prison. He escaped but later died in a Michigan jail. All of the youths served at least six years in prison, even Leroy Wright and Eugene Williams aged twelve and thirteen, who were later allowed off on the condition that "they leave the state of Alabama never to return."[44] Andrew Wright was the last of the prisoners paroled, nineteen years later in 1950.

[43] Statement of Judge James E. Horton, New York *World Telegram*, April 6th, 1933, in ibid., pp. 223–24.

[44] Ibid., p. 377.

The Scottsboro case, coming as it did in the midst of the greatest economic depression in American history, discouraged many thoughtful blacks. The judicial system seemed hopeless. The one intriguing aspect—Communist championship of the cause of racial equality—lacked conviction. The Reds seemed far more interested in advancing their own political fortunes than in assisting the welfare of the Scottsboro boys.

Fortunately, a new national leader emerged who seemed to promise progress through political action. Franklin D. Roosevelt had served creditably as governor of the most powerful state in the Union. His New York record favored the underprivileged; perhaps his presidency would champion the cause of second-class citizens regardless of color.

No administration in the twentieth century prior to that of FDR held much hope for American blacks. Theodore Roosevelt had looked promising but had been a tragic failure. Taft had a good personal record, but he proved to be a weak president. Wilson had greatly disappointed almost everyone, although knowledgeable black leaders had warned this was likely to be the case. His antiblack record caused American race relations to sink to a new low. The presidents during the 1920's—Harding, Coolidge, and Hoover—were not antiblack so much as simply antigovernment. They largely abdicated governmental responsibilities of any kind.

Franklin D. Roosevelt came to power when all Americans, white and black, sought a way out of the Depression. His comfortable majority in the 1932 election included the votes of many blacks. But these votes were cast more in the hope that his New Deal would supply economic reforms than in the belief that social equality was near.

The New Deal proved to be good economically for blacks as well as other underprivileged groups. But beyond economic reforms little real change occurred because blacks had virtually no political power at the start of the New Deal. One person, Oscar DePriest, had been elected to the U.S. House of Representatives in 1928. He was the only black member of either house of Congress. He served as the first black member to take a seat since 1901, the year that George White retired, the sole surviving leader from the black representation days following the Civil War.

President Roosevelt earned some respect in minority circles with his use of a "Black Cabinet" or "Black Brain Trust." The group included Robert C. Weaver, who became a racial adviser in the Department of the Interior; Eugene K. Jones of the Urban League, who served in the Department of Commerce; Lawrence Oxley, who became head of a division in the Department of

Labor; Mary McLeod Bethune, who was Director of the Division of Negro Affairs in the National Youth Administration; Abram Harris, who advised the NRA; Rayford Logan, who worked in the office of Inter-American Affairs; and Ira Reid, who was a consultant for the Social Security Board. By 1946 blacks in the federal service came to about 200,000; they had constituted only about 50,000 at the start of the New Deal. In addition FDR desegregated federal facilities in a reversal of the policies of the Wilson administration.

Moreover, blacks took hope from the genuine concern shown by the first lady. Eleanor Roosevelt, a personal friend of Mary McLeod Bethune, invited the National Council of Negro Women to tea at the White House. She traveled in and out of the country and demonstrated real interest in the plight of blacks. Sometimes she offended white racists with her unorthodox actions and made enemies in many quarters. In one highly publicized incident, Mrs. Roosevelt made a point of being photographed with two black ROTC students at Howard University who escorted her to the speaker's platform.

The apocryphal stories of the "Eleanor Clubs" stemmed from the first lady's friendship with Mary Bethune and other blacks. A whisper campaign across the country insisted that black women had organized into "Eleanor Clubs" and were standing together for impossible, atrocious social change. The slogan of the clubs supposedly argued for "A White Woman in Every Kitchen by 1943."[45] Allegedly, any black maid would walk off her job if her white employers said anything critical of the president or his wife.

A Florida version held that no black woman would accept a job in a white home without first finding out the views of the white head of the house. If those views opposed the Roosevelts, the position went begging. In 1942 a rumor spread that the Eleanor Clubs were unionizing black maids and demanding the outrageous sum of $8 per week as a minimum wage. Black males allegedly evidenced sympathy for the Eleanor Clubs when they wore zoot suits.

Many accused Eleanor Roosevelt of stirring up racial hatred; her husband received even more vicious attacks. One common piece of doggerel popular among racists placed the following words in the president's mouth: "You kiss the niggers and I'll kiss

---

45 Howard W. Odum, "Race and Rumors of Race," in Gilbert Osofsky, ed., *The Burden of Race: A Documentary History of Negro-White Relations in America* (New York: Harper & Row, 1967), p. 402.

the Jews, and we'll stay in the White House as long as we choose."[46]

But FDR basically disappointed the hopes of those who sought profound social change. The president was a politician who presided over a loose coalition of Northern liberals, big-city bosses, and Southern conservatives, many of whom held racist views and practically all of whom enjoyed major power in Congress. The president shrank from attacking the white problem in any but a superficial manner. As a result, he established a meager record in the field of civil rights.

This record can be illustrated by the fate of the Costigan-Wagner Anti-Lynching Bill of 1935. The bill sought to apply fines on counties where lynchings took place and jail terms for public officials who allowed such to happen. Walter White of the NAACP had been working for ten years on this imperative item, but when it actually got to Congress, he could not even get in to see President Roosevelt to discuss his support. White finally got Mrs. Roosevelt to intervene and she arranged a meeting.

Senator "Cotton Ed" Smith of South Carolina then led a Southern Democratic attack against the bill with a wide-swinging defense of states' rights and local self-government which suggested lynching was needed to protect women from beastly assaults.

When White finally got his audience with the president he described his frustrations in the following words: "The . . . conference was on the south portico of the White House on a warm spring Sunday in 1935. I found Mrs. Sara Delano Roosevelt and the President's wife on the porch, but the President had been delayed in returning from a cruise on the Potomac River. . . . Shortly afterward the President arrived in exuberant good spirits. As was his custom when he wished to avoid discussing a subject he told many gay and amusing anecdotes to postpone an anticipated ordeal. But finally I was able to bring the conversation to the . . . filibuster."

FDR then advanced a variety of arguments to the effect that the bill was unconstitutional. White countered his views. The president insisted that his wife must have been priming White. "Laughing, the President turned to his mother to say, 'Well, at least I know you'll be on my side.' "

"The president's mother shook her head and expressed the opinion that she agreed with Mr. White.

"Being a good loser, the President roared with laughter and confessed defeat.

---

[46] Leaflet distributed during Philadelphia transit workers strike, 1944, in ibid., p. 401.

"But I gained from the visit only a moral victory, because the President was frankly unwilling to challenge the Southern leadership of his party," White reported.

" 'I did not choose the tools with which I must work,' he told me. 'Had I been permitted to choose them I would have selected quite different ones. But I've got to get legislation passed by Congress to save America. The Southerners by reason of the seniority rule in Congress are chairman or occupy strategic places on most of the Senate and House committees. If I come out for the anti-lynching bill now, they will block every bill I ask Congress to pass to keep America from collapsing. I just can't take the risk.' "[47]

Increasingly, blacks became disillusioned with the New Deal. The black press consistently criticized the administration, partly because FDR's news conferences excluded black editors and reporters. A striking evidence of this black disillusionment with "the Dirty Deal," as some militants called it, took place in 1935 in Harlem, the most famous black community in the world. A severe riot of the modern variety occurred. Previous riots were largely white-led assaults against blacks and their property. The Harlem riot was a black-led attack on whites and their property, particularly white property which had any slum lord aspect.

As usual, the touch-off incident involved the police. A black boy caught stealing a penknife from a store on 125th Street ran from the police unharmed. But rumors got around that he had been roughly handled and even that he had been killed. Crowds rushed into the streets and for all the night of March 19 the black mobs rioted and looted. No similar public exhibition of pent-up black rage had ever taken place in America before. Most of the stores which operated in Harlem were white-owned; many had no black employees. The mobs destroyed more than 200 stores during the rampage.

When the news of the rioting spread, Mayor Fiorello La Guardia went to the disturbed areas with Walter White of the NAACP and tried to restore calm. After twenty-four hours of nightmare the attacks subsided. Two blacks died and dozens were injured; about $2 million worth of damage resulted. A commission headed by E. Franklin Frazier studied the event and concluded that the lawlessness grew out of "resentments against racial discrimination and poverty in the midst of plenty."[48]

As the Depression continued, American blacks suffered par-

---

[47] Account of interview by Walter White, *A Man Called White,* in ibid., pp. 408–11.
[48] Statement of E. Franklin Frazier in John Hope Franklin, *From Slavery to Freedom* (New York: Alfred A. Knopf, 1969), p. 540.

ticularly severely. By 1935 one in four struggled on meager federal relief. The situation did not improve significantly until World War II eventually stimulated the nation's economy.

World War I began at a time when the citizenship status of blacks had reached a crisis point. Economically weak, politically disfranchised, socially separated, they struggled to survive. The war brought new hopes for social mobility but the policies of the Wilson administration blunted these hopes. In the postwar era the mass of whites continued to be insensitive to the tragedy of racism at work. Marcus Garvey's black nationalism attracted many desperate supporters but to most it seemed an unlikely solution. The coming of the Depression created difficulties for all Americans; to blacks it meant further bitter frustration in a social structure that seemed about to collapse.

Even as all hope appeared lost, World War II emerged to create new social unrest and open fresh opportunities for genuine reform. Thoughtful blacks saw the new war, as they had seen World War I, as a time for forcing social change but on this occasion they determined to succeed. The nation has yet to emerge from the new era which began in the turmoil created by involvement in World War II.

# World War II and Its Aftermath

# 8

AMERICAN blacks supported the nation in large numbers during World War II; some were drafted; many enlisted. In contrast to the period prior to World War I when few blacks found the international situation a matter of concern, many had become sensitive to the menace of fascism starting with the Italian conquest of black Ethiopia in 1935. In 1936 the National Negro Congress issued an appeal for help for Ethiopia in its efforts to defend itself against the Italian attack. Hitler's racist policies placed blacks well down on the ethnic scale and the long-term implications of his attitudes clearly threatened all minority groups. The Führer had refused to appear on the reviewing stand during the 1936 Olympics in Berlin when an American black named Jesse Owens received four gold medals. Owens' fellow blacks, Ralph Metcalf, John Woodruff, and Cornelius Johnson, also won gold medals for the United States along with snubs from the Third Reich. Joe Louis, defeated by Max Schmeling, a German Nazi, in 1936, became an American national hero when he knocked Schmeling out in less than one round in New York City in 1938. The Louis–Schmeling fight attracted great attention, especially among blacks, and served to widen the Nazi–black cleavage.

When war broke out in 1939, only about 5,000 blacks served in the U.S. Regular Army and less than a dozen black officers held commissions. The Selective Service Act of 1940 forbade discrimination in both drafting and training men, but in practice authorities ignored the provision. All military forces and facilities remained segregated. As in previous wars, the nation assigned blacks, for the most part, to menial support functions rather than active combat units. Nearly 50 per cent of black servicemen received nothing but menial assignments, whereas only some 20 per cent of whites were thus limited.

Walter White describes a painful scene in 1942 in North Africa. The commanding officer asked him to speak to 6,000 black soldiers who had just been reassigned from combat units to port battalions with orders to unload ships. The blacks had been trained for combat and went overseas with high morale. At the time they received reassignment uncommitted white units were available to do the work, as were large numbers of Italian prisoners of war. Morale in the black units went down close to zero. White could find nothing worthwhile to say and described his own speech as "feeble and ineffective."[1] In the Navy blacks probably suffered the most demeaning discrimination, being limited to service as cooks or stewards' mates, but the Army and Air Force also severely inhbited black advancement. The Marines had never admitted blacks into that all-volunteer, elite fighting corps.

By war's end more than a million blacks had served in the armed forces, about half of them in overseas posts. Draft boards became integrated for the first time and generally operated on a fairer basis than in the past. Eventually, all branches of the services opened their ranks to blacks, but confined them to segregated units. Although their pay, quarters, and equipment matched the whites', blacks often suffered through lonely assignments burdened with social ostracism and the galling condescension of supremacist-minded whites.

Black units, in spite of segregation, fought hard and well. The 761st Tank Battalion, for example, served in six countries in Europe and was one of the key defense units at the Battle of the Bulge in December 1944. The 332nd Air Combat Unit, commanded by Colonel, later General, Benjamin O. Davis, Jr., won high praise everywhere. Eighty of its pilots received Distinguished Flying Crosses. A large black contingent, 10,000 troops, constituted a major work force in the construction of the Ledo Road in Burma. Under repeated Japanese attack, they worked to build a life line to China, alternating shovels and rifles as the need arose.

But the white myth which defined blacks as inferior soldiers remained the common view. The fact that blacks fought in segregated units made it easy to criticize, on racial grounds, if a black group failed in some degree. For example, the 92nd Division fighting in Italy received heavy criticism when it gave up some ground. One official report of the Secretary of War placed the main blame for the losses on the low educational level of a major portion of the division, but the report, quoted out of context,

---

1 Walter F. White, *A Rising Wind* (New York: Doubleday, Doran and Co., 1945), p. 77.

raised old stories of black cowardice in the face of enemy attack. The rumors gained wide currency among white troops and damaged black morale. On balance, the 92nd actually established a good record, including a highly effective crossing of the Arno River under fire; individuals in the division received 12,000 decorations and citations.

On various occasions white units retreated under heavy enemy attack, and even wilted entirely. For example, several white divisions in Eisenhower's attack army in Tunisia cracked apart and fell back in a demoralized rout early in 1943. But no one seemed to conclude that whites could not fight.

No scholarly, objective analysis has concluded other than that American blacks supported the nation in World War II. But, as in so many national experiences, status as second-class citizens forced blacks to operate from a complex and even contradictory position. The country had been brutally attacked at Pearl Harbor; vicious foreign regimes threatened freedom everywhere; racist philosophies motivated the Nazi and Fascist enemies. Obviously, all Americans felt a compulsion to stand with the nation in its time of need.

Yet America still practiced discrimination, segregation, exploitation, and oppression. Many blacks saw little to choose between the new enemy abroad and the old enemy at home. As one black writer put it, "Our war is not against Hitler in Europe but against the Hitlers in America."[2] Letters from black soldiers to the NAACP reveal the pressures felt by minority group servicemen. One black soldier wrote, "Just carve on my tombstone, Here lies a black man killed fighting a yellow man for the protection of a white man." Another said, "I am a Negro soldier 22 years old. I won't fight or die in vain. If I fight, suffer or die it will be for the freedom of every black . . . man to live equally with other races. . . . If the life of the Negro in the United States is right as it is lived today, then I would rather be dead."[3]

Incredible incidents served as background for such bitter comments. On a crowded troop train going through Texas, authorities fed black soldiers, isolated in a corner behind a Jim Crow curtain, while in the main section of the dining car white soldiers ate side by side with German prisoners of war. The galling insult became widely known and even found its way into a poem.

---

[2] Letter in Pittsburgh *Courier,* December 21, 1940, in Richard M. Dalfiume, "The 'Forgotten Years' of the Negro Revolution," Bernard Sternsher, ed., *The Negro in Depression and War* (Chicago: Quadrangle Books, 1969), p. 302.

[3] Various letters from black soldiers to the NAACP in Gilbert Osofsky, ed., *The Burden of Race: A Documentary History of Negro-White Relations in America* (New York: Harper & Row, 1967), pp. 414–15.

*On a train in Texas German prisoners eat*
*With white American soldiers, seat by seat,*
*While black American soldiers sit apart*
*The white men eating meat, the black men heart.*
*Now, with that other war a century done,*
*Not the live North but the dead South has won,*
*Not yet a riven nation comes awake.*
*Whom are we fighting this time, for God's sake?*
*Mark well the token of the separate seat.*
*It is again ourselves whom we defeat.*[4]

Discriminatory incidents only slightly less humiliating occurred everywhere. As in World War I a substantial percentage of military bases operated in the South, but military and civilian authorities avoided confronting segregationist practices in all parts of the country.

Individual black soldiers frequently faced an almost daily personal fight in order to maintain their humanity. Sammy Davis, Jr., received his draft notice and landed in an outfit with a bigot for a sergeant and numerous white supremacists as his "buddies." He found himself in a fist fight every day or two because he refused to take a subservient stance. "I had scabs on my knuckles for the first three months in the Army," he recalled. "I fought clean, dirty, any way I could win. They were the ones who started the fights and I didn't owe them any Queensberry rules."[5] Another black soldier who suffered similar treatment predicted, "A new Negro will return from the war—a bitter Negro if he is disappointed again. He will have been taught to kill, to suffer, to die for something he believes in, and he will live by these rules to gain his personal rights."[6] Still another said, "Those of us who are in the armed services are offering our lives and fortunes, not for the America we know today, but for the America we hope will be created after the war."[7]

In sharp contrast to black gloom regarding the racial situation, whites felt little concern. During 1941 the Office of War Information conducted an opinion survey on "White Attitudes Toward Negroes" which demonstrated the low priority given to the race question by the majority. OWI polled more than 3,500 whites nationwide and found little difference between geographic sec-

---

[4] From *Take Away the Darkness,* by Witter Bynner. Copyright 1947 by Witter Bynner. Reprinted by permission of Alfred A. Knopf, Inc.

[5] Sammy Davis, Jr., *Yes I Can* (New York: Farrar, Straus, 1965), pp. 33–34.

[6] Letter from black soldier to NAACP in Gilbert Osofsky, ed., *The Burden of Race: A Documentary History of Negro-White Relations in America* (New York: Harper & Row, 1967), p. 415.

[7] Ibid., p. 420.

tions of the nation on important questions. The survey showed that whites believed blacks had opportunities, that race relations would change little after the war and that, insofar as discrimination still existed, blacks themselves were to blame for lack of initiative and effort. The OWI report concluded, "The situation is definitely not one of a prejudiced South arrayed against a liberal–tolerant North. In every region, the majority feel that Negroes should go to separate schools, eat in separate restaurants, live in separate parts of town, and consistent majorities admit that it would really make a difference to them if Negroes of equal education and income moved into their neighborhood."[8]

Some black leaders frankly used the war crisis to gain leverage for social change. Disappointing experience during World War I, when pressures to reduce the restrictions of second-class citizenship had been largely suspended, suggested the necessity of taking advantage of the special opportunities created by wartime conditions. The black revolution of the 1950's and 1960's began with some of the less publicized events of World War II. One historian has termed the war period "The Forgotten Years"[9] of the equal-rights movement. No better example could be advanced than that of the maneuvering which surrounded the issuance of Executive Order 8802.

When the war began in Europe in 1939 the United States still suffered unemployment from the Depression. Even with war production reducing the army of the unemployed, some 5 million whites remained without jobs in 1940. Blacks who went to find work in expanding industry met with mixed success. Unlike the situation at the start of World War I the nation faced no labor shortage. Blacks, who still received significantly lower wages than whites, found many opportunities closed to them for reasons of discrimination. Business leaders refused to employ blacks or underemployed them; often, such hiring discrimination resulted from *sub rosa* union pressure or white labor threats to cause trouble if blacks received jobs or were upgraded from the menial, janitorial, and service functions to which companies generally assigned them. The national government had yet to eliminate discrimination in its own programs, let alone stand strongly against injustice in private business. Boulder City and Norris, two government towns built near major dams, refused to admit blacks

---

8 Office of War Information Report in E. David Cronon, ed., *Twentieth Century America: Selected Readings*, Vol. II (Homewood, Ill.: Dorsey Press, 1966), pp. 270–71.

9 Richard M. Dalfiume, "The 'Forgotten Years' of the Negro Revolution," in Bernard Sternsher, ed., *The Negro in Depression and War* (Chicago: Quadrangle Books, 1969), pp. 298 ff.

as residents. And the Federal Housing Authority would not approve government insurance for home loans to blacks who sought to live outside traditional minority group neighborhoods anywhere in the country.

A remarkable man named Asa Philip Randolph, head of the Pullman Porters union, who had a long record of opposition to America's racial practices, again emerged as the militant leader favoring genuine change. He and other blacks, chiefly drawn from the NAACP, determined they would force President Roosevelt to use federal power to guarantee equal opportunity. In the spring of 1941 many blacks experienced job discrimination in war plants. A well-publicized comment by the president of North American Aviation that, "regardless of their training as aircraft workers, we will not employ Negroes in the . . . plant. It is against company policy,"[10] simply made public the general policy of the entire rapidly expanding aircraft industry. Randolph determined his course of action; he decided that if the nation failed to correct the situation, blacks would march on Washington and demonstrate to the world their country's hypocrisy in calling for freedom abroad while practicing discrimination at home.

Under the cry "Let the Negro Masses Speak," Randolph urged: "Let us tear the mask of hypocrisy from America's Democracy. Negroes cannot stop discrimination in National Defense with conferences of leaders and the intelligentsia alone. Whatever Negroes get in jobs and vocational training opportunities, they must fight for. Nothing will be given them. We would rather die on our feet fighting for Negroes' rights than live on our knees as half-men, as semi-citizens begging for a pittance. Let the Negro masses march! Let them swarm from every hamlet, village and town; from the highways and byways, out of the churches, lodges, homes, schools, mills, mines, factories and fields. Let them come though the winds blow and the rains beat against them, when the date is set.

"We call not upon our white friends to march with us. There are some things Negroes must do alone. This is our fight and we must see it through."[11]

Randolph and his aides planned carefully. He first gained the support of leading blacks like Walter White, Mary McLeod Bethune, and others. Some feared the then daring idea of an all-black confrontation with the presidential head of the white

---

[10] Gilbert Osofsky, ed., *The Burden of Race: A Documentary History of Negro-White Relations in America* (New York: Harper & Row, 1967), p. 392.
[11] A. Philip Randolph, "Let the Negro Masses Speak!" in ibid., pp. 392–96.

power structure. Undeterred by cautious counsel from some quarters, Randolph issued his call for the "March on Washington for Jobs in National Defense and Equal Integration in the Fighting Forces of the United States." He chose July 1, 1941, as the confrontation date.

A war of nerves between Randolph and the administration followed. Randolph maintained, without clear assurance of success, that the black masses would indeed follow him to Washington. President Roosevelt, not certain that Randolph could produce his army of disaffected blacks yet uneasy in ignoring the tense situation, jockeyed for time. The pressures built up; the poker game was played out. At the president's urging, Randolph and White met with leading liberals like Eleanor Roosevelt, Mayor Fiorello La Guardia, and others in New York City. The whites urged caution and gave assurance that something could be done if only Randolph would eliminate the march. He refused and insisted upon an audience with FDR himself. Mrs. Roosevelt again urged that the march be called off, arguing that it would do more harm than good. Randolph calmly corrected her, insisting not only that it would do good, but that it had "already done some good; for if you were not concerned about it you wouldn't be here now." At this point the first lady shifted ground and pointed out that the black marchers would not find places to eat or sleep in segregated Washington. Randolph replied that they would march into the "hotels and restaurants and demand service." He left the meeting in downtown Manhattan and by the time he got back to his Harlem office, a telegram had arrived urging him to come to Washington to discuss the march plan with the president.

The great confrontation took place on June 18 at the White House. Randolph, Walter White of the NAACP, and Arnold Hill of the Urban League met with FDR, the Secretary of War, the Secretary of the Navy, and several other Cabinet officers. The president, as usual, charming, began with various stories, but Randolph broke into one of his anecdotes rather bluntly and said, "Mr. President, time is running on. You are busy. We want specifically to talk to you about the problem of jobs for Negroes in defense industries. Our people are being turned away at factory gates because they are colored. They can't live with this thing. What are you going to do about it?"

FDR replied, "Now you're quite right, Phil. I am going to do something about it. Call off this march of yours and we'll do something. Questions like this have sociological implications. They can't be gotten at with hammers and tongs. They can't be settled with marches."

Randolph said that neither could they be "settled with good intentions."

FDR then asked how many would march. Randolph replied, "100,000." FDR looked at him, not sure of the degree to which the union leader sought to bluff him. The president turned to Walter White, who gave the same answer; FDR stared at *him*. No one knows for certain whether the march would really have attracted 100,000 blacks. The 1963 version of the march idea drew a quarter of a million persons, but quite a few whites took part. Probably Randolph could not have gotten 100,000 persons, but he would have come close enough to create much adverse publicity for the United States.

FDR said, "We cannot have a march on Washington. We must approach this problem in an analytical way."

Randolph rejoined, "Then, Mr. President, something will have to be done at once."

FDR replied, "Something will be done, but there must be no public pressure on the White House."

But Randolph refused to compromise. "Mr. President," he said, "something must be done now!"[12]

Within a week Roosevelt issued Executive Order No. 8802. The president's action ruled against all racial discrimination in the hiring of workers in defense industries or government bureaus. The directive applied to all work involving government contracts and created a committee on Fair Employment Practices to implement the new order.

Randolph then terminated plans for the March on Washington for the duration of the war. Interestingly, some of his younger militants, such as Bayard Rustin, who in the 1960's would be charged by youthful blacks with insufficient militancy, criticized Randolph for backing down on the march threat. Randolph kept the MOW organization together in a loose grouping and led it to a second great victory after the war, the desegregation of the armed forces. Eventually the March on Washington contributed to the turning-point events of 1963.

Executive Order 8802 and the FEPC it established did not reduce discrimination appreciably. In one perspective, therefore, the MOW movement failed to reach its objective. Nevertheless the 1941 march threat marked a major turning point in the equal-rights struggle. Randolph's successful gambit convinced many blacks that they must become aroused in support of their own cause. A subtle change of attitude occurred; the further progress

---

12 Account given in Lerone Bennett, Jr., *Confrontation: Black and White* (Baltimore: Penguin Books, 1966), pp. 149–51.

of the postwar era depended upon this indispensably necessary increase in black confidence.

Although the 1941 struggle for jobs presaged postwar social change on a broad scale, the average black continued to suffer from discrimination and the average white continued to be unaware of the magnitude of the problem. No better example of this generalization can be found than that of the wide-scale continuance of urban race riots during the war. Various cities suffered outbreaks usually involving white resistance to black entry into new job classifications. Serious conflicts occurred in Mobile, Beaumont, Newark, Philadelphia, El Paso, and New York City. The most severe riot took place in Detroit, where the usual racial tensions had been heightened by the incoming of rural whites who streamed north in search of war jobs. From 1940 to 1943 the city experienced a large population influx, nearly half a million persons, of whom some 50,000 were black. The new minority group members found themselves crowded into several small black neighborhoods, the most impacted being the inaccurately named Paradise Valley.

Three incidents during 1943 in the Detroit area preceded the riot and showed the underlying racial hostility which threatened to destroy the city. The Sojourner Truth Federal Housing project was the scene of a tense white–black confrontation. The trouble began when whites refused to allow blacks to enter the housing project which ironically bore the name of a great black preacher, abolitionist, and feminist. Troops eventually enforced desegregation of the development. The second incident took place at Selfridge Field, an army base near Detroit. The commanding officer, a white, got into an altercation with a black soldier who had come to serve as his driver; in the melee the soldier was wounded. The commanding officer said that he had given orders that no black should be assigned to this job. The third incident took place at a Packard auto plant when 20,000 white union men went on strike after three blacks had been promoted for superior work on the assembly line.

On June 20, 1943, a hot night, a black and a white man got into a fist fight coming out of the Belle Isle city park. The exchange took place on a bridge across the Detroit River. Groups of blacks and whites became involved and the crowds leaving the park quickly got caught up in the contest. Wild rumors flooded the city, carried by both whites and blacks. The stories, similar in nature, usually involved assaults on women and children; the color of the speaker determined the color of those assaulted.

Black residents in Paradise Valley began to attack whites who came in or near the area. Whites congregated in Cadillac Square, stopped streetcars, pulled blacks off the cars, and beat them. Both blacks and whites, depending on the area, attacked war workers coming off shifts in plants. Some people were assaulted before they even realized that a race riot was in progress. A mob of blacks seized John Holyak, a fifty-nine-year-old white worker whose son was then in a Japanese prisoner-of-war camp. They threw him down and kicked him to death. Sam Mitchell, a black veteran of World War I, escaped from a crowd that rushed into the streetcar in which he was riding. As he fled several shots struck him. Still living, he appealed to two white policemen for help; they held his arms while the white mob continued to beat him.

One white reporter risked his life to visit Paradise Valley while the riot was still in progress. He found blacks going "berserk" and destroying every store which failed to display a sign indicating the owner to be black. A sixteen-year-old white boy told another reporter that he had been with a group of two hundred whites who specialized in assaulting blacks wherever they could find them. "We killed eight of 'em," he said. "I didn't kill any myself, I was too scared. I lost my nerve I guess, but my pals did. I saw knives being stuck through their throats and heads being shot through, and a lot of stuff like that—it was really some riot. They were turning cars over with niggers in them, you should have seen it."[13] A white student described a scene which she observed from a bus window. "I saw one Negro being chased down street by a gang of young whites with knives. He was gray with fear, saliva drooling, shirt torn open, gasping. Whites were raving with hate. They probably caught him—they were gaining ground when I saw them."[14] But the bus pulled away before she learned the ending to the unforgettable sequence. Still another participant, a nineteen- or twenty-year-old white youth, said of his part, "I took the day off from the tool shop so I could be in the thick of it downtown. Jesus, but it was a show! We dragged niggers from cars, beat the hell out of them, and lit the sons-of-bitches' autos. I'm glad I was in it! And those black bastards damn well deserved it."[15]

After three days of violence, President Roosevelt used troops to restore order. Twenty-five blacks and nine whites lay dead; hundreds had been seriously injured, more than a million dollars

13 Office of War Information, Special Memorandum, "Opinions in Detroit Thirty-Six Hours After the Race Riots," June 30, 1943, in E. David Cronon, ed., *Twentieth Century America: Selected Readings*, Vol. II (Homewood, Ill.: Dorsey Press, 1966), p. 273.

14 Ibid., p. 274.

15 Account given in Alfred M. Lee and Norman D. Humphrey, *Race Riot: Detroit, 1943* (New York: Octagon Books, 1968), p. 80.

worth of property was destroyed. Once again the casualty figures belie the stereotyped white view that blacks are a violent and brutish people. Seventeen of the dead blacks had been killed by the police; no whites died at the hands of the officers. Gerald L. K. Smith, the racist, anti-Semitic, superpatriotic radio preacher in Detroit whose inflammatory rhetoric had helped stir up the trouble, blamed the riot on Communists who had allegedly incited the blacks. He urged the city to adopt rigid segregation similar to the policies of the Union of South Africa.

In April 1945, as the war drew to a close, FDR suddenly died and left the presidency to an ex-senator from Missouri, Harry S Truman. A compromise choice at the Democratic National Convention in 1944, Truman had been ill informed and largely ignored by the inner circles of the Roosevelt administration. For example, he did not know about the Manhattan Project which developed the atomic bomb. When he assumed the duties of the presidency he said that he felt as if the world had fallen on him. He also expressed the view that at least a million persons were more qualified than he to be president. Early evidence suggested he might be correct. But as he gained experience, he did a truly remarkable job, both in foreign and domestic affairs. His motto "The Buck Stops Here" suggested a man willing to take strong executive action. He possessed two vital ingredients of great leadership: knowledge of his country's history and courage. In the end he faced as many great decisions as any president, and in the field of equal rights he provided the breakthrough for a new era. He was the first American president to take a strong stand against the color line and to follow that stand with needed action.

In the fall of 1946, following a White House meeting with Walter White and other black leaders, Truman appointed a distinguished biracial President's Committee on Civil Rights. The black leaders had arranged the meeting against a background of increased mob violence involving blacks. Six persons had been lynched during the year, one for house breaking, one for stabbing a man in a fight, one for allegedly stealing a saddle, and three against whom no charge whatsoever had been brought. The presidential committee issued a famous report, "To Secure These Rights," which called for strong national efforts toward equal justice on a broad front. The committee concluded that moral, economic, and international considerations compelled a change in America's long-standing policy of permitting whites to impose second-class status on blacks. "There are times," the commissioners wrote, "when the differences between what we preach about civil rights and what we practice are shockingly illustrated by individual outrages. There are times when the whole structure of our ideology is made ridiculous by individual instances. And there are certain continuing, quiet, omnipresent practices which do irreparable damage to our beliefs."[16] Truman also created an education committee and their report pointed toward major change in the nation's schools. Finally, Truman undertook to desegregate the armed forces.

In this he had the active support of Asa Philip Randolph. Truman asked the Congress to continue the draft to assure strong national forces in the unfolding Cold War with the Soviet Union. Randolph, Rustin, and others immediately announced they would oppose the law and urge millions of blacks to refuse to register and serve unless the Congress also established equal rights in the armed forces. They concentrated their energies through the "League for Nonviolent Civil Disobedience Against Military Segregation."

Truman called Randolph and the other black leaders to a White House discussion. Randolph in a scene reminiscent of his contest with Roosevelt over jobs, said, "Negroes are sick and tired of being asked to shoulder guns in defense of democracy abroad until they get some at home. They are prepared to resort to civil disobedience and refusal to register for the draft if it means serving in a Jim Crow Army."

Truman, nettled by the remark, replied, "I wish you hadn't said that. I don't like it. I'm doing the best I can. You know what I have asked Congress to do. . . . I don't like it at all."[17] But Randolph calmly stood his ground and educated the president to the emerging new reality of American race relations. Black leaders like Randolph had no intention of allowing the nation to return to prewar racial assumptions. A desperate conviction that freedom must come now supplied high motivation to his group. Truman, to his credit, recognized the justice of their arguments.

Randolph also educated the Congress, including Senator Wayne Morse of Oregon, who then served on the Armed Services Committee. In an exchange with Morse, Randolph strongly opposed segregation in the military and said, "I personally pledge myself to openly counsel, aid and abet youth, both white and Negro . . . in an organized refusal to register and be drafted."

Morse replied, "It may lead to indictments for treason and very serious repercussions."

Randolph answered, "We are willing to pay that price. . . . I

16 President's Committee on Civil Rights, 1947, "To Secure These Rights," in Albert P. Blaustein and Robert L. Zangrando, eds., *Civil Rights and the American Negro* (New York: Washington Square Press, 1968), pp. 375–79.

17 Account given in Lerone Bennett, Jr., *Confrontation: Black and White* (Baltimore: Penguin Books, 1966), p. 164.

believe any of you men would raise hell . . . if you felt the indignities and injustices that are suffered by Negroes in America.
I am prepared to oppose a Jim Crow Army until I rot in jail."[18]

In this context Truman issued his famous Civil Rights Message of February 2, 1948 in which he drew upon all the experiences of his administration in the equal-rights fight. In the early
phases of an election year in which his renomination by his
party was by no means assured. Truman had the courage
to present a ringing affirmation of the original American creed
of true equality for all citizens. He alluded to the belief in equal
justice under law, which both the Declaration of Independence
and the Constitution affirm. He then noted that "there are still
. . . flagrant examples of discrimination, which are utterly contrary to our ideals. Not all groups of our population are free from
the fear of violence. Not all groups are free to live and work
where they please or to improve their conditions of life by their
own efforts. Not all groups enjoy the full privileges of citizenship
and participation in the Government under which they live.

"We cannot be satisfied until all our people have equal opportunities for jobs, for homes, for education, for health, and for
political expression, and until all our people have equal protection under the law.

"The protection of civil rights is the duty of every government
which derives its powers from the consent of the people. This is
equally true of local, state and national governments."[19]

Truman then called specifically for a Permanent Commission
on Civil Rights, a Joint Congressional Committee on Civil
Rights, a Civil Rights Division in the Justice Department, a law
against lynching, federal action to protect the right to vote, a
national Fair Employment Practices Commission, elimination of
all discrimination in public transportation, and final desegregation of the armed forces.

No president, before or since, urged a more comprehensive
equal-rights program. Mr. Truman closed the message with these
words: "If we wish to inspire the peoples of the world whose
freedom is in jeopardy, if we wish to restore hope to those who
have already lost their civil liberties, if we wish to fulfill the
promise that is ours, we must correct the remaining imperfections
in our practices of democracy. We know the way. We need only
the will."[20]

---

18 Ibid., p. 165. See also *Congressional Record*, 80th Congress, 2nd Session,
April 12, 1948, p. 4313, and *New York Times*, April 1, 1948, pp. 1, 10.

19 Truman's "Civil Rights Message," February 2, 1948, 80th Congress, 2nd
Session, House Doc. No. 516 in Henry S. Commager, ed., *Documents of American History*, Vol. II (New York: Appleton-Century-Crofts, 1968), pp. 542–43.

20 Ibid., p. 544.

The president fought to fulfill his promises but unfortunately the Congress opposed him on most of his ideas, thus reflecting the traditional white reluctance to face the reality of second-class citizenship in America. Had the sentiment in Congress been different, the course of history might have been altered. Acceptance of the mechanics of the Truman program followed up with the vigorous, executive leadership of which he was capable, might have wrought major social change before black frustrations built to the pressure point of the 1970's.

Fortunately, some elements of the program did succeed. For example, in spite of strong opposition the armed forces gave up their segregationist rules. Prominent persons like Dwight D. Eisenhower testified against the desegregation plan on the grounds that the morale of white soldiers would be undermined. One ranking officer insisted that integration proposals could not possibly work because whites would refuse to participate in a bi-racial army. "There may be," he wrote, "some super-tolerant people that would join a Negro outfit, but their numbers would be few. Other whites that would join a Negro outfit would be the same class of whites that would live in a Negro community."[21] President Truman insisted that the change must be made and A. Philip Randolph won another victory. When desegregation came, white and black soldiers quickly adjusted to the new system; gloomy predictions regarding the lowering of morale turned out to be erroneous.

President Truman's continued insistence upon needed change in the field of civil rights drew support from liberals but alienated many persons with traditional views. When the Democratic party met in Philadelphia in July to nominate its candidate for president it was seething and divided. President Truman and the administration hoped to avoid an open split and attempted to ease through on the matter of equal rights. Truman had already clearly demonstrated a willingness to move in new directions, but he saw no purpose in making such a pointed issue of the civil rights question that the Southern wing of the party would feel threatened and leave the convention.

However, events overran the administration plan. On the night prior to consideration of the platform a black delegate, George Vaughn, challenged the majority report of the Credentials Committee. In a dramatic speech Vaughn urged that the convention refuse to seat the Mississippi delegation. At the climax of his remarks he raised a clenched fist and referred to the millions of

---

21 Memo from William Hastie to Secretary of War, June 13, 1942, in Richard J. Stillman, II, ed., *Integration of the Negro in the U.S. Armed Forces* (New York: Frederick A. Praeger, 1968), p. 28.

blacks who had been forced to leave the South because of the vicious racism practiced there. Boos from Southern delegations met his words and immediately many Northern representatives sought the floor to give him support. But the chairman went through with a swift voice vote which accepted the majority report and seated the Mississippi delegation.

White liberals and black delegates met that night in an excited conference which did not break up until dawn. During the discussions, the brash young mayor of Minneapolis, Hubert Humphrey, agreed to make a key speech in support of a strong civil rights plank in the platform. The substitute motion commended President Truman for actions already taken, but insisted that the party and the nation must finally face up to the larger question —equal rights for all. Humphrey stirred the convention with his words. He said that the Democratic party should move itself "out of the shadows of states' rights and walk forthrightly into the bright sunshine of human rights." To those who argued that he was rushing the matter he insisted "we are 172 years too late."[22] In the exciting roll call vote which followed, the strong plank won in a close vote 651½ to 582½. The Humphrey initiative ruptured the party and the right-wingers walked out to nominate J. Strom Thurmond of South Carolina for president on the Dixiecrat ticket. Truman had feared clear Democratic affirmation of the liberal position might reduce the party's chances of victory in November, However, once Humphrey's group had forced the point the president made civil rights a major issue in the campaign.

Nevertheless, the left-wing Democrats could not accept Truman's leadership, particularly in foreign affairs, and went over to ultraliberal Henry Wallace. The Wallace Progressive party included the Communists, and radical blacks like Paul Robeson and Ben Davis promoted the cause. Perhaps, in 1948, the Communist party would have made significant inroads into American politics had it not been for the stand which Humphrey took at Philadelphia and Truman projected during the election. The campaign proved to be one of the most unusual in American history. Strong emotions, chiefly growing out of the civil rights issue, erupted into violence at times. One vice-presidential candidate was arrested in Birmingham, Alabama, for entering a church through the "colored" door.

Truman, deprived of both the left and right wings of his party, seemed a certain loser, but in spite of all the odds against him, he

---

22 Transcript copy of speech supplied to author by Hubert Humphrey. See also Irwin Ross, *The Loneliest Campaign* (New York: Signet, 1968), pp. 118–22. (Originally published by New American Library, New York, 1968.)

won. Foreign policy, declining farm income, the dull campaign of Republican candidate Dewey of New York, played a part in the Truman victory, but the equal-rights issue emerged as the key factor. For the first time American blacks voted almost unanimously for the Democratic nominee and provided the margin of victory in many close states.

Truman continued to fight for equal rights. When he left office voluntarily in 1952, much still remained to be done, but a new era had opened. In one of his final speeches, made at Howard University in 1952, Truman urged completion of a civil rights program backed by the "full force of the Federal Government." Only thus, he argued, could the nation end discrimination against minorities. He predicted that the closer the nation came to full justice "the stronger, more vigorous and happier" it would be.[23]

Doubtless Mr. Truman's estimate will eventually prove true. However, the continued racial malaise that the nation has suffered suggests that a considerable distance remains to be traversed before the harmony of a just society becomes a reality. Yet progress has been made in selected areas of national existence; probably no better example can be cited than that of the world of sports. Prior to the war, virtually no blacks had access to athletic opportunity; since 1945 practically every phase of sporting activity has been opened to them.

It has become fashionable in some black militant and radical white circles to ridicule the matter of change in the world of sports. On the one hand, critics accuse white America of using the black athlete in the traditional role of entertainer. On the other side the same opposition charges the black athlete with selling himself to the white purpose.

America has always been a sports-oriented nation. Partly because of affluence most Americans play at some sport; they also watch sports avidly. Television has vastly increased the sporting emphasis, especially for men. Indeed, some women have come to feel that men arrange matters to insure that all leisure time is spent in either observing sports on the field or in the living room. Sports appeal to both sides of human nature—the understanding and the will—the intellect and the emotions—the brain and the heart. Babe Ruth, Red Grange, Knute Rockne, Bill Tilden, Bobby Jones, Tom Harmon, Eric Tipton, Lou Gehrig, Jo DiMaggio, and numbers of other stars long served to focus American attention on the life values of dedication to the hard trail to sporting success. Generations of American boys looked up to the stars as

---

[23] Speech of President Truman, June 13, 1952, *New York Times*, June 14, 1952, p. 10.

models for life. Because the sports color bar remained virtually total, young people of both races had only white stars to admire. In 1945, Satchel Paige, probably the greatest pitcher in baseball history, who had frequently mowed down white stars in exhibition games, had never played baseball in the major leagues. Paul Robeson, one of the greatest college football players of all time, briefly made the line-up of a professional team, but increasing racism in the 1930's closed this rapidly growing sport to black athletes. Every year thousands of American males of great talent graduated from high schools (and a few from colleges), but never had an opportunity to play anything but high-grade semiprofessional sports, because they happened to have been born black.

Individual sports such as boxing had sometimes given way to black strength. The great heavyweight champions like Jack Johnson and Joe Louis, and some like American fight history's greatest boxer, Ray Robinson, demonstrated the potential of the black athlete. Eight blacks have been heavyweight champions of the world. But team sports, dominated by whites, remained off limits to American blacks. The situation involved a continuous public affront to black humanity. Despite ridicule of black "firsts" the breakthrough in the world of sports served as a significant precursor to the black revolution of the 1950's and 1960's.

In this period of change Jackie Robinson will always stand as a leader along with Branch Rickey, the white general manager of the old Brooklyn Dodgers baseball team. Racism entered baseball in 1867, when the National League banned blacks. The boycott remained firm until 1901 when John McGraw of the Baltimore Orioles tried to smuggle Charles Grant in as an American Indian. McGraw failed.

Rickey purchased Robinson's contract from the black Kansas City Monarchs and, after a brief seasoning in the International League at Montreal, brought him to Brooklyn. Robinson had been a brilliant all-round athlete in Pasadena, California. He sat in a segregated balcony when he went to the movies, swam in the city pool only on black Tuesdays and played at the YMCA on the one segregated black night each week.

But he had never psychologically accepted second-class status. Repeated incidents in his school career showed him to be unwilling to permit whites to demean him. During World War II, Robinson, a commissioned officer, refused to move to the back of a bus on an army base, thereby precipitating a celebrated case which he finally won, although he lost his command position and his unit went overseas without him.

When he came to the Dodgers in 1947, he and Rickey worked out a strategy for Robinson's behavior on the field. Assuming that he would meet with abuse, he and Rickey agreed that he would not fight back against the barrage of bigotry, but would play the first season, regardless of the provocation. Some teams, and many white players, did accept Robinson without question. But certain teams, numerous white players, several managers, and thousands of fans reacted quite differently. On several occasions, opposing teams refused to take the field unless Robinson was removed from the line-up. The traditional fear of job holders that someone else might take a job away from them may have been a minor factor in the threatened boycotts. If some white players could have foreseen the tremendous influx of outstanding black ball players, they might actually have fought harder against Robinson than they did. But unquestionably racism lay behind the strike threats, and fortunately organized baseball refused to allow them to succeed. Ford Frick, president of the National League, warned the potential strikers that they would be dealt with immediately and firmly. "I do not care if half the League strikes," he said. "Those who do so will encounter quick retribution. All will be suspended and I don't care if it wrecks the National League. . . . [We] will go down the line with Robinson, whatever the consequence. You will find if you go through with your intention that you will have been guilty of complete madness."[24] Frick's strong stand probably changed no bigot's heart, but it did curb prejudiced behavior. If every influential person consistently followed this pattern the race problem would disappear.

The Philadelphia Phillies proved to be the most obscene in their anti-Robinson stand partly because they lacked leadership. They rode Robinson, who played third base, unmercifully; "nigger" was one of the milder epithets used. In spite of all the extra pressure, Robinson's brilliant performance won him "Rookie of the Year" honors. Financially the Dodgers benefited through a 400 per cent increase in attendance. Robinson was later named "Most Valuable Player" and eventually became the first black to enter baseball's Hall of Fame, at Cooperstown, New York.

Black stars quickly came to dominate the rosters of many clubs. A look at the records of 1968, an Olympic Year, suggests a virtual black monopoly on top honors in the world of sports. Some examples are the following:

> Alcindor v. Hayes: college basketball
> Russell v. Chamberlain: professional basketball

---

[24] Account given by Andrews S. N. Young, "Great Negro Baseball Stars," in Lettie J. Austin, Lewis H. Fenderson, and Sophia P. Nelson, eds., *The Black Man and the Promise of America* (Glenview, Ill.: Scott, Foresman and Co., 1970), p. 421.

Gibson, Flood, and Brock (Cards) v. Horton (Tigers): World
   Series opponents, baseball
Lee Elder: golf
Arthur Ashe: tennis
OJ Simpson: college football
Leroy Kelley, Gale Sayers, Don Perkins, Bob Hayes: pro
   football

Controversy swirled around two black members of the U.S.
Olympic Team, John Carlos and Tommie Smith, who stood on
the victory stand during the playing of the Star Spangled Banner,
with bowed heads and raised fists, in the black power salute. Officials suspended them from the team and sent them home, but an
unforgettable photograph went around the world and exposed
the continued racism of the U.S. to further discussion and cen-
sure. A black boycott of the Olympic games seemed likely at one
point, but Carlos and Smith preferred to demonstrate their dis-
approval in a more direct fashion. Many Americans condemned
them as unpatriotic but who can define patriotism for another?
Can a patriot remain silent when injustice needs exposure?

But the Carlos-Smith raised-fist incident projects well beyond
the immediate postwar period in American history. An amazing
variety of once incredible events occurred following 1945 which
together form the outline of a social revolution. In retrospect,
clearly the war years provided fluid situations into which black
Americans in increasing numbers moved to alter their own
destiny and that of their nation. White Americans, frequently resisting the change, nevertheless permitted it to go slowly forward,
sensing at last, perhaps, that the American dream was indeed
indivisible.

# Equal-Rights Revolution of the 1950's and 1960's

# 9

In many ways the Eisenhower era has come to seem like a throwback to the slower pace of the nineteenth century. The furious movement of the 1960's stands in stark contrast to the rather pastoral feeling of the 1950's. Eisenhower came to power in 1952 as a result of the confluence of a variety of factors. The nation had tired of the dragging problems of the postwar period; disgust with the Korean War, Communist subversion, and petty corruption in government pointed to an Eisenhower victory. Ike's giant reputation as a winning personality convinced many white Americans that their problems would disappear if he became president. The general and his politically more astute advisors did nothing to alter this impression. Indeed, Eisenhower probably believed that simple, old-fashioned honesty in government mixed with abandonment of New Deal type restraints on business would return the nation to a happy state. Certainly nothing Eisenhower said or did during the 1952 campaign suggested any degree of real concern for the burning social issue of the day—equal rights for the nation's black citizens.

In spite of the heat of the civil rights issue in the election of 1948 and many important changes during the Truman administration, the question of equal rights played a strictly subordinate role in 1952. Yet the tone of the 1960's might have been hinted at by the heavy black vote, not for Ike, but for his Democratic opponent, Adlai Stevenson. Most black districts across the nation went for Stevenson with majorities as high as nine to one. Ike swept into office against a stream of black votes cast for Truman's political heir. And before long Eisenhower found it impossible to ignore the implications of this reality. This nineteenth-century-oriented, small-town, lily-white, religious conservative was forced to become involved in the greatest social revolution of the twentieth century.

His involvement, and the country's immersion, in the equal-rights revolution grew out of one of the most important judgments ever to emerge from an American court. The background of this decision included a famous college and two lawyers. The school was Howard University and the lawyers were Charles Hamilton Houston and Thurgood Marshall. Marshall attended the Howard Law School in the 1930's when Houston served as vice-dean. Houston set himself a goal, the creation of a "West Point of Negro leadership." Houston had looked upon the national scene and found great opportunities. He concluded that a cadre of brilliant black lawyers must be trained to break the system of segregation and second-class citizenship by working through the courts to enforce the Constitution of the United States.

Houston was tough and demanding. On the first day of a new term he would grimly tell his students to look at the person on each side carefully, because by the end of the year, "two of you will not be here."[1] Marshall, one of his most talented pupils, later gave Houston credit for bringing about the Supreme Court decision of 1954.

Since World War I the NAACP had been struggling to break the restrictions of second-class citizenship with the legal approach. The organization had enjoyed some success but on many occasions had been unable to win through. Marshall, in a 1935 case, forced the University of Maryland to admit to its law school a black student named Donald Murray (*Donald G. Murray* v. *University of Maryland*). This was the first in a long string of Marshall-led efforts to open the American school system to blacks. Because the public schools of the United States are the most significant and influential social institution, Houston, Marshall, and others sought to break open the entire educational structure step by step.

The intervention of World War II delayed the process but the pace quickened after the war ended. One day in 1945, Marshall, Walter White, W. H. Hastie, and others held a meeting in New York City. They decided to accelerate their attack on the legal barriers to equal educational opportunity. At that particular moment they knew nothing about the situation in Topeka, Kansas, nor did they see the details of the various challenges which lay before them.

It might be worth noting that many whites gave money to the effort. And beyond money, some white lawyers worked on the

---

[1] Lerone Bennett, Jr., *Confrontation: Black and White* (Baltimore: Penguin Books, 1965), pp. 185–86.

NAACP staff. A few sensitive whites have always been aware of the severe nature of the white problem in America. But the real thrust came from blacks headed by Thurgood Marshall, chief lieutenant in Houston's "West Point" cadre of legal minds.

The Marshall forces effected an interesting switch in tactics during the postwar era. During the 1930's and before, blacks had sought *equal* educational opportunities; now they demanded access to the *same* facilities. Ironically, by switching the approach they quickly won the earlier fight. From 1945 to 1954 whites responded to the black attack on educational segregation by conceding the previous battle and funding equal, separate schools. New buildings for blacks received prime attention and much money shifted for the first time into other aspects of black education. But Marshall continued the assault upon separation by race.

*Sweatt* v. *Painter,* 1950, supplied the judicial preliminaries to the landmark ruling of 1954. The University of Texas Law School denied access to Henry M. Sweatt, a qualified black. Sweatt insisted that the separate black facilities as provided by the state in no way equaled those for whites and therefore he must be admitted directly into the university law school. When he won the case the law school accepted him and he graduated without major incident. That same year another court decision forced Oklahoma authorities to dismantle the special cubicles which had been constructed for George W. McLaurin, in the corner of each classroom of the university's graduate school. News pictures of this ludicrous situation may have convinced many persons that the separation fight had been lost. But the Texas legislature refused to believe it and scrambled to create all-black Texas Southern University as an alternative to integration.

The 1954 decision grew out of five cases in four states and the District of Columbia. The case of Oliver Brown's daughter in Topeka, Kansas, ironically involved less painfully discriminatory aspects than the others. But his name became affixed to the historical judgment of which one source has concluded, "Probably no decision in the history of the Court has directly concerned so many individuals."[2] Marshall and John Davis presented the two sides; they concluded their arguments in March 1954. The United States government spoke in support of the black plaintiff.

Many persons debated the likely outcome of the Court's deliberations. Some leaders predicted serious happenings if *Plessy* v.

---

[2] Albert P. Blaustein and Robert L. Zangrando, eds., *Civil Rights and the American Negro: A Documentary History* (New York: Washington Square Press, 1968), p. 415.

*Ferguson* were overturned. There will be, one said, "riots, strikes, bloodshed, and even lynchings."[3] Was this a threat of violence? Another official termed the Court's decision an "unthinkable evil" which should be opposed at all costs. "We shall never submit," he said "to the . . . mixing [of] the races in the classrooms of our schools."[4]

The all-white membership of the Supreme Court deliberated for weeks. Chief Justice Earl Warren, unquestionably one of the great judicial leaders of the Court's history, read the unanimous decision on May 17, 1954. With Marshall and other black lawyers present, and a full, quiet chamber, Warren reviewed the case as the tension in the room mounted. Then, he discussed the central aspect of the decision:

"Today," he said, "education is perhaps the most important function of state and local governments. Compulsory school attendance laws and the great expenditures for education both demonstrate our recognition of the importance of education to democratic society. It is required in the performance of our most basic public responsibilities, even service in the armed forces. It is the very foundation of good citizenship. Today it is a principal instrument in awakening the child to cultural values, in preparing him for later professional training, and in helping him to adjust normally to his environment. In these days, it is doubtful that any child may reasonably be expected to succeed in life if he is denied the opportunity of an education. Such an opportunity, where the state has undertaken to provide it, is a right which must be made available to all on equal terms.

"We come then to the question presented: Does segregation of children in public schools solely on the basis of race, even though the physical facilities and other 'tangible' factors may be equal, deprive the children of the minority group of equal educational opportunities? We believe that it does. . . .

"We conclude that in the field of public education the doctrine of 'separate but equal' has no place. Separate educational facilities are inherently unequal."[5]

That evening NAACP activists held a victory party in the association's New York offices. Laughter and lightheartedness

3 Senator Herman Talmadge of Georgia in Lerone Bennett, Jr., *Confrontation: Black and White* (Baltimore: Penguin Books, 1965), p. 188. See also *New York Times*, May 18, 1954, p. 20.

4 Governor Marvin Griffin of Georgia, *New York Times*, November 7, 1954, p. 79.

5 *Brown* v. *Board of Education of Topeka, Kansas*, Supreme Court of the United States, 347 U.S. 483 (1954), in Albert P. Blaustein and Robert L. Zangrando, eds., *Civil Rights and the American Negro: A Documentary History* (New York: Washington Square Press, 1968), pp. 436–37.

predominated. Marshall, however, walked from group to group in a glum manner saying, "You fools go ahead and have your fun, but we ain't begun to work yet."[6] Marshall's prediction was correct. Yet, as Lorone Bennett, Jr., has noted, a sixteen-year-old black girl in a segregated school in Virginia also expressed something of the spirit of the times with a more optimistic view. Her teacher read the Court decision aloud to the class and then had the students go back to work. Barbara Trent and others wept. "We went on studying history," she recalled, "but things weren't the same, and will never be the same again."[7]

The decision in *Brown* v. *the Board of Education of Topeka, Kansas,* aroused tremendous hope in the minds of black Americans. All of the bleak years from the death of Black Reconstruction through the enforced separation of *Plessy* v. *Ferguson* to the lynch-riots of World War II seemed about to recede into unpleasant memories. But events did not quite work out this way.

The Court offered the hope of freedom yet nothing seemed to happen. After a time, Louis E. Lomax observed, "The Supreme Court school desegregation decision was an electric thing, coming as it most certainly did, just as the Negro was at the breaking point. Negro soldiers had come home from a war against Hitler's race madness only to face incredible insults and police brutality at the hands of the nation they had risked their lives to defend. Later other Negroes were filtered back from Korea.

"It would be impossible for a white person to understand what happened within black breasts on that Monday. An ardent segregationist called it 'Black Monday.' He was so right, but for reasons other than the ones he advances: That was the day we won; the day we took the white man's laws and won our case before an all-white Supreme Court with a Negro lawyer, Thurgood Marshall, as our chief counsel. And we were proud. But we were also naive.

"'The people of the South will never accept this monstrous decision.' Mississippi Senator James Eastland cried. 'I predict this decision will bring on a century of litigation.' "[8] This prediction may not prove precisely true, but within a short period of time, black America seethed with unrest. Discontent at the slow pace of school desegregation spread. Disillusionment set in. Direct action beckoned. Violence lay ahead.

An old female resident of Mississippi said that "we colored

---

[6] In Lerone Bennett, Jr., *Confrontation: Black and White* (Baltimore: Penguin Books, 1965), p. 189.

[7] In ibid., p. 189.

[8] Louis E. Lomax, *The Negro Revolt* (New York: Signet, 1963), pp. 84–85. (Originally published by Harper & Row, New York, 1962.)

people ain't nothing but a bundle of resentments and sufferings going somewhere to explode."[9] The explosion which has come to be called the black revolution was precipitated by a white man but started by a black woman. The action began on December 1, 1955, in Montgomery, Alabama. Perhaps it is symbolic that the revolt began in the original capital of the Confederacy.

The city of Montgomery then segregated everything including the bus lines. Buses were divided in the middle, white in front, black in back. And the city authorities in effect made every bus driver, all of whom were white, a police officer as well as a bus driver. The city ordinance directed members of each race to sit in the proper group section; there had long been no open friction, merely smoldering resentment. One cause of the resentment stemmed from the driver's practice when buses became crowded. At such times whites could move into the back section and displace seated blacks. The drivers enforced this rule with varying degrees of arrogance.

On this warm December day, Mrs. Rosa Parks, a mild-mannered person who worked as a seamstress, sat in one of the front rows of the black section. When the bus stopped at the Empire Theater, eight or ten whites got on and the seats in the white section filled. The driver ordered the blacks in the front rows of the black section to move to the rear and stand. Three Negroes got up and obeyed. Rosa Parks, whose feet were tired, remained in her seat. She had reached the point of open defiance.

The bus driver came back and snarled at her to move. She refused. He then called the police and they arrested her. Word of her jailing swept the black community and within twenty-four hours a mass meeting took place. The Reverend L. Roy Bennett shouted, "This is no time to talk; it is time to act."[10] Violence threatened.

But discussion followed and the majority decided to attempt a one-day black boycott of the bus lines. They agreed to make the effort on the following Monday, December 5, 1955. A tremendous task lay before them. The city's blacks made up approximately 75 per cent of the bus riders and the absence of such a group would be noticed. But effective boycotts require planning and, above all, mass communication. No member of the general meeting which made the decision to boycott knew certainly that the matter could be arranged in a single week end.

A young Montgomery minister, only twenty-six years of age,

---

9 In ibid., p. 92.
10 In Martin Luther King, Jr., *Stride Toward Freedom* (New York: Ballantine Books, 1958), p. 37.

who had come from Crozer Theological Seminary in Pennsylvania to his first ministry, reluctantly agreed to try to organize the effort. A fantastic sequence followed and a major equal-rights leader emerged. Martin Luther King, Jr., saw to the printing and distribution of some 7,000 leaflets describing the reasons for the boycott. One semiliterate black maid gave a copy to her white employer, who turned it over to her husband. He sent it to the Montgomery *Advertiser,* and they gave it front page publicity. Probably this freak happening made the boycott a success.

On Monday about 95 per cent of the city's blacks walked to work or stayed home. That night another mass meeting agreed upon the following mild requests and issued them in the name of the newly formed "Montgomery Improvement Association."[11]

1. Black bus riders would be given courteous treatment.
2. Bus riders would be seated as they boarded, blacks from the back of the bus toward the front and whites from the front toward the back. No one would be asked to move if the bus became crowded.
3. Black bus drivers would be employed on predominantly black routes.

These were hardly revolutionary or even radical demands. In fact the executive committee of the local branch of the NAACP at first refused to endorse the boycott because they felt the demands did not go far enough. NAACP leadership favored outright insistence upon immediate desegregation of the bus lines. Later the NAACP elected King as president of the Montgomery chapter and supported the boycott. What had been originally planned for a single day of refusal to ride stretched into weeks. Blacks walked, rode in car pools, or waited calmly while white employers drove into the ghettos to bring maids and butlers, gardeners and clerks to and from work. The boycott continued for 385 days and the city bus line went bankrupt; the decline in revenue totaled approximately $750,000. Downtown merchants lost thousands more from reduced business activity.

City officials took action to break the boycott. The mayor appealed to whites to stop chauffeuring blacks to and from work. Police arrested car-pool drivers for trivial offenses; some they locked up. King, first arrested for driving 30 miles per hour in a 25-mile zone, spent time in jail. Actually he had stopped his car at the time of his initial arrest to let three black riders out at their corner. The officers took the minister, who rapidly emerged

11 Ibid., pp. 46 and 52.

as the symbol of black defiance, to the police station, booked him, and locked him up. But even as they took his fingerprints, a crowd of blacks gathered outside. The jailer became frightened and released him shortly. He was later arrested and jailed for violating an old city ordinance against boycotts.

Court hearings on the boycott included testimony from twenty-eight black witnesses who had experienced abuse by the white bus drivers. Operators referred to them as "niggers," "black cows," and "black apes." Many of the bus drivers made the blacks pay their fare at the front door, then dismount and go to the rear door to enter the bus. Sometimes they drove off with the fare money before the black rider could reach the rear door. Mrs. Martha Walker told of the day her husband, who was blind, was still getting off the bus when the driver slammed the door on his leg and drove off dragging him down the street. She screamed and managed to get the bus to stop. But her complaint to the company for redress for her husband's injury brought no action.

The most shocking incident was related by Mrs. Stella Brooks. Her husband boarded a bus one day, paid his fare, and was ordered to get out and climb in the rear door. He saw that the bus was so crowded that he would not get a seat and told the driver he would get off and walk. But when he asked for the return of his dime the driver insolently refused. An argument followed. Brooks stayed on the bus and the driver called a policeman. The officer lost his head after Brooks still insisted that his money be returned, drew his revolver, and shot the black man. Brooks later died of his wounds.

Finally, on appeal, the United States Supreme Court declared the Montgomery racial laws unconstitutional and official city resistance to desegregation ceased. Authorities ordered the line to comply with the Court's instructions, and told the drivers to obey. Six drivers resigned at once. Others gave only minimal acceptance to the new concept.

King rode a bus on the first day of desegregation and suffered no incident. However, his home had been bombed a few days earlier and later it was bombed again. Many times night riders shot into the desegregated buses, causing several injuries. On the night of January 9, 1957, four black churches and two ministers' homes were bombed. White supremacy groups viewed the bus boycott as a crucial test. One leaflet advocated the abolition of the black race with "proper methods" including the use of "guns, bows and arrows, slingshots and knives." The boycott according to this group had submitted whites to "oppression" and "degradation" by "black, slimy, juicy, unbearable stinking niggers."[12] But eventually things calmed down on the Montgomery bus lines.

They have not calmed down in the nation since. Martin Luther King became the early champion of the direct action phase of the integration revolution. And his highly idealistic yet confrontation-minded Southern Christian Leadership Conference has continued, even past his death, to be an important element in the equal rights struggle.

The Supreme Court decision of 1954 followed by the Montgomery bus boycott of 1955 deeply disturbed the Southern white power structure. The North continued complacent in the comfortable assumption that all was reasonably well; de facto segregation and widespread discrimination in Northern cities had yet to be forced upon the nation's conscience. But in the South, fear spread through white minds. Most Southerners could hardly conceive of local blacks doing what they did during the Montgomery bus boycott. This action, following the Supreme Court decision which many Southern whites judged to be the work of either the Communist party or the devil, led to increased growth of the KKK, the White Citizens Councils, and the John Birch Society. The last group eventually spawned an ineffective movment to impeach Earl Warren. "The South says never" became the common cry.

This cry took its most eloquent expression in the Southern Manifesto, which most Southern congressmen signed. The supporters included the entire delegations from Alabama, Arkansas, Georgia, Louisiana, Virginia, Mississippi, and South Carolina. Senator Richard Russell of Georgia wrote the final draft of the Manifesto, although the impetus for this approach came from crusty Senator Harry F. Byrd of Virginia.

No doubt most of the sponsors expressed their sincere convictions. But a few quotes from the document reveal the depth of the paternalistic misjudgments which they rendered.

"The unwarranted decision of the Supreme Court in the public school cases," they said, "is now bearing the fruit always produced when men substitute naked power for established law. . . . Parents should not be deprived by Government of the right to direct the lives and education of their own children. . . . This unwarranted exercise of power by the Court, contrary to the Constitution, is creating chaos and confusion in the States principally affected. It is destroying the amicable relations between the white and Negro races that have been created through 90 years of patient

---

[12] White Citizens Council leaflet in James Peck, *Freedom Ride* (New York: Simon and Schuster, 1962), p. 55.

effort by the good people of both races. It has planted suspicion where there has been heretofore friendship and understanding. . . . Outside agitators are threatening immediate and revolutionary changes in our public school systems. . . . We pledge ourselves to use all lawful means to bring about a reversal of this decision which is contrary to the Constitution and to prevent the use of force in its implementation."[13]

The decade of the 1950's, calm on the surface, writhed beneath. The Southern Manifesto expressed the views of the least blatantly racist elements of the white majority. Less restrained bigotry erupted into violence all across the nation. Between 1955 and 1959 racial conflict ended a half dozen lives, injured nearly 100 persons and damaged dozens of homes and public buildings. Roy Harris, president of the White Citizens Councils, sparked a significant portion of these incidents. He went from place to place calling for the election of public officials on the single consideration—"Who's the strongest man for segregation?"[14] Such leaders as Ross Barnett of Mississippi, Orval Faubus of Arkansas, Gene Talmadge of Georgia, and George Wallace of Alabama emerged to sound the call for racial reaction.

Who can estimate how many persons, black and white, felt intimidated by the situation? To the white supremacist, violent events occurred because the Supreme Court acted unjustly and the Montgomery blacks pushed for too much. Yet equal opportunity for education and decent treatment should be the birthright of every American. To seek such surely constitutes a minimum request! Racial violence in the period can be traced to a single cause, white insistence upon two classes of citizenship. Social change inevitably produces tension. The violent white reaction to black-led social change flowed from the natural human tendency to protect advantage. Freedom cannot be received; it must be won.

Frederick Douglass once stated the matter eloquently: "If there is no struggle there is no progress. Those who profess to favor freedom, and yet deprecate agitation, are men who want crops without plowing up the ground. They want rain without thunder and lightning. They want the ocean without the awful roar of its many waters. This struggle may be a moral one; or it may be a physical one; or it may be both moral and physical; but it must be a struggle. Power concedes nothing without a demand.

---

[13] Declaration of Constitutional Principles, March 12, 1956, 84th Congress, 2nd Session, *Congressional Record,* 1956 in Gilbert Osofsky, ed., *The Burden of Race: A Documentary History of Negro-White Relations in America* (New York: Harper & Row, 1967), pp. 491–94.

[14] In ibid., p. 494.

It never did and never will. . . . Men may not get all they pay for in this world; but they must certainly pay for all they get."[15]

As recently as October 1969, George Wallace pontificated on the subject of likely violence if the Supreme Court tried to carry through its decision to end the period of "deliberate speed" and order immediate desegregation of public school systems in all parts of the nation. Wallace again placed blame for tension on the Court rather than on the real cause—continued white refusal to accept black humanity.

While events flowed forward toward increased racial tension, President Eisenhower assumed a passive role. He never publicly spoke for the rightness of the Brown decision and privately indicated that the Court made an error which caused trouble in the country. The president stressed his belief in the impossibility of changing hearts with laws or decisions. Martin Luther King later responded that the law may not change the heart, but it can restrain the heartless. King had respect for Eisenhower's sincere, personal belief in racial justice, but he assessed his public stance in the following manner: Eisenhower "had no ability to translate . . . [his personal belief] to the public, or to define the problem as a supreme domestic issue. I have always felt that he failed because he knew that his colleagues and advisers did not share his views, and he had no disposition to fight even for cherished beliefs. Moreover, President Eisenhower could not be committed to anything which involved a structural change in the architecture of American society. His conservatism was fixed and rigid, and any evil defacing the nation had to be extracted bit by bit with a tweezer because the surgeon's knife was an instrument too radical to touch this best of all possible societies."[16] Eisenhower's neutral stand encouraged whites who opposed change and led his administration into racial trouble. When the Little Rock, Arkansas, crisis erupted he was forced to use the power of the federal authorities to uphold the Court's decision to desegregate the schools.

As in the Montgomery bus boycott, the Little Rock crisis was precipitated by a white man but started by a black woman. Governor Orval Faubus, a demagogue from the Arkansas back country, became a national figure overnight through his insistence that Daisy Bates would never integrate a school system in the state of Arkansas. Mrs. Bates, who served as head of the local chapter of

---

[15] Philip S. Foner, ed., *The Life and Writings of Frederick Douglass* (New York: International Publishers, 1950), Vol. II, p. 437.

[16] Martin Luther King, Jr., *Why We Can't Wait* (New York: Signet, 1964), p. 143. (First published by Harper & Row, New York, 1963.) For revealing comment by Eisenhower see *New York Times*, April 3, 1948, p. 3.

the NAACP, had a strong will, which she pitted against that of Governor Faubus. She once insisted, "We've got to decide whether its going to be this generation or never."[17]

The Montgomery bus boycott had been dramatic, but less so than the school crisis in Little Rock. In Montgomery no blacks sought to enter a previously closed white preserve. They simply withdrew their patronage and waited. In Little Rock they tried to enter a place from which they had been excluded and the face-off created the most pointed federal–state confrontation in four generations.

On the morning of September 24, 1957, six high school-age girls and three boys, neatly dressed, escorted by some parents and adults, sought to enter Central High School in downtown Little Rock. Since hundreds of students were then entering the building for the new term these nine should not have stood out. However, their black skin made them the target of hate stares. Howling mobs screamed at them as they walked along accompanied by Mrs. Bates. Curses and spit followed. White high school students took part, but adults originated most of the abuse. When the black students reached the door, members of the Arkansas National Guard, called out by the governor to deny the students the entrance they sought, blocked the way.

One of the girls, Elizabeth Eckford, tried to slip between two of the guardsmen. They blocked her path with their bayonets and snarled at her to get back. The crowd of some 500 angry whites began to taunt her. They called her a "black bitch." Someone yelled, "Get her! Lynch her!" Frightened, the young student made her way to a nearby bus stop and slumped down on the bench to wait to make her escape from the dangerous nightmare in which she found herself. Benjamin Fine, education editor for the *New York Times,* sat down beside her, put his arm around her, and tried to comfort her. The mob became even more menacing. One person shouted, "Get a rope and drag her over to this tree." Mrs. Grace Lorch, wife of a professor at Philander Smith College, came upon the scene and scolded the mob. They shouted back, "Another nigger-lover. Get out of here." Amidst the tension the city bus arrived and Mrs. Lorch got on with Elizabeth. Deprived of their prey, the crowd turned upon Fine and threatened to lynch him. One middle-aged woman said, "Grab him and kick him in the balls." A white girl screamed in his face and called him a "dirty New York Jew." Eventually Fine made his escape unharmed, although his experience had so unnerved him

---

[17] Daisy Bates, *The Long Shadow of Little Rock* (New York: David McKay, 1962), p. 70.

that he could not tell it in detail for some weeks. Elizabeth Eckford went into semishock, from which she recovered slowly, having been psychologically seared, probably for life.[18]

President Eisenhower had previously stated that he did not see any circumstance under which he would use federal troops to enforce the Supreme Court order. Yet, on September 25, after many agonized conferences, the president federalized the National Guard and ordered it to protect the rights of the nine blacks by admitting them to the school of their choice. Little Rock Central High School was thus integrated by Eisenhower's action. Although no one died in the process, considerable mob violence occurred and the troops remained on duty at the school throughout the academic year. Governor Faubus, for all his bravado, shrank from actual physical opposition to the power of the federal government. Thus Little Rock constituted an important step in the process of confrontation; but the ultimate action of physical opposition by a governor to federal authority had yet to be undertaken. This came in Mississippi.

In 1958 Daisy Bates, who was personally vilified and whose home was bombed, received the Spingarn Medal issued by the NAACP. She got the honor along with the nine brave students who took big steps in support of black pride. The NAACP, suffering an internal crisis at the time, did not plan to include Mrs. Bates in the award ceremony because her militant stand worried some conservatives. The nine students refused the honor until she too was included.

History tends to focus upon the crisis points of human evolution. The exigencies of time and space lead toward emphasis of only a few elements in the equal-rights revolution of the 1950's and 1960's. A distorted image may emerge giving the impression that only a few high spots counted. Obviously it should be kept in mind that many small steps taken between the milestones, by individual citizens and groups some white, mostly black, contributed to the confrontation crisis. The less dramatic efforts to effect social change deserve their due. Yet the crisis points establish new plateaus and open fresh opportunities for further advance.

One crisis point can scarcely be undervalued in its impact. The sit-in movement, or "hamburger war" as later militants have sometimes belittled it, accomplished two advances. First, it aroused American youth, particularly young blacks, to commit themselves personally to the equal-rights struggle. Second, it made direct confrontation of discriminatory practices plausible every-

---

[18] Ibid., pp. 70–71.

where in the country, from the smallest hamlet to the largest urban complex.

Probably no one will be able to say exactly at what moment the idea of a sit-in movement first germinated. Jack Newfield concludes that the winter of 1960 was crucial. Many students in colleges across the country debated the slow pace of change through endless hours of dormitory bull sessions. School de-segregation was "going forward" at the rate of approximately 1 per cent per year. Thus, by 2054, the job would be completed with "all deliberate speed." In more than forty counties in the South no black voter was registered. In at least twenty counties white registration exceeded the size of the white population. Mack Charles Parker and Emmett Till had been lynched, but no convictions followed. Blacks in the Mississippi Delta, replaced by machines, existed at the starvation line. Unemployment for black youths ran over 30 per cent in many cities of the North.

On Sunday night, January 31, 1960, four college freshmen— Ezell Blair, Jr., David Richmond, Franklin McCain, and Joseph McNeill—all seventeen or eighteen years of age, three from North Carolina, one from Washington, D.C., sat discussing the situa-tion in a room in Scott Hall on the campus at segregated Agri-cultural and Technical College at Greensboro, North Carolina. Blair later said that they "spent a lot of time discussing the segre-gated situations we were exposed to. . . . It just didn't seem right that we would have to walk two miles to town, buy notebook paper and toothpaste in a national chain store, and then not be able to get a bite to eat and a cup of coffee at the counter." Finally Joe McNeill said, "We've talked about it long enough. Let's do something."[19] Entirely on their own, they decided to act the next day.

At about 4:45 the following afternoon, February 1, 1960, they went into the F. W. Woolworth Co. ten cent store on North Elm Street in downtown Greensboro. Each bought a tube of tooth-paste and then quietly went over and sat down at the lunch counter. A Negro woman who worked in the kitchen went over to them and scolded, "You know you're not supposed to be in here." She later told reporters that the four students were "ig-norant" and a "disgrace to their race."[20]

But the students ignored the Negro woman and quietly asked

---

[19] Jack Newfield, *A Prophetic Minority* (New York: Signet, 1967), p. 36. The account of the sit-in movement and later SNCC activities owes much to New-field's effective treatment. See especially Chapter 3, "The Beginning," Chapter 4, "Amite County," and Chapter 5, "SNCC." (First published by New Ameri-can Library, New York, 1966.)

[20] Ibid., p. 36.

for a cup of coffee. The white waitress politely answered, "I'm sorry but we don't serve colored here." McCain answered, "I beg your pardon, but you just served me at a counter two feet away. Why is it that you serve me at that counter and deny me at another? Why not stop serving me at all counters?" The manager came over as a small crowd started to gather. He said, "I'm sorry but we can't serve you because it is not the local custom."[21] The four students took out books and quietly sat at the counter without any coffee until 5:30, when the store closed.

The next day twelve more students joined the original four and the third day the number of sit-ins swelled to fifty, including some black high school students and some white co-eds from Women's College in Greensboro. No one got served, but with the increase in numbers they began to block service for others as they quietly sat and read their assignments. Woolworth's and other stores in the downtown Greensboro area were the targets during the initial week of the new movement.

College campuses around the nation are remarkably interconnected. News of concern to young people flashed by the mass media almost instantly triggers telephone calls between students who either contact their friends or communicate with leadership counterparts in student organizations. Student protests during the decade of the 1960's have frequently demonstrated the effectiveness of this informal network connecting American campuses. By the end of the first week news of the sit-ins had aroused substantial student interest all across the nation. The attention of the country was further heightened when, on Friday, a number of white students, with Confederate flags as their symbol of disagreement, began to heckle and jostle the sit-ins. They cursed and spat and otherwise threatened the black students and their increasingly numerous white allies.

The contrast between the two groups shocked the sensitive, even many who believed firmly in continued racial segregation. The Richmond *News Leader,* scarcely noted for its liberal stand on the race question, editorialized on February 22: "Many a Virginian must have felt a tinge of wry regret at the state of things as they are, in reading of Saturday's sit-downs by Negro students in Richmond stores. Here were the colored students, in coats, white shirts, ties and one of them reading Goethe and one was taking notes from a biology text. And here, on the sidewalk outside, was a gang of white boys come to heckle, a ragtail rabble, slack-jawed, black jacketed, grinning fit to kill, and some of them,

---

God save the mark, were waving the proud and honored flag of the Southern States in the last war fought by gentlemen."[22]

As usual, television provided the major emotional impact with its news clips contrasting the polite, nonviolent, sit-in students reading books with the duck-tailed, leather-jacketed, tough-looking whites who snarled, shook chains, and dumped catsup down backs. Some of the sit-ins were pushed off the stools; a few were slugged. By Saturday, tension in Greensboro had reached considerable heights. Managers at both the Woolworth and the Kress stores closed up as a result of the large crowds of sit-ins and counterdemonstrators.

The following week sit-ins began to occur all over the Carolinas. The movement affected Durham, Raleigh, Charlotte, Winston-Salem, High Point, Salisbury, and Concord, North Carolina, and Rock Hill and Orangeburg, in South Carolina. From there the pattern jumped to Hampton, Richmond, and Portsmouth, Virginia, and Nashville, Tennessee. In Nashville the white resisters developed a new tactic, stubbing cigarettes out on the necks of the sit-ins. Police arrested and jailed eighty-one Fisk University students for participating in a sit-in near the campus.

But the movement grew in strength and took on new forms. Students from Clafflin University and South Carolina State College marched into downtown Orangeburg on March 14 some 700 strong. Many carried Bibles. Police using tear gas and fire hoses broke up the march. The harsh streams of water knocked many students down; some were hurt. Authorities arrested approximately 500 and placed 350 of them in a chicken-wire stockade after the jails had been filled. Newspapers carried accounts with pictures of the students huddled together singing "God Bless America" in the subfreezing temperatures.

The sit-in students stung the conscience of America. Within two months sixty-five cities in twelve states had been the scene of major demonstrations. During the first year approximately 50,000 young people participated in sit-ins, stand-ins, kneel-ins, wade-ins, in all parts of the country. In the North, where facilities had long been operated on a desegregated basis, protests took the form of picketing. Chain stores that maintained segregated facilities in other parts of the country had to handle large crowds of chanting, sign-carrying pickets.

Harold Flemming, then the white director of the Southern

---

22 Editorial in Richmond *News Leader*, February 22, 1960, in Howard Zinn, *SNCC: The New Abolitionists* (Boston: Beacon Press, 1965), p. 27.

Regional Council, a liberal group, said of the sit-in movement: "Just as the Supreme Court decision was the legal turning point, the sit-ins were the psychological turning point in race relations."[23] Ralph McGill, white editor of the Atlanta *Constitution*, later wrote, "The sit-ins were, without question, productive of the most change. . . . No argument in a court of law could have dramatized the immorality and irrationality of such a custom as did the sit-ins. No force brought change as quickly as they. . . . The sit-ins reached far out into the back country. They inspired adult men and women . . . to support the young students in the cities. Not even the Supreme Court decision on schools in 1954 had done this."[24]

In 1948 William Faulkner, probably the greatest modern writer from the South, prophetically suggested a solution to the race problem in his novel *Intruder in the Dust*. Faulkner described actions of two boys, one black and one white, who refused to accept the ancient racial customs of the region and risked their lives to save a black prisoner from a lynch mob.

The sit-in approach to social change had succeeded before in history, even in America. Gandhi used it in India, of course, to gain freedom from the British, but the auto workers also used it in Detroit in the 1930's to force recognition of their union and the Congress of Racial Equality had used it on a small scale in Chicago and St. Louis in the 1940's. Yet it took students to make it a great weapon. Ezell Blair, one of the originators, said later, "It seems as if it's all a dream since the first sit-in although deep back in my mind I thought it would grow."[25]

In early 1961 a then forty-year-old black leader named James Farmer, resigned from the Board of Directors of the NAACP to become the National Director of the Congress of Racial Equality. CORE was a comparatively militant equal-rights organization founded by blacks and whites during World War II in an effort to supply a more rapid alternative to the legalistic approach of the NAACP which younger blacks had begun to question.

Until America destroys second-class citizenship in its every vestige, the fight requires various approaches. The NAACP has played a crucial role, but so have other organizations, even some which have adopted questionable ideologies. Farmer believed a fresh thrust must be attempted; he took up his new job on February 1, 1961, just one year after the beginning of the student sit-ins.

---

[23] Jack Newfield, *A Prophetic Minority* (New York: Signet, 1967), p. 38.
[24] Ralph McGill, *The South and the Southerner* (Boston: Little, Brown, 1963), pp. 16–17.
[25] Jack Newfield, *A Prophetic Minority* (New York: Signet, 1967), p. 39.

Actually, the sit-in movement had aroused so much emotional response all over the nation that the leadership of equal-rights groups everywhere felt compelled to take initiatives which would match the obvious commitment of the students. Direct confrontation of discrimination became the order of the day. An organization or leader who could not get involved lost credibility.

On March 13, 1961, CORE announced sponsorship of a series of "freedom rides" throughout the South to confront discrimination in interstate commerce. The effort can be compared to the Montgomery bus boycott, but with a major difference. Instead of refusing to ride, CORE leaders proposed to ride buses on an equal basis and to enter all bus stations, restaurants, and other facilities and use them freely. Thus, they planned to force the discrimination question in the very heart of the rural South. The red-necks would be faced down directly by small groups of blacks and whites who would deliberately break law or custom in hostile country under threat of mob action and dependent upon the scarcely just Southern law enforcement system.

The freedom rides began on May 4. Actually, similar rides had taken place earlier on a few Southern trains, but this constituted the first attempt to confront discrimination on the country's bus lines, a more difficult target. The bus riders took far larger risks measured by the greater isolation of a bus operated by a single driver. The first group contained only thirteen persons, six white and seven black.

As the group moved south hostilities began. On May 7 a dispute in Danville, Virginia, over lunch counter segregation was settled peacefully. On May 8 one of the black riders tried to get his shoes shined in Danville; the police arrested him for the attempt, even though a black man ran the shoe shine stand. On May 9 authorities closed the bus terminal in Rock Hill, South Carolina, rather than involve themselves in a tense situation. On May 10 police arrested two more riders for trespassing; after questioning and harassing them the authorities released them; the rider previously arrested also rejoined the group. On May 12 the riders found all facilities in Augusta, Georgia, open for their full use. The next day they also used all facilities in Athens, but Atlanta officials closed the bus station before they arrived.

By this time national publicity had made the freedom ride a crucial test. Alabama red-necks gathered to meet the challenge. On May 14 at Anniston a mob attacked the bus. They refused to allow the passengers to leave the vehicle and sliced the tires, which went flat several miles out of Anniston. Six car loads of white thugs tried to get on the bus to assault the riders. A courageous state official, Eli Cowling, blocked the doorway. The mob then set the bus on fire. Everyone inside had to leave and twelve went to the hospital suffering from smoke inhalation; the bus was completely destroyed by the fire.

But the ride continued the next day on another bus and the brutal climax came at Birmingham, where a mob assaulted the riders when they tried to enter the Greyhound station. One of the riders described the sequence in the following words: "As we entered the white waiting room and approached the lunch counter, we were grabbed bodily and pushed toward the alleyway leading to the loading platform. As soon as we got into the alleyway and out of sight of onlookers in the waiting room, six of them started swinging at me with fists and pipes. Five others attacked . . . [the rider just ahead]. Within seconds, I was unconscious on the ground."[26] He required fifty-three stitches in his scalp but did live to tell of the experience. Miraculously, everyone escaped death but the white bigots injured many.

Police in Anniston had made no arrests but they had been on the scene. The police in Birmingham, then directed by Eugene "Bull" Connor, pointedly stayed away from the area around the bus station, in spite of freedom-ride publicity and rumors that racists planned violence. Connor told reporters that he had been unable to supply protection because too many of his men had leave for Mother's Day. On May 15 the Greyhound drivers refused to operate the buses with the riders in them, and the group had to give up its original plan to travel all the way to New Orleans.

Attorney General Robert Kennedy took an active part in trying to obtain protection for the riders, but Governor Patterson of Alabama, who considered the riders to be rabble, rarely made himself available even for telephone communication. Patterson announced grandly, "We are going to do all we can to enforce the laws of the state on the highways and everywhere else, but we are not going to escort these agitators. We stand firm on that position."[27]

Subsequent freedom rides precipitated even more vicious situations, made worse by the duplicity of local officials. For example, on one occasion after mobs brutalized six riders, police arrested all of the integrationists, but not a single one of the white racists. On May 20th RFK ordered federal marshals to carry out their public responsibilities. Only Floyd Mann, Alabama Public Safety Director, attempted any real action to protect the riders. The rest of the members of the Alabama governmental structure avoided

---

26 James Peck, *Freedom Ride* (New York: Simon and Schuster, 1962), p. 128.
27 Louis E. Lomax, *The Negro Revolt* (New York: Signet, 1963), p. 150.

offending the white racist sentiments of the majority of their constituency. Governor Ross Barnett of Mississippi wired support to Governor Patterson urging him to continue resisting usurpation of power by the federal authorities.

Eventually federal marshals and National Guard troops restored order and made it possible for the freedom riders to complete their objectives—desegregation of all interstate transportation facilities. Robert Kennedy announced that federal pressure to eliminate discrimination would continue until the rights of all citizens had been assured. Federal officials carried out their assignment even to protection for a group of riders representing the American Nazi party who came in a "hate bus" to complicate the situation.

The freedom rides galvanized the country in a manner almost comparable to the sit-in movement on which they had been patterned. CORE's actions, joined officially by SCLC and SNCC and unofficially by some of the locals of the NAACP, broke through crusty traditions and opened yet another revealing insight into the ugly nature of the white problem in America. Some 4,000 persons acting in this courageous, yet simple manner brought CORE to the front of the civil rights movement. The NAACP's conservative stand in the freedom ride crisis caused it to lose strength as many moved into CORE; for the first time its membership became predominantly black. Louis Lomax once described CORE's contribution to the equal-rights revolution in these words: "The genius of CORE . . . [was] its insistence that direct mass action is the only way for Negroes to realize the practical results of the towering legal decisions the NAACP won."[28]

But while CORE continued its work, a new organization began to challenge the leadership role. The Student Nonviolent Coordinating Committee had evolved from the high idealism of young people inspired by the gentle leadership of Martin Luther King, Jr. Following the success of the Montgomery bus boycott, several dozen students and young persons just out of college began working for the Southern Christian Leadership Conference. A small, Atlanta-born white girl named Jane Stembridge went to the office of the SCLC to help coordinate youth actions. Robert Parris Moses, a black youth from Harlem who held a master's degree from Harvard, joined her there and the two of them served as the central pivot around which a biracial group of idealists gathered to discuss their future role in the equal-rights struggle. In October 1960, after the surging success of the sit-in movement, more than 200 delegates formed the Student Nonviolent Coordi-

---

28 Ibid., p. 158.

nating Committee. Julian Bond, who later became communications director of the new group, assisted the work of this organizational meeting.

SNCC devoted itself to action but through nonviolent means. The statement issued by the organization's founders contained the following idealistic sentiment: "Through non-violence, courage displaces fear. Love transcends hate. Acceptance dissipates prejudice; hope ends despair. Faith reconciles doubt. Peace dominates war. Mutual regards cancel enmity. Justice for all overthrows injustice. The redemptive community supercedes . . . immoral social systems."[29]

Bob Moses traveled through the black belt and decided that potential voting power must be harnessed by conducting vigorous registration campaigns. Members of SNCC went eagerly at the problem with phrases like "appealing to conscience" and the "genuine spirit of love" paramount in their thinking. Idealistic young people, both black and white, tested their belief that unselfish leadership and hard work can accomplish even that most difficult of tasks—changing human attitudes. The historian James Harvey Robinson once wrote, "We are incredibly heedless in the formation of our beliefs, but find ourselves filled with an illicit passion for them when anyone proposes to rob us of their companionship. . . . The result is that most of our so-called reasoning consists in finding arguments for going on believing as we already do."[30] The young workers of SNCC faced this reality with all of its violent implications. In one state after another they were harrassed, abused, beaten, given unequal justice, and in some cases murdered. Violence forced the SNCC leadership to review the assumptions on which the organization operated.

The SNCC experience in Amite County, Mississippi, where the county seat bears the ironic name Liberty, exemplifies the type of testing to which the SNCC approach was put. It was a cruel, one-sided fight. When SNCC began its voter registration drive there in 1961, Sheriff Daniel Jones, whose father headed the local KKK, controlled all the important power centers in the governmental structure. The movement nicknamed the county the Ninth Circle of Hell; Sheriff Jones contributed to this image. Only one black citizen had previously been officially registered to vote in the county, but the SNCC people never found him.

Alone, Bob Moses went into Amite County and organized the

---

[29] Statement of Purposes of SNCC in Joanne Grant, ed., *Black Protest: History, Documents and Analyses* (Greenwich, Conn.: Fawcett, 1968), pp. 289–90.

[30] James Harvey Robinson, *The Mind in the Making* (New York: Harper and Bros., 1921), pp. 40–41.

SNCC effort there. Few persons active in the equal-rights struggle have exhibited greater courage. Dick Gregory once introduced Moses to a huge audience at Berkeley as a "man who to me and to many people, will stand up among the greatest human beings who have ever walked the face of the earth."[31]

The campaign got off to a modest start in July 1961, and a few blacks registered to vote. Then night riders shot one of the new registrants and Moses had to deal with the fears of the black population as well as harrassment and repression from the white power structure. In August Moses suffered violence. Billy Jack Caston, a cousin of Sheriff Jones, assaulted Moses, who, consistent with the SNCC philosophy, refused to defend himself with counterviolence. But shortly after the assault Moses took a simple action which no black man had ever done in Amite County before. He filed charges against Caston and followed them with full testimony in open court. The jury acquitted Caston, with 100 armed whites milling outside threatening the court; Moses received a police escort to the county line.

Undaunted, he soon returned accompanied by another young black named Travis Britt. Together they renewed the voter registration drive. Britt recorded the following description of his experience at the county courthouse in Liberty when he was waiting to help a black farmer to register: "A tall white man, about middle-aged, wearing a khaki shirt and pants stepped up to me and asked, 'Boy, what's your business?' at which point I knew I was in trouble. The clerk from the hallway came to the backdoor leading to the courthouse with a smile on his face and called to the white man, 'Wait a minute, wait a minute.' At this point the white man . . . hit me on my right eye. Then I saw this clerk motion his head as if to call the rest of the whites. They came and all circled around me and this fellow . . . hit me on my jaw, and then on my chin. Then he slammed me down; instead of falling I stumbled onto the courthouse lawn. The crowd (about 15, I think) followed, making comments. He was holding me so tight around the collar, I put my hands on my collar to ease the choking. This set off a reaction of punches from this fellow they called Bryant: I counted fifteen; he just kept hitting and shouting, 'Why don't you hit me, nigger?' I was beaten into a semi-conscious state. My vision was blurred by the punch to the eye. I heard Bob yell to cover my head to avoid any further blows to my face. . . . Bob took me by the arm and took me to the street, walking cautiously to avoid any further kicks or blows. The Negro fellow that had

---

[31] In Jack Newfield, *A Prophetic Minority* (New York: Signet, 1967), p. 52.

been taking the registration test gave up in the excitement, and we saw him in his truck. . . ."[32]

The beatings continued and in September, Herbert Lee, a black farmer, father of nine children, attempting to qualify for the most fundamental right of citizenship, was shot and killed. His murderer, E. H. Hurst, a white man, calmly came up to Lee while the latter sat in the cab of his truck and shot him as he stepped into the street. A number of witnesses observed the shooting. Lee fell out of the truck into the gutter and lay in his own blood with flies swarming around him for some two hours. Finally the coroner came and later that afternoon, a coroner's jury ruled that Hurst killed Lee in self-defense. The black witnesses feared to testify to the truth. One of them later told the FBI the full story, but by then a grand jury had found Hurst innocent. A sheriff's deputy learned about the FBI testimony, denounced Louis Allen, the witness, and struck him with a flashlight, breaking his jaw. The deputy received no punishment but on the night of Friday, January 31, 1964, some person or persons killed Louis Allen in the front yard of his home with three blasts from a shotgun. Mississippi authorities have never solved the murder.

Herbert Lee became a minor hero of the voting rights movement and was put into a song, "Never Turn Back," which served as the "We Shall Overcome" of the SNCC. The final verse goes:

> *We have hung our heads and cried*
> *Cried for those like Lee who died*
> *Died for you and died for me*
> *Died for the cause of equality*
> *No, we'll never turn back*
> *No, we'll never turn back*
> *Until we've all been freed*
> *And we have equality*
> *And we have equality.*[33]

Moses saw the voter registration movement almost die out a dozen times, mostly through the grip of fear which paralyzed the adult citizens of the black belt. He was in and out of jail, often threatened by both the authorities and individual whites. Fortunately, he gained the dedicated support of hundreds, some of whom exhibited the same high courage which Moses always displayed. Sam Block, gaunt, black son of a Cleveland laborer, serves as one example of the incredible bravery then necessary to sustain any momentum against the frighteningly abusive white power

---

[32] Ibid., p. 56.
[33] Ibid., p. 58.

structure. On one occasion in Greenwood, Mississippi, the sheriff ordered Block to leave town before morning. Block calmly replied, "If you don't want to see me here, you better pack up and leave, because I'll be here."[34]

Moses stuck doggedly to the task and eventually sparked the movement which led to the Mississippi Summer Project in which Schwerner, Goodman, and Chaney were murdered. The SNCC efforts also led to the creation of the Mississippi Freedom Democratic party which first attracted national attention at the convention in Atlantic City in 1964, and which since has grown to the point where the entire political structure of the black belt is changing. In May 1971 the Voter Education Project in Atlanta, Georgia, counted nearly 650 black officials in the eleven Southern states. They include mayors, sheriffs, constables, town marshals, judges, and dozens of city councilmen and state legislators.

The Mississippi Freedom Democrats have influenced the course of national politics. The Democratic party, which for so long allowed whites to control its Southern wing, has begun to change significantly. As the *New York Times* put it: "The day of the lily-white delegations . . . is over. The Democrats from the rest of the country have finally lost patience with the exclusion of Negroes from party affairs in the South and with the blatant trickery employed by the white supremacy faction."[35] In 1968 the antiwar riots in Chicago obscured the amount of genuine change which had come to the Democratic delegations from all parts of the country. Blacks sat in virtually every group and the representation from Mississippi approximated the population division in that state. The 1972 nominating convention will be even more democratically based; the implications of these changes in the Democratic party obviously affect the Republican party as well.

But whereas SNCC can observe significant shifts for the better resulting from its efforts, the pressure through which the organization had to pass brought fundamental change to SNCC itself. Truly, the story of SNCC's conversion into the violence-minded Student Coordinating Committee marks one of the genuine tragedies of modern American history. Idealistic young people, black and white together, set forth on a noble crusade. They sought no destruction except that of ancient oppressions. They wanted no power except the legitimate voting rights of each citizen. They desired no conspiracy but rather a gentle brotherhood between people of all races. Howard Zinn, one of the historians of the SNCC movement, has termed these dedicated

---

34 In Howard Zinn, *SNCC: The New Abolitionists* (Boston: Beacon Press, 1965), pp. 85–86.
35 *New York Times*, August 27, 1964, p. 32.

young people "a ragged, incorruptible front line in the struggle to abolish racism in the United States."[36] Of them all it might be said, as Bob Moses said of one, they took on "the deep hates and deep loves which America and the world reserve for those who dare to stand in a strong sun and cast a sharp shadow. . . ."[37]

White power, fearful of any moves toward genuine equality, struck at these young blacks and their white allies with the ulti-mate means by which fearful majorities traditionally defend their exploitative position—violence. Federal authorities passively allowed the process to go forward despite many requests from SNCC leaders for protection. Justice Department representatives largely limited themselves to note taking and report writing. The insensitivity of the power structure turned young blacks like Stokely Carmichael and H. Rap Brown from nonviolence to violence. The process made cynics of significant numbers of able black leaders and drove a wedge not only between SNCC and the nation but between the whites and blacks who had attempted to work out a common destiny. If America one day ends in a racially rooted civil holocaust, one of the important turning points will have been reached when bigotry drove the Student Nonviolent Coordinating Committee into revolutionary opposition. As one white member of SNCC put it, "I curse this country every day of my life because it made me hate it, and I never wanted to."[38]

Jack Newfield, another of the historians of the SNCC move-ment mused, "Perhaps these desperate pioneers, who created the sit-ins, the freedom rides, the freedom parties, the summer proj-ects, the whole superstructure of myth that illuminated the free-dom movement for one historical moment, perhaps they now believe that only their own final destruction can somehow prove to the non-white majority on this planet, the utter wretchedness of the nation they tried so long to reform and redeem."[39]

Newfield's view may be too apocalyptic in tone but the young idealists of SNCC created strong currents for change; these cur-rents have affected many persons and the end results have by no means been fully realized. One Mississippian, doubtless affected by the new spirit of independence which SNCC tried so hard to foster in the area's blacks, set upon a personal course which precipitated the ultimate test between the power of the nation and the state. James Meredith proved able to forge his own his-

36 Howard Zinn, *SNCC: The New Abolitionists* (Boston: Beacon Press, 1965), p. 216.
37 Ibid., p. 76.
38 Comment of Mendy Samstein in Jack Newfield, *A Prophetic Minority* (New York: Signet, 1967), pp. 73–74.
39 Ibid., p. 82.

toric turning point through his successful integration of the University of Mississippi, ultimate symbol of white segregation.

The background to the Meredith–Mississippi Case lay not only at Little Rock, Arkansas, but at Tuscaloosa, Alabama, where University of Alabama authorities failed to uphold the rights of a beautiful black student named Autherine Lucy. In 1954, when Lucy went to court to gain admission to the state's most important institution of higher learning, some white students on the Alabama campus attempted to persuade the president and other members of the administration to accept the transition peacefully. Charles Morgan, a white student from Birmingham who had never lived anywhere but in the South, led the enlightened effort. He later gained national attention for speaking out in favor of the desegregation of Birmingham during the 1963 campaign and was driven from his legal practice as a result. University officials assured Morgan and his fellow students that their efforts would succeed and that Autherine Lucy, when she appeared for entrance, would be properly received.

However, the administration, although it may have been sincere in this assurance, did nothing to guard against mob violence. When Lucy appeared, officials allowed her a room on campus and registered her for classes, but an angry mob of white students accompanied by town adults forced her to flee for her life.

The fear-ridden administration then suspended her for what was termed her own safety. A federal court ordered that she be reinstated but the trustees, under threat of further mob violence, pemanently expelled her. They charged her with making defamatory remarks against the university. Actually she said that the administration had not done anything to block mob violence, an entirely accurate statement. Lucy never got back into the University of Alabama; mob violence had successfully blocked admittance of a black student to the state university system. By implication the same result could be forced upon all public schools.

Perhaps Alabama would not have provided a sufficiently acid encounter in any case. Maybe the ultimate test of federal vs. state authority vs. mob violence had to come in Mississippi. Ole Miss had never knowingly admitted a black student, although apparently a mulatto once gained entrance and graduated in the early 1900's.

James Meredith, an intense and able Mississippi Air Force veteran, decided that he could not get the kind of education he needed in the black colleges of his native state. Wishing to go to school at the University of Mississippi he proceeded to file the necessary papers and begin the long process of using the courts to force his admission. All evidence indicates that he made the decision on his own, although he later got assistance from the NAACP and other civil rights organizations.

When the federal courts ordered the college to admit him, Governor Ross Barnett assumed power over the state university and announced that no black student would ever darken his alma mater. The Kennedy administration decided to use national marshals, and if necessary, troops, to protect Meredith's rights and the integrity of the federal system. The confrontation began on the night of September 30, 1962, when Meredith arrived on campus escorted by a group of U.S. marshals. At this point a mob made up of students and a large number of white adults virtually took over the campus for an all-night session of violence. Meredith tried to sleep in his dormitory room while the marshals attempted to hold off the mob on the lawn outside.

Governor Barnett, who had tried to block the procedure but failed, now withdrew police power. Suddenly all the state troopers got into their cars and left the scene, leaving the badly outnumbered marshals to face the crowd alone. At this point the mob went almost completely mad. Two persons were killed, dozens injured, and the marshals were in danger of being overrun. Attorney General Robert Kennedy, under orders from the president, sent troops and they restored an uneasy peace.

Troops (and police) are not necessarily bad or on the wrong side. It depends who is giving the orders and to what purpose. In this case troops were indispensably necessary to bring about that amount of law and order which would insure the rights of a human being who happened to be black and who was seeking that which he had every right to seek, an education in a public college. Initially the Kennedy administration hesitated to apply the needed amount of counterforce to block mob success. Once the situation became overheated, however, federal power showed a superb balance of control with restraint. Troops stayed in the area and marshals remained on campus. Meredith slept in an apartment protected by six marshals throughout the year. Some of them accompanied him to class. Subsequently he graduated from Ole Miss, as have a number of black students since.

President Kennedy gave one of his greatest speeches as an outgrowth of the Meredith situation. Both he and his brother learned much from the experience as did other whites. Magnificently thorough television coverage of the Meredith-Mississippi case caused many Americans to make an emotional committment to the equal-rights fight for the first time in their lives.

On June 12, 1963, after a further antiblack action by Governor Wallace of Alabama, President Kennedy pledged himself to the effort. He said in part, "This nation was founded by men of many nations and backgrounds. It was founded on the principle that all men are created equal, and that the rights of every man are diminished when the rights of one man are threatened.

"Today, we are committed to a worldwide struggle to promote and protect the rights of all who wish to be free. And when Americans are sent to Vietnam or West Berlin we do not ask for whites only.

"It ought to be possible, therefore, for American students of any color to attend any public institution they select without having to be backed up by troops. It ought to be possible for American consumers of any color to receive equal service in places of public accommodation, such as hotels and restaurants, and theaters and retail stores without being forced to resort to demonstrations in the street.

"And it ought to be possible for American citizens of any color to register and to vote in a free election without interference or fear of reprisal.

"It ought to be possible . . . for every American to enjoy the privileges of being American without regard to his race or his color.

"In short, every American ought to have the right to be treated as he would wish to be treated, as one would wish his children to be treated. But this is not the case.

"The Negro baby born in America today, regardless of the section or the state in which he is born, has about one-half as much chance of completing . . . high school as a white baby, born in the same place, on the same day; one-third as much chance of becoming a professional man; twice as much chance of becoming unemployed; about one-seventh as much chance of earning $10,000 a year; a life expectancy which is several years shorter and the prospects of earning only half as much.

"This is not a sectional issue. Difficulties over segregation and discrimination exist in every city, in every state of the Union, producing in many cities a rising tide of discontent that threatens the public safety. . . .

"We are confronted primarily with a moral issue. It is as clear as the American Constitution. The heart of the question is whether all Americans are to be afforded equal rights and equal opportunities; whether we are going to treat our fellow Americans as we want to be treated.

"If an American, because his skin is dark, cannot eat lunch in a restaurant open to the public; if he cannot send his children to the best public school available; if he cannot vote for the public officials who represent him, if, in short, he cannot enjoy the full and free life which all of us want, then who among us would be content to have the color of his skin changed and stand in his place?

"Who among us would then be content with the counsels of patience and delay? One hundred years of delay have passed since President Lincoln freed the slaves, yet their heirs, their grandsons, are not fully free. They are not yet freed from the bonds of injustice; they are not yet freed from social and economic oppression.

"And this nation, for all its hopes and all its boasts, will not be fully free until all its citizens are free.

"We preach freedom around the world, and we mean it. And we cherish our freedom here at home. But are we to say to the world—and much more importantly to each other—that this is the land of the free, except for the Negroes; that we have no second-class citizens, except Negroes; that we have no class or caste system, no ghettos, no master race, except with respect to Negroes."[40]

President Kennedy went on to call upon Congress to write the necessary laws and the people of the country to put them into effect, as a moral obligation. It was indeed a powerful speech as any who heard it given will attest. It should have moved an entire people. But rhetoric, no matter how high-toned, remains an abstraction until individuals put it into effect in their own lives. Even after Kennedy asked for action Congress resisted making the change.

Little that was really new occurred except in places where brave individuals forced discriminatory practices into open confrontation with their spirit and their bodies. George Wallace, a small-minded politician with a big white following in Alabama and elsewhere in the nation, said in his inaugural address: "I draw the line in the dust and toss the gauntlet before the feet of tyranny and I say segregation now, segregation tomorrow, segregation forever."[41]

Martin Luther King, Jr., Ralph Abernathy, and other black leaders, in and out of the SCLC, decided that the time had come to confront discrimination in its most blatant center, Birmingham, Alabama. They chose the city for a major negative reason—its obscene injustice under the leadership of Bull Connor—and for a

---

[40] Speech of President Kennedy, June 12, 1963, in Gilbert Osofsky, ed., *The Burden of Race: A Documentary History of Negro-White Relations in America* (New York: Harper & Row, 1967), pp. 564–70.

[41] Peter M. Bergman and Mort N. Bergman, eds., *The Chronological History of the Negro in America* (New York: Mentor, 1969), p. 579. See also Martin Luther King, Jr., *Why We Can't Wait* (New York: Signet, 1964), p. 50.

powerful positive reason—the integration work of the Reverend Fred Shuttlesworth through the Alabama Christian Movement for Human Rights.

The carefully planned campaign of confrontation marches began in April 1963, just after Albert Boutwell, a "moderate," was elected mayor. Soon blacks filled the jails with protestors including Shuttlesworth, Abernathy, and King. The movement quietly insisted that the power structure of the city accept four simple changes:

1. Desegregation of lunch counters, rest rooms, fitting rooms and drinking fountains in variety and department stores in the downtown area.
2. Hiring and upgrading of Negroes on a nondiscriminatory basis in the business district.
3. Dropping of all charges against anyone jailed for demonstrating against the unjust laws of the city.
4. Creation of a biracial committee to work out a timetable for desegregation in other areas of Birmingham.

These demands hardly seem revolutionary, but they evoked a tremendous reaction from Connor and the white supremacists. They met the black marchers with sentry dogs, fire hoses, cattle prods, and police brutality. And the first turning point in the campaign came when television showed the ugly face of discrimination to the world. Still the desegregation campaign lagged. The decisive turning point came when the movement called upon parents to allow students to participate. At first the high school and junior high blacks entered the effort. Eventually elementary school children walked in brave protest into Connor's crowd-control equipment and into his jails.

King, arrested again, wrote his eloquent "Letter from a Birmingham Jail," one of the truly great documents of American history. In due course it should receive reverence equal to that granted the Declaration of Independence, the Constitution, the Gettysburg Address, and other statements regarding the sacredness of human freedom. King wrote in response to white clergymen who had spoken critically, accusing the desegregation movement of "poor timing." Some excerpts from King's letter provide penetrating insight into the entire scope of the SCLC campaign:

"You deplore the demonstration taking place in Birmingham," King wrote, "but your statement, I am sorry to say, fails to express a similar concern for the conditions that brought about the demonstrations.

"I am not afraid of the word 'tension.' I have earnestly opposed violent tension, but there is a type of constructive, nonviolent tension which is necessary for growth.

"While Mr. Boutwell is a much more gentle person than Mr. Connor, they are both segregationists, dedicated to maintenance of the status quo.

"We have not made a single gain in civil rights without determined legal and nonviolent pressure. . . . Privileged groups seldom give up their privileges voluntarily.

"Freedom is never voluntarily given by the oppressor; it must be demanded by the oppressed. Frankly, I have yet to engage in a direct-action campaign that was 'well timed' in the view of those who have not suffered unduly from the disease of segregation.

"Justice too long delayed is justice denied.

"We have waited more than 340 years for our constitutional and God-given rights.

"There are two types of laws; just and unjust. I would be the first to advocate obeying just laws. One has not only a legal but a moral responsibility to obey just laws. I would agree with St. Augustine that 'an unjust law is no law at all.'

"A just law is a man-made code that squares with the moral law or the law of God. An unjust law is a code that is out of harmony with the moral law. . . . An unjust law is a human law that is not rooted in eternal law and natural law. Any law that uplifts human personality is just. Any law that degrades human personality is unjust.

"Segregation is not only politically, economically and sociologically unsound, it is morally wrong and sinful.

"We should never forget that everything Adolf Hitler did in Germany was 'legal' and everything the Hungarian freedom fighters did in Hungary was 'illegal.'

"In your statement you assert that our actions, even though peaceful, must be condemned because they precipitate violence. But is this a logical assertion? Isn't this like condemning a robbed man because his possession of money precipitated the evil act of robbery?

"Progress never rolls in on wheels of inevitability; it comes through the tireless efforts of men willing to be co-workers with God.

"Injustice must be rooted out by strong, persistent and determined action.

"Let us all hope that the dark clouds of racial prejudice will soon pass away and the deep fog of misunderstanding will be lifted from our fear-drenched communities, and in some not too distant tomorrow the radiant stars of love and brotherhood will shine over our great nation with all their scintillating beauty."[42]

Finally, after days of close confrontation, the white business community, the city government, and the black demonstrators arranged a truce. The protestors' demands were met. Isolated incidents of violence continued, including the bombing of a church and the murder of four black girls several months later. Doubtless basic attitudes remained much the same, but the campaign had created a measure of forward motion.

In October 1969 the Association for the Study of Negro Life and History, a biracial organization, met in peace in the Tutwiler, reportedly the best hotel in Birmingham. Bull Connor was long since retired from public office. The white mayor and white governor went out of their way to welcome the scholars and at least a superficial harmony prevailed.

King's success in the Birmingham campaign raised him to a position of unquestioned leadership in the black revolution. Whites found his nonviolent approach acceptable; blacks, encouraged by King's willingness to confront discrimination, supported this American Gandhi in large numbers. But, ironically, even as King seemed at the very pinnacle of success, currents counter to his approach ran strong; his moment in history had already peaked.

A complex of causes contributed to this situation. King had yet to attack the basic aspects of discrimination. Freedom to buy a "Coke" or try on a dress in the stores of downtown America had little to do with the right to obtain a job, a home, or an education on a truly equal basis. The racism which permeated American institutions supplied whites with fundamental, continuous advantages with which nonviolent marches had little to do. King awakened the country to the possibilities of effective protest against racial injustice, but more militant black approaches were required to force white America to face the realities of the power equation. The black ghettos of the nation's urban centers contained millions of persons who watched and listened, and for the most part approved of what King was doing. But these same millions knew also that the cycle of poverty and despair which encircled them had receded hardly at all. They stood ready to listen to other, more revolutionary voices.

Few whites sensed the situation. Instead, many joined what appeared to them to be the grand culmination of the "Negro

[42]Abridged from "Letter from Birmingham Jail"—April 16, 1963—in *Why We Can't Wait* by Martin Luther King, Jr. Copyright © 1963 by Martin Luther King, Jr. Reprinted by permission of Harper & Row, Publishers, Inc., and Joan Daves.

revolt"—the March on Washington. In the summer of 1963 Asa Philip Randolph's long delayed demonstration finally took place. Bayard Rustin, a close co-worker of Randolph's from the early 1940's, headed the movement which grew to encompass most black leadership groups and many liberal whites as well. Approximately a quarter-million persons marched in the Capitol city on the appointed day, after months of planning which involved a great deal of attention to means by which violence could be avoided. The crowd included approximately 60,000 whites. The administration gave the movement its blessing; President Kennedy received the leaders at the White House.

And at the Lincoln Memorial a peaceful, biracial multitude listened to many noble words. Martin Luther King probably gave the most memorable and moving speech of his career: "Now is the time to make justice a reality for all of God's children," he said. "There will be neither rest nor tranquility in America until the Negro is granted his citizenship rights. The whirlwinds of revolt will continue to shake the foundations of our nation until the bright day of justice emerges." King then spoke out against racial separation. "The marvelous new militancy which has engulfed the Negro community must not lead us to distrust all white people," he said, "for many of our white brothers as evidenced by their presence here today have come to realize that their destiny is tied up with our destiny."

King also indicated that much remained to be done. "There are those who are asking the devotees of civil rights, 'When will you be satisfied?' We can never be satisfied as long as the Negro is the victim of unspeakable horrors of police brutality. We can never be satisfied as long as our bodies, heavy with the fatigue of travel, cannot gain lodging in the motels of the highways and the hotels of the cities.

"We can never be satisfied as long as our children are stripped of their selfhood and robbed of their dignity by signs saying 'for whites only.' We cannot be satisfied as long as the Negro in Mississippi cannot vote and the Negro in New York believes he has nothing for which to vote."

King climaxed the speech with his eloquent vision of the future which appealed to moderate blacks and liberal whites as the ideal expression of peaceful resolution of the racial crisis in America. "I have a dream that one day this nation will rise up and live out the true meaning of its creed. 'We hold these truths to be self-evident, that all men are created equal.'

"I have a dream that one day on the red hills of Georgia the sons of former slaves and sons of former slaveowners will be able to sit down together at the table of brotherhood.

"I have a dream that my four little children will one day live in a nation where they will not be judged by the color of their skin, but by the content of their character."[43]

The nation reacted to the march on Washington in an overwhelmingly favorable manner. One has to turn back to Booker T. Washington's appearance at the Atlanta Exposition in 1895 to find a time when the American press responded to a racial situation with an equally unanimous expression of approval. Many believed that the so-called "colored problem" in the United States, which had troubled the Republic for more than 200 years, would soon disappear.

But a few questioned the value of the March on Washington. Malcolm X, for example, scorned it as a white-manipulated "farce on Washington."[44] Had white America listened to his viewpoint, optimism regarding the significance of the march would have been considerably reduced. And, apart from black militants, objective appraisals recognized that the march had not accomplished much by way of genuine social change. It may have had an indirect effect and it may have drawn additional whites into the struggle for social justice, but Lerone Bennett's observation probably came close to the mark:

"As a morale booster, the March was a stunning success," he wrote. "But as an exercise in leadership, it was something less than scintillating. The March was not coordinated with anything that followed it. It led nowhere and was not intended to lead anywhere. *It was not planned as an event within a coherent plan of action.* As a result, the March was a stimulating but detached and isolated episode."[45]

More active protest beckoned those who saw the reality—that the fundamental social structure under which blacks struggled, had yet to be altered in significant degree. The final and more violent phase of the black revolution was about to open. Two stunning murders in 1963 may have speeded the process.

The first one occurred on the night of June 12, 1963. A man, returning to his home after an exhausting day of work as Field Secretary of the NAACP in Mississippi, parked his car in his driveway and slowly began walking toward his front door. The current series of demonstrations against segregation had kept him going at an exhausting pace for some weeks, and he frequently missed supper with his family.

---

[43] Speech of Martin Luther King, Jr., August 29, 1963, in Frank Freidel and Norman Pollack, eds., *American Issues in the Twentieth Century* (Chicago: Rand McNally, 1969), pp. 426–27.

[44] Malcolm X, *Autobiography* (New York: Grove Press, 1965), p. 281.

[45] Lerone Bennett, Jr., *Confrontation: Black and White* (Baltimore: Penguin Books, 1966), p. 243.

His wife, having just seen President Kennedy's great speech on civil rights, dozed. Her two children still watched television. She later recalled the events of her husband's horrible murder in the following words. "Darrell heard the car first. 'Here comes Daddy.' We listened to the familiar sound of the car. I roused myself as the tires reached the gravel driveway, stretched, and then heard the car door close. I wondered what Medgar would have to say about the speech, and I sat up on the bed.

"A shot rang out, loud and menacing. The children, true to their training, sprawled on the floor. I knew in my heart what it must mean.

"I flew to the door, praying to be wrong. I switched on the light. Medgar lay face down at the doorway drenched with blood.

"I screamed, went to him, calling his name.

"There was another shot, much closer, and I dropped to my knees. Medgar didn't move.

"The children were around me now, pleading with him. 'Please Daddy, please get up!'

"Behind Medgar on the floor of the carport were the papers he had dropped and some sweatshirts. Crazily, across the front of one, I read the words, 'Jim Crow Must Go!' In his hand, stretched out toward the door, was the door key. There was blood everywhere."[46]

Medgar Evers, shot by a coward from ambush, never regained consciousness. His death caused a brief period of national remorse. That fall, some Americans recalled the Evers murder when another coward crouched behind boxes in a building overlooking a street in Dallas, Texas, and killed the president of the United States.

Following Kennedy's death Lyndon Johnson appealed for passage of the Civil Rights Act of 1964 in the memory of those who had fought for justice. The Senate finally voted to end debate, the first time that the upper house applied cloture to a civil rights measure since adoption of the rule in 1917. Minority Leader Everett Dirksen of Illinois said, in supporting the law, "This is an idea whose time has come. It will not be stayed. It will not be denied."[47] The bill placed on the statute books a broad series of provisions touching many aspects of American life.

Ironically, the 1964 law strongly resembled the short-lived act

[46] Mrs. Medgar Evers with William Peters, *For Us, the Living* (Garden City, N.Y.: Doubleday, 1967), p. 302.

[47] Albert P. Blaustein and Robert L. Zangrando, eds., *Civil Rights and the American Negro: A Documentary History* (New York: Washington Square Press, 1968), p. 525.

of 1875 which had also attempted to solve the white problem in America with legislative action. In 1875 the Congress had insisted that "all persons within the jurdisdiction of the United States shall be entitled to the full and equal enjoyment of the accommodations, advantages, facilities and privileges of inns, public conveyances on land or water, theaters, and other places of public amusement."[48] The 1964 act includes the following provision: "All persons shall be entitled to the full and equal enjoyment of the goods, services, facilities, privileges, and advantages . . . of any place of public accommodation . . . such as any inn, hotel, motel . . . restaurant . . . theater, sports arena, stadium or other place of . . . entertainment."[49] Study of the white response to black emancipation suggests a bad dream in which the same evil scenes repeat themselves.

The Civil Rights Act of 1964, although it failed to solve the white problem, did provide the legal structure on which a just society must be built. The eighty-nine-year gap in American legislation had finally been filled. Harry S Truman had led the way in the civil rights field. John F. Kennedy, little aware of the race problem at the start of his administration, learned rapidly and made significant contributions not only in the Meredith–Mississippi case but in other situations.

But Lyndon B. Johnson proved to be the most unusual president of all. A Texan who had racist backgrounds and who, in the first phases of his fantastic public career, opposed black progress, moved white America to a closer understanding of the depths of the problem than any previous occupant of the White House. Once he escaped from his Texas constituency and wielded the power of the presidency he accomplished remarkable things. Johnson, a man difficult to defend before many groups, deserves honors as the one who, more than any other president in American history, advanced the cause of equal rights. In addition to serving as the legislative leader in the passage of the mild Civil Rights Act of 1957, the first significant piece of legislation in the field since 1875, Johnson should receive major credit for the Act of 1964, the Voting Rights Act of 1965, the Open Housing Act of 1968, and other federal initiatives to enforce the Constitution of the United States.

Some of his words have an eloquent ring. "Nothing," he said, "is more freighted with meaning for our own destiny, than the revo-

---

48 Civil-Rights Act, March 1, 1875 in Henry S. Commager, *Documents of American History*, Vol. I (New York: Appleton-Century-Crofts, 1963), p. 536.
49 78 Stat. 241, 1964 in Albert P. Blaustein and Robert L. Zangrando, eds., *Civil Rights and the American Negro: A Documentary History* (New York: Washington Square Press, 1968), pp. 528–29.

lution of the Negro American. In far too many ways American Negroes have been another nation; deprived of freedom, crippled by hatred, the doors of opportunity closed to hope." The president announced, "We seek not just freedom but opportunity— not just legal equity but human ability—not just equality as a right and a theory, but equality as a fact and a result." "All of us must overcome the crippling legacy of biogtry and injustice . . . [and] 'We shall overcome!' "[50]

If America does overcome its racist past, it will owe much to the leadership supplied by persons like Harry Truman, Daisy Bates, Robert Parris Moses, James Farmer, Medgar Evers, James Meredith, Martin Luther King, Jr., Ezell Blair, Julian Bond, John F. Kennedy, and Lyndon Johnson. It will also owe a tremendous debt to the powerful personality of a brilliant militant who supplied crucial thrust to the accelerating pace of the black revolution.

During the 1960's Malcolm Little rose to grace the national scene as he spoke for increasing millions of American blacks no longer willing to wait patiently for white America to accept the truth. No person ever caught the real meaning of the phrase "Freedom Now" in quite so central a fashion as did this man who rose from poverty and degradation to lead a people.

Malcolm X's childhood in Michigan was blotched with horror. His father died in a mysterious accident when Malcolm was a boy. Many felt that he had been murdered by brutal whites who hated him for his unwillingness to take a subservient position. His mother, driven insane by the pressures of life after her husband's death, ended in an asylum. Her young son observed her humiliating mental degeneration. "Society" placed him in a home, and he did well in school earning high grades and serving as president of his class. But racist teachers in secondary school discouraged him from trying to become a lawyer. Possessed of a brilliant mind he quit school and drifted downwards to dope, pimping, and theft, in Boston and Harlem.

Arrested for burglary, he went to prison, where he educated himself by wide reading. He studied the English language through copying the dictionary page by page in long hand. He also joined the Black Muslim movement and emerged as one of this separatist group's most powerful spokesmen.

---

[50] Excerpts from President Johnson's speech at Howard University, June 4th, 1965, in ibid., pp. 559–66; and excerpts from President Johnson's message on Voting Rights Bill, March 15, 1965, in Peter M. Bergman and Mort N. Bergman, eds., *The Chronological History of the Negro in America* (New York: Mentor, 1969), p. 591. (Originally published by New American Library, New York, 1969.)

During his Muslim period he denounced whites as devils and demanded that blacks stand up for their rights. He argued that nonviolence was all right in its place, when social conditions were really fair and equal, and opposed violence as a way of life. But he advocated the Old Testament view: an eye for an eye and a tooth for a tooth. "Be peaceful, be courteous, obey the law, respect everyone" he said, "but if someone puts his hand on you [to exploit you] send him to the cemetery."[51] The white press consistently presented him as a racist in reverse and a violence monger. Yet he spoke such plain truth as to make American blacks (and a few whites) face the reality of the racial wrongs in America as they never had done before. He warned whites that the injustice, violence, and brutality of the past cannot be continued. To blacks he said, rise up, stand tall, throw off a second-class mental outlook, and take charge of your destiny.

After a disagreement with Elijah Muhammad he went to Mecca and became an orthodox Muslim rather than a follower of the personality cult which characterizes the American version of Islam. In the end, fanatical followers of Elijah Muhammad murdered Malcolm X in a hotel in Harlem. But his power lives on.

Ossie Davis caught Malcolm X's spirit best with powerful words spoken in eulogy at his funeral: "Malcolm was our manhood, our living, black manhood," Davis said. "This was his meaning to his people. And in honoring him, we honor the best in ourselves. . . . And we will know him then for what he was and is—a Prince—our own black shining Prince—who didn't hesitate to die, because he loved us so."[52] Later Davis explained his reasons for eulogizing a man most Americans had seen as a purveyor of violent hatred. "Malcolm—whatever else he was or was not—Malcolm was a man! White folks do not need anybody to remind them that they are men. We do! This was his one incontrovertible benefit to his people. . . . Malcolm said . . . get up off your knees and fight your own battles . . . Malcolm . . . was refreshing excitement; he scared hell out of the rest of us, bred as we are to caution. . . . But Malcolm knew that every white man in America profits directly or indirectly from racism, even though he does not practice it or believe in it. He also knew that every Negro who did not challenge on the spot every instance of racism, overt or covert, committed against him and his people, who chose instead to swallow his spit and go on smiling, was an Uncle Tom

51 Malcolm X, "Message to the Grass Roots," in *Malcolm X Speaks* (New York: Grove Press, 1965), p. 12.
52 Epilogue Chapter by Alex Haley, in Malcolm X, *Autobiography* (New York: Grove Press, 1965), pp. 450–51.

and a traitor, without balls or guts, or any other commonly accepted aspects of manhood!"[53]

The main thrust of the social revolution of the 1960's found its source in the proud message of Malcolm X. As one black woman said to a reporter at his funeral, "I'm paying my respects to the greatest black man in this century."[54] And history should eventually record that Malcolm X deserves a place among the greatest men of American history. White and black alike will doubtless come to see him in this light. He supplied the indispensable charisma by means of which the ideals of a revolutionary élan are reduced to practical actions.

Still, progress continued to be painfully slow. Each area, each city seemed to need confrontation campaigns. Such repetitious actions heavily drained the strength and talent of black leaders. Counsels for patience and delay found little favor in circles where Malcolm's message had been heard. Malcolm died in February 1965. Martin Luther King and other moderate leaders were then preparing a new campaign targeted on Selma, Alabama. They followed a familiar pattern, but nonviolence as a basic tactic had ceased to appeal to a significant number of black Americans. The "moderate" leadership was in close danger of losing control of the black revolution to the alienated, embittered leaders of the second civil war in America.

SCLC and SNCC began a fairly traditional antisegregation campaign in Selma with the usual marches and other confrontation tactics. But the nation became horrified by the brutal manner in which the Alabama state police crushed a freedom march on the Edmund Pettus bridge outside Selma on March 7, 1965. Television again supplied the emotional impact. Whites and blacks, stung into action, either went to Selma to finish the campaign and then march on Montgomery or made plans to attack discrimination frontally in their own communities. A new militancy heightened tensions.

Even relatively conservative organizations like the NAACP began to move toward direct action. Roy Wilkins announced that black Americans were "furious over the brutal attack by Alabama State Police on . . . [the] freedom march at Selma. Like the citizens of Nazi-occupied France, Holland, Belgium, Denmark, and Norway, Negroes must either submit to the heels of their oppressors or they must organize, underground if necessary to

[53] Ibid., pp. 453–55.
[54] Ibid., p. 449.

protect themselves from the oppression of Governor Wallace and his storm troopers."[55]

Struggles occurred in almost all groups involved in the equal-rights fight. The militants moved to the fore. Selma supplied something of a turning point. After Selma, more often than not, race confrontations erupted into violence.

Into a volatile situation, Stokely Carmichael, a young militant, injected the expression *black power*. Immediately, the concept seemed to clarify the struggle for many blacks even as it confused, angered, and frightened whites. Black leaders, including Richard Wright, W. E. B. Du Bois, and Adam Clayton Powell, had used the term before, but a special dynamism stemmed from the youthful, hell-with-the-system, burn-it-down-if-necessary approach of Carmichael. The setting often supplies the extra ingredients necessary to begin a real revolution. Carmichael, as noted, had started as a nonviolent leader in the early, integrationist phases of the SNCC movement. But his repeated experiences with brutal repression changed him fundamentally. When James Meredith attempted his lone "March Against Fear" in Mississippi from the Tennessee border to Jackson and was shot by a white man from ambush, others came forward to continue the march. Out of this march came the slogan which caught the imagination of the country, carrying hope to some, fear to many.

Martin Luther King, Jr., described the dramatic moment in these words: "As we approached . . . Greenwood large crowds of old friends and new turned out to welcome us. At a huge mass meeting that night, which was held in the city park, Stokely [Carmichael] mounted the platform and after arousing the audience with a powerful attack on Mississippi justice, he proclaimed: 'What we need is black power.' Willie Ricks, the fiery orator of SNCC, leaped to the platform and shouted, 'What do you want?' The crowd roared, 'Black Power.' Again and again Ricks cried, 'What do you want?' and the response 'Black Power' grew louder and louder, until it had reached fever pitch."[56]

The concept is both simple and complex. To be black in America has traditionally meant to be powerless; to be white has carried the power implication, although not all whites have, of course, exercised equal amounts of power. To the black-power advocate the American system is a power system and the only

[55] Lerone Bennett, Jr., *Confrontation: Black and White* (Baltimore: Penguin Books, 1965), p. 252.

[56] Martin Luther King, Jr., *Where Do We Go From Here: Chaos or Community?* (New York: Bantam Books, 1968), p. 34. (First published by Harper & Row, New York, 1967.)

way to survive and prosper in that system is to have a full share in the power equation.

Black power has both political and economic components. Effective unification of black people in their own struggle depends upon black control of the vital aspects of black existence. This control would be exercised to compel federal authorities to enforce the Constitution and all laws which provide for equal justice. In the process of demanding freedom, blacks would upgrade their own image and become fully self-sufficient.

As the black-power concept became popular, whites, no matter how "liberal," "tolerant," or "well intentioned," became increasingly superfluous in the black community and in equal-rights organizations. To the black-power advocate, the role of whites lay with other whites and in white communities. The role of blacks lay in establishing, by direct action when necessary, the power needed to control their own destiny.

One youth beautifully described the essence of black power in replying to a question from a white regarding the racial contributions of the mayor of a major city, known for his liberal efforts. "Yeah, sure, Jerry Baby's [Detroit Mayor Jerome P. Cavanagh's] done a few things for us. . . . But that's just it, man. We're tired of having people do things for us. We want to do things for ourselves. I mean this isn't way down yonder in New Orleans any more, and we don't need any nice old plantation sugar daddy to take care of us. We're going to help ourselves whether whitey likes it or not. And that's just what Jerry Baby and all those nice white liberals don't like. They're willing to share some of the corn and taters with us, but when it gets right down to the nitty-gritty of power, they aren't sharing anything."[57]

In Carmichael's phrasing, "It's 'time out' for nice words. It's time black people got together. We have to say things nobody else in this country is willing to say and find the strength internally and from each other to say the things that need to be said. . . .

"If you are born in Lowndes County, Alabama, Swillingchit, Mississippi, or Harlem, New York, and the color of your skin happens to be black you are going to catch it. The only reason we have to get together is the color of our skins. They oppress us because we are black and we are going to use that blackness to get out of the trick bag they put us in. Don't be ashamed of your color. . . .

"The extremists in this country are the white people who force us to live the way we live. . . .

---

[57] Alfred M. Lee and Norman D. Humphrey, *Race Riot* (New York: Octagon Books, 1968), p. x.

"We are going to use the term 'Black Power' and we are going to define it because Black Power speaks to us. We can't let them project Black Power because they can only project it from white power and we know what white power has done to us. We have to organize ourselves to speak from a position of strength and stop begging people to look kindly upon us. We are going to build a movement in this country based on the color of our skins that is going to free us from our oppressors and we have to do that ourselves."[58]

"Black Americans have two problems: they are poor and they are black. . . .

"Ultimately, the economic foundations of this country must be shaken if black people are to control their lives. The colonies of the United States—and this includes the black ghettos within its borders, north and south—must be liberated. For a century, this nation has been like an octopus of exploitation, its tentacles stretching from Mississippi and Harlem to South America, the Middle East, southern Africa, and Vietnam; the form of exploitation varies from area to area but the essential result has been the same—a powerful few have been maintained and enriched at the expense of the poor and voiceless colored masses. This pattern must be broken. As its grip loosens here and there round the world, the hopes of black Americans become more realistic. For racism to die, a totally different America must be born. . . .

"Integration is a subterfuge for the maintenance of white supremacy. . . .

"No one ever talked about 'white power' because power in this country is white. . . .

"Black people do not want to 'take over' this country. They don't want to 'get Whitey,' they just want to get him off their backs as the saying goes. . . . The white man is irrelevant to blacks, except as an oppressive force. Blacks want to be in his place, yes, but not in order to terrorize and lynch and starve him. They want to be in his place because that is where a decent life can be had. . . .

"The love we seek to encourage is within the black community, the only American community where men call each other 'brother' when they meet. We can build a community of love only where we have the ability and power to do so; among blacks.

"As for white America, perhaps it can stop crying out against 'black supremacy,' 'black nationalism,' 'racism in reverse,' and begin facing reality. The reality is that this nation, from top to

---

[58] From speech by Carmichael in Chicago, July 28, 1966, in Gilbert Osofsky, ed., *The Burden of Race: A Documentary History of Negro-White Relations in America* (New York: Harper & Row, 1967), pp. 629–36.

bottom, is racist; that racism is not primarily a problem of 'human relations' but of an exploitation maintained—either actively or through silence—by the society as a whole. . . ."

But Carmichael warned "the rebuilding of this society, if at all possible, is basically the responsibility of whites—not blacks. We won't fight to save the present society, in Vietnam or anywhere else. We are just going to work, in the way we see fit, and on goals we define, not for civil rights but for all our human rights."[59]

The turgid events of the 1960's must be seen against some understanding of this Black Power movement.

The long hot summers of the 1960's unfolded a pattern of revolt in American black ghettos which troubled the nation more deeply than the oratory of all speakers black and white. The Harlem Riot of 1935 provided an early model for the type of violent, antienvironment riots which began to take place with regularity all around the country during the mid-1960's. It is difficult to single out the one riot which most caught the imagination of the majority of long-frustrated blacks, but a good case can be made for the Watts, Los Angeles, violence of 1965.

In August, in Watts, a segregated area in the city of Los Angeles, two white policemen stopped a car driven by a twenty-one-year-old black named Marquette Frye. Frye had been drinking and got into an argument with the officers. A crowd gathered; words, spit, and physical resistance followed; Frye and several others were taken to jail. The incident proved to be the event needed to arouse thousands in the community. For six days the area rocked with revolt. Chaos came to control the entire scene; shooting, stoning, burning, and looting destroyed both lives and property. Thirty-four persons, thirty-one of them black, died, twenty-three of them as a result of police gunfire. More than a thousand were hospitalized. City police and some 14,000 National Guard troops arrested approximately 3,500 persons. The enraged mobs completely destroyed 200 businesses and left 400 others in substantial ruin. Property damage totaled $40 million, the great majority owned by blacks.

During the first hours of the rioting many black leaders tried to cool the situation with appeals for nonviolence but the focus soon shifted. Bitter young blacks who felt they had nothing to lose forced the community into an understandable transfer of attention from symptoms to causes. They argued that if unrest existed as a result of the Frye arrest, the solution lay not in calm-

---

ing matters down but in exposing the underlying conditions which created the discontents. As the McCone Commission later concluded, "the depth and the seriousness of the situation were not accurately appraised in the early stages."[60]

The shocking intensity of the riot revealed pent-up frustration which can only be compared to that which punctuated the Atlantic slave trade in the eighteenth century. During the terrible middle passage, entire shiploads of Africans, chained in between deck compartments less than two feet high, sometimes went mad and destroyed each other in the process.

An American observer of one such disaster in 1829 described the scene on a slave trader which his ship had just overtaken: He expressed horror at the "state of this vessel for conveying human beings," but more experienced witnesses told him that they had frequently seen worse. "The height sometimes between decks was only eighteen inches," he wrote "so that the unfortunate beings could not turn round or even on their sides, the elevation being less than the breadth of their shoulders; and here they are usually chained to the decks by the neck and legs. In such a place the sense of misery and suffocation is so great that the Negroes, like the English in the Black Hole at Calcutta, are driven to a frenzy. They had on one occasion taken a slave vessel in the river Bonny; the slaves were stowed in the narrow space between decks and chained together. They heard a horrible din and tumult among them and could not imagine from what cause it proceeded. They opened the hatches and turned them up on deck. They were manacled together in twos and threes. Their horror may be well conceived when they found a number of them in different states of suffocation; many of them were foaming at the mouth and in the last agonies—many were dead. A living man was sometimes dragged up, and his companion was a dead body; sometimes of the three attached to the same chain, one was dying and another dead. The tumult they had heard was the frenzy of those suffocating wretches in the last state of fury and desperation, struggling to extricate themselves. When they were all dragged up, nineteen were irrecoverably dead. Many destroyed one another in the hopes of procuring room to breathe; men strangled those next to them, and women drove nails into each other's brains."[61]

---

60 McCone Commission Report in Gilbert Osofsky, ed., *The Burden of Race: A Documentary History of Negro-White Relations in America* (New York: Harper & Row, 1967), p. 618.

61 The Reverend R. Walsh, "Notices of Brazil," 1829, in Henry S. Commager and Allen Nevins, eds., *The Heritage of America* (Boston: Little, Brown, 1951), pp. 453–54.

Much has been said and written about the wrongness of riot-ing. Even more has been said about the senselessness of destroying one's own block and of how black neighborhoods suffer more than white and so forth. Do these comments explain the ghetto riots? Or did one bitter young black express a more cogent viewpoint when he said, "I ain't got nothing to lose if I get killed burning this damnation down."[62] Another astute observer has noted that "Riots are ugly, but they are not meaningless. They cry out profoundly for understanding and corrective action."[63]

Eldridge Cleaver records a revealing description of the reaction to Watts by the black inmates in Folsom prison: "As we left the Mess Hall Sunday morning and milled around in the prison yard, after four days of abortive uprising in Watts, a group of low riders (Los Angeles nickname for ghetto youth) from Watts assembled on the basketball court. They were wearing jubilant triumphant smiles, animated by a vicarious spirit by which they too were in the thick of the uprising taking place hundreds of miles away to the south in the Watts ghetto.

" 'Man!,' said one, 'what they doing out there? Break it down for me, Baby.'

"They slapped each other's outstretched palms in a cool salute and burst out laughing with joy.

" 'Home boy, them Brothers is taking care of Business,' shrieked another ecstatically.

"Then one low rider, stepping into the center of the circle formed by the others, rared back on his legs and swaggered, hunching his belt up with his forearms as he'd seen James Cagney and George Raft do in too many gangster movies. I joined the circle. Sensing a creative moment in the offing, we all got very quiet, very still, and others passing by joined the circle and did likewise.

" 'Baby,' he said, 'they walking in fours and kicking in doors; dropping Reds (a barbiturate called Red Devils) and busting heads; drinking wine and committing crime, shooting and looting; high-siding (cutting up) and low-riding, setting fires and slashing tires; turning over cars and burning down bars; making Parker (Chief of Police) mad and making me glad; putting an end to that "go slow" crap and putting sweet Watts on the map—my black ass is in Folsom this morning but my black heart is in Watts.' Tears of joy were rolling from his eyes."[64]

62 Nathan Wright, Jr., *Let's Work Together* (New York: Hawthorn Books, 1968), p. 94.

63 Elmo Ellis in Alfred M. Lee and Norman D. Humphrey, *Race Riot* (New York: Octagon Books, 1968), p. xiv [sic].

64 Eldridge Cleaver, *Soul On Ice* (New York: Delta, 1968), pp. 26–27. (Originally published by McGraw-Hill, New York, 1968.)

This close identification with the rioters could not, in Folsom Prison, be easily turned into sympathetic actions, but the attractions for many young blacks of such a course can be seen from the record of similar outbreaks which occurred in other areas even while Watts still writhed. Violence erupted in San Diego, Pasadena, Pacoima, Monrovia, Long Beach, and San Pedro. The McCone Commission found no cause to believe that these outbreaks had been planned by some pre-established decision-making process; they took place spontaneously as a consequence of long-standing grievances.

The mayor blamed the governor and the governor blamed the mayor. A big investigation followed; the McCone Commission rendered a report. Some conservatives and right-wingers blamed the incident on the communists. But built-up frustration in the black community growing from the conditions provided the central cause. Although Watts was at least as good as most ghetto areas for housing, one fifth of the homes were dilapidated. The area contained one sixth of Los Angeles' half-million blacks, held there by discriminatory practices in other parts of the city.

Residents also suffered from job scarcity. Four times more congested than the rest of the city, Watts' unemployment ran higher than 30 per cent. Many of the unemployed had no hope of holding a good position because they lived too far from industries with available jobs. The situation could scarcely have been more conducive to riot; those who advocated violence gained an audience regardless of their particular organization or point of view.

After Watts, a series of riots, more or less on the same pattern, shook the nation. Cambridge, Maryland; Tampa, Florida; Cincinnati, Ohio; Atlanta, Georgia; Newark, New Jersey; Detroit, Michigan; Philadelphia, Pennsylvania; Cleveland, Ohio; and many other places erupted. In the process, hundreds died, thousands were injured, millions of dollars' worth of property was damaged or destroyed.

The Detroit Riot of July 1967, probably the single most destructive racially based clash in American history, left major sections of that city in the condition typical of a modern war.

About 3:45 A.M. one Sunday morning police raided a drinking club called the United Community and Civil League. Instead of finding just a few patrons, the police discovered eighty-two blacks celebrating the homecoming of two Vietnam veterans. As they took the patrons to the station for booking, a crowd began to gather. Some rocks were thrown; incidents of violence spread. Police reinforcements appeared. Looters broke into the first store at about 6:00 A.M. A full-scale riot began.

John Conyers, Jr., a black member of the U.S. House of Representatives, had no success in attempting to bring calm to the neighborhood. Constituents shouted him down for defending the Establishment even though his record as an uncompromising black leader held solid throughout the district. Even black-owned stores began to be looted. "Soul Brother" signs rarely stopped the crowd which became increasingly ugly and unwilling to listen to any calm voice, black or white. Congressman Conyers noticed a black woman with a baby in her arms, who "was raging [and] cursing 'whitey' for no apparent reason."[65] The endless imposed inhibitions had finally driven the people to fury and the woman simply expressed the rage which she had restrained for so long.

If any significant portion of America has ever been at the brink of genuine, mass revolution, the city of Detroit must have been that area in the summer of 1967. As one report put it: "A spirit of carefree nihilism was taking hold. To riot and to destroy appeared more and more to become ends in themselves. Late Sunday afternoon it appeared to one observer that the young people were 'dancing amidst the flames.' "[66] One black man threw a fire bomb into a store at the end of his own street. The wind was high. Within a few minutes the fire jumped from roof to roof and within the hour the entire block burned out of control. The ninth house to catch fire was owned by the man who threw the bomb.

As the riot ran its course, enraged blacks drove firemen from burning buildings rather than allow them to put down the flames, even though the areas affected were mostly peopled by blacks. Fourteen thousand National Guard, and federal troops, restored order. One observer felt the city to be "saturated with fear."[67] Reports of sniper and rifle fire led troops and police to retaliate. Eventually forty-three persons, most of them black, died in the riot. Machine guns, mounted on armored jeeps, and tanks rolled through the streets. "Peace" finally came after 1,250 fires, 2,000 injuries, 7,200 arrests, and $44 million in property damages.

Once again the nation created a special commission to investigate the ghetto riots. President Johnson directed the Kerner Commission to determine what happened, why it happened, and what could be done to prevent it from happening in the future. The Kerner Commission report may yet prove to be simply one more ineffective effort. Indeed, President Johnson gave only slight attention to the report and many blacks consider it to be

---

[65] Kerner Commission, *Report of the National Advisory Commission on Civil Disorders* (New York: Bantam Books, 1968), p. 89. (Originally published by E. P. Dutton, New York, 1968.)

[66] Ibid., p. 91.

[67] Ibid., p. 99.

an empty document. Yet the Commission did produce a direct statement of historic reality which has gained a certain currency and which may yet prove to be a turning point, not in black rioting, but in white thinking about the real cause of riots in America, namely, white racism. The Commission, scarcely a radical group, included Governor Otto Kerner of Illinois, Mayor John Lindsay of New York, Senator Fred R. Harris of Oklahoma, and Herbert Jenkins, the Chief of Police in Atlanta, Georgia. The two blacks on the commission were Senator Edward Brooke of Massachusetts and Roy Wilkins of the NAACP.

These men, white and black together, reached the correct conclusion. White racism has always been the cause of America's social problem. Separate and unequal societies mar the nation's record. "Discrimination and segregation," they wrote, "have long permeated much of American life; they now threaten the future of every American." The authors added, "What white Americans have never fully understood, but what the Negro can never forget—is that white society is deeply implicated in the ghetto. White institutions created it, white institutions maintain it, and white society condones it."[68]

The document should be viewed by every white American. Tom Wicker, in writing an introduction to the report, stated, "Reading it is an ugly experience but one that brings, finally, something like the relief of beginning. What had to be said has been said at last, and by representatives of that white, moderate, responsible America that, alone, needed to say it."[69] He added, ". . . the importance of this report is that it makes plain that white, moderate, responsible America is where the trouble lies."[70]

If America can solve its white problem the solution to other social ills—foreign war, poverty, urban decay, environmental pollution—will also be within our grasp. But if the nation cannot find the way to a racially just society, efforts to solve other problems will become mere academic charades.

---

68 Ibid., pp. 1–2.
69 Ibid., p. xi.
70 Ibid., p. v.

# Epilogue

# 10

As the preceding chapters in this book attempt to show, the white problem has long troubled the United States. No social question has roots which go deeper or extend further back in time. Yet even after slavery, after the Civil War, after the brutal repressions of the Reconstruction era, after the sorry refusal of whites to accept blacks as neighbors, after the racially imposed humiliations of the two world wars, after the long history of exclusion, exploitation, and oppression, American whites find it difficult to accept the charge that the national record has been fundamentally marred by racism.

An interesting example of the widely divergent racial assumptions of blacks and whites can be seen in the results of a 1970 survey of friction in the American Army in Germany. The Pentagon, troubled by repeated accounts of racial incidents among occupation troops, sent a team of investigators to study the situation. But most of the questioners were white and they made little progress in getting at the facts. One black sergeant, irritated by the line of questioning to which he was submitted, remarked, "What's the problem, what's the problem? Hell . . . [the white man] knows the problem! He *is* the problem!"[1]

As recently as the fall of 1969 the Harris Survey again demonstrated that whites question the validity of the accusation that they acquiesce in the continuation of a discriminatory system of second-class citizenship for blacks. Harris asked a sample of blacks and whites across the nation a variety of questions regarding discrimination. Interviewers sought to determine whether the respondents felt that discrimination continued in housing, jobs, hotel and motel accommodations, quality education in public

---

[1] *New York Times*, November 23, 1970, pp. 1, 26.

schools, fair wages, entry into labor unions, and general treatment as human beings. The results varied slightly from question to question, but whites as a whole did not believe blacks to be in serious difficulty. Although a similar survey a few years ago found more than 60 per cent of whites agreeing that blacks still suffered major discrimination, the 1969 sampling revealed that this large majority had fallen to less than half, some 46 per cent, and that 43 per cent of whites felt discrimination had been eliminated. Not surprisingly, but strikingly, blacks strongly disagreed. Only 4 per cent felt the problem had ended, whereas 84 per cent continued to believe that they suffered because of their race.

Obviously one view must be incorrect, or substantially so. Equally obviously, this book concludes that the white perspective is in need of considerable alteration. Only through sweeping change in white attitudes can the racial problem in America be solved. Yet a stream of evidence suggests that whites do not really understand the situation. A classic example of this white myopia occurred in Asbury Park, New Jersey, during July 1970. Like other coast cities, tourists and summer residents take over most of the beaches and attractive housing areas. A few blocks back from the ocean, second-class neighborhoods begin, often peopled largely with blacks who supply the menial service functions which support the city's vacation-oriented life.

On Wednesday, July 8th, 1970, headlines in major east coast newspapers carried news of racial violence in Asbury Park. After several nights of confrontation, police fired upon the crowds and wounded forty-six black citizens. No deaths occurred, doubtless partly because the police fired shotguns only. Authorities estimated that property damage, mostly in black areas, would run to over $1 million. As "law and order" returned to the city, the white mayor commented upon the sequence of events. He indicated that he was "very much" surprised at the outbreak of racial trouble in his town. "We didn't know," he added, "of any tensions that were building." And then he made the following revealing observation. "The beachfront, thank goodness, hasn't been affected."[2]

The "beachfront" of American race relations has for too long been an area untouched by genuine white understanding of the real nature of the problem. Any teacher who attempts to deal with the issue of second-class citizenship will come upon striking examples of white deficiencies in this regard. While most white college students express tolerant opinions, and few really qualify as racial bigots, a frighteningly high percentage clearly reveal themselves as mere distant observers of the American racial

---

[2] *Philadelphia Evening Bulletin,* July 8, 1970, p. 19.

scene, lacking in anything but the most superficial estimates of the depths of the problem which exist. An unfortunate mixture of paternalism and petulance characterizes these superficial views.

As an outgrowth to reading and discussing books like Michael Harrington's *The Other America* and Charles Silberman's *Crisis in Black and White,* I asked a recent class of mine to write a brief essay indicating personal solutions to the problems of poverty and race in America. One sincere white student observed, "I feel the whole solution to the problem lies in education of the Negro and white man. There should be a health corps which visits Negro homes constantly and shows them how to use a little soap and water. There should be funds to help Negroes paint up and clean up their property. . . . Low income housing is a good idea, but Negroes must be taught how to live in them. If they are not it will look like a second ghetto. . . . The list of ways to help the Negro is unending, but the biggest asset is education which I feel will be the only salvation for them."[3]

The fantastic condescension of this honest answer must be apparent to all but a tiny fraction of American whites who seriously reflect upon it. In my experience it is typical. The great majority of white students in the average white school hold similar views, learned largely from their parents.

I often begin a course by asking students to submit questions for discussion during the semester. Some of the questions submitted by blacks indicate a measure of confusion regarding the situation around them. A few recent examples: "Why do white people seem to resent black people getting together? Have the riots in cities such as Watts and Newark helped to win support for blacks from whites or have they alienated the majority of whites? Why do some white people hold prejudices against black people when they give no reasons for their views?"

Yet the degree of white bewilderment seems far more extensive. The following illustrations reveal more about the questioner than he or she realized: "Why do some blacks fall back on their color as a means for defense against criticism, unemployment, and so forth, but then turn around and say, 'black is superior to white'? Why do blacks feel they want the privileges of whites and when they get some they misuse them; do they feel this is the only way to gain power? Why do blacks feel that everything should be handed to them on a silver platter? Why didn't blacks react to their situation sooner?"

Or perhaps the following classic comment might be taken as a prototype for all the rest. The only thing missing is the phrase,

---

[3] Exam paper in author's possession. Name withheld.

"Some of my best friends are. . . ." "First, I must say" the questioner wrote, "that I am wholeheartedly in favor of the actions
the black people have taken in order to be recognized. But why
must there be prejudices to begin with? And why don't blacks
realize that other ethnic groups have had to fight for recognition?
Some blacks talk as though they were the only group in the world
that has had to fight for their rights. I don't feel that those blacks
are justified in their thinking or in what they are doing."[4]

Assumptions play a terribly important part in all human behavior. A child who assumes that a furry caterpillar will be an
interesting object to taste and puts one in his mouth will probably have an experience different from the one he expected. A
defensive halfback who assumes that the approaching end will
break to the outside because his initial move is in that direction
may have an embarrassing moment when the game films are reviewed on Monday. A president who assumes that no great foreign power would risk trying to place long-range missiles on an
island close to the shores of his nation will be required to make a
major commitment to restore the military balance in the area. All
have gained new sets of assumptions which will guide their behavior in fresh situations.

The national creed insists that all citizens should receive equal
treatment and most Americans make some attempt to put this
into effect in their own actions toward others. Yet assumptions
regarding racial superiority and inferiority weigh heavily against
the genuine application of this national creed. In the best of
times whites, as a whole, have difficulty seeing the ugly realities
of the system of second-class citizenship which works continuously
against black advancement. They have been conditioned by the
culture to think that all citizens have an equal chance and their
assumptions hold them back from clear understanding of the
actual situation, let alone planning for its improvement. In times
which are not so good, when sirens wail, fists fly, stores are looted
and buildings burned, the "gut reactions" of numberless whites,
take whatever form they will, tend towards assumptions of black
trouble-making, unreliability, dishonesty, fearsomeness, vicious-
ness, and inferiority. In such circumstances the blacks involved
appear to most whites to be conducting themselves in an un-
American manner.

No doubt some of them are. Blacks as a whole seem no more
immune than any other ethnic group in producing their share of
deadbeats who seize opportunities to further themselves unjustly

---

[4] Student questions submitted during school years 1969–1970 and 1970–
1971, in author's possession.

at someone else's expense. Yet black opposition to the restrictions of second-class citizenship has run for so long and taken such a variety of forms that more fundamental questions must be answered. If since 1619 blacks have been demonstrating their dissatisfaction with certain aspects of American life, perhaps they, as a people, do not belong within the country. On the other hand, maybe the nation's life itself needs alteration. The American creed rules out a caste system. Citizens who demonstrate against such might indeed be properly judged to be the more truly American than those who accuse them of lack of patriotism.

Knowledge must precede change. The task of self-education on the race question stands like a seemingly immense mountain blocking further progress. Many blacks, especially the young, educated militants, have given up and seek total separation from the majority, although the practical difficulties in such a move receive little attention. Blacks with separatist tendencies avoid troubling themselves about America's problems because America has for so long not troubled itself about black problems. The cause appears hopeless to many on both sides of the racial line.

However, amazingly rapid changes can take place even in the minds of persons long committed to another view. On a recent occasion, a serious-looking white student came to see me after class. He had paid close attention from the beginning of the semester, but had not until that day taken any part in class discussions. The topic for the period had been the *Autobiography of Malcolm X*. This student had several times made observations which showed clearly not only that he had done the assignment, but that he was profoundly moved by it. He told me, "Sir, you did not know it and may not believe it, but I was one of the most ardent white supremacists on this campus before I took this course. In fact, I heard about what you have been doing from other students and signed up for the course with the idea that I would expose the fraud that you were perpetrating." He added, "It simply has not worked that way. The course had been getting to me before, but when I read Malcolm X, I was completely swung over to acceptance of the charge that America has been racist at its core." Those who have read Malcolm X will realize what a major change had taken place in this student's thinking. No one accepts criticism as harsh as that made by Malcolm unless he is convinced that the charges are substantially true. As we parted the student said, with complete sincerity, "this book and this course have changed my entire life."

A few weeks later even more striking evidence of the power of knowledge to effect rapid change in attitude came to my attention. I had given a lecture to an adult education group. My topic was "The White Problem in America," and along with the generalizations and specifics which I presented I urged them to read certain books. In addition to Malcolm X, I mentioned Carmichael and Hamilton's *Black Power* and Grier and Cobbs' *Black Rage*. A few weeks after the lecture some students were conducting a poll of public opinion in the nearby town. The questions covered a variety of civic issues, but racial considerations loomed large. One respondent, a handsome woman in her early seventies, gave increasingly liberal answers to the racial questions. The interviewer thought that from her appearance, home, and affluent neighborhood, she might have viewed racial matters the other way; when the interview ended, he drew her into further conversation. She frankly admitted that a short time before she might have given much different responses, but that she had heard a lecture at the college on "The White Problem" which had encouraged her to read some books. She had just finished the last one and found to her excitement that her whole thinking had changed. As she put it, "I have come to realize that my entire life I have been living a lie."

The United States during its existence as a nation has been living a lie.

But necessary change in attitude could come far more quickly than most assume if the proper things are done by a sufficiently large number of people. This thought raises the question, "What precisely must be done?" No one can present an exact formula which will be equally applicable to everyone. The suggestions which follow, and which conclude this book, have grown out of many discussions with students. Frequently they ask, "But what can I do?"

To blacks I advise, do more of what most of you are doing now. Continue to unify and to struggle. Refuse to accept any affront. Oppose every vestige of discriminatory action. Confront society. If necessary, as a last resort, in a given situation, use that amount of resistance required to insure that the American constitutional creed applies to all. And while you are doing so, realize the power of education—not just on the racial question or on black culture—but on every aspect of life. The man or woman who controls knowledge possesses the capital of the present and of the future, and capital is power. One hundred years ago, power in America lay largely with those who owned the land. Fifty years ago, power lay with those who held positions of influence in industry. But today power rests with those who have education.

I urge that every black student in school today should work ten times harder than any white, not with any Booker Washington approach, assuming that by the demonstration of excellence in learning he will be "allowed" into the mainstream of national life, but with the militant thought that those who control knowledge will control the future in this country and elsewhere around the globe. The strikingly high degree of influence in the emerging nations exerted by those who have education demonstrates the validity of this view.

Advice to white students involves a somewhat more complex formula. I urge upon them also, of course, the power of knowledge. But, in addition, I insist that only through their efforts will America change where it has to change the most—within the white majority. One astute black observer has correctly noted that, "The key to meaningful resolution is in the hands of that large majority of whites who conceive of themselves as liberal, moderate, and decent human beings. It is a cold hard fact," he continues, "that the many flagrant forms of racial injustice North and South could not exist without their acquiescence."[5]

Every segment of white society, every institution, bureau, business, union, association, in a word, every aspect of white society must be studied and where injustice exists, it must be exposed and changed. This does not imply that the process will change the minds of all whites regarding the nature of the white problem in America. But if justice be placed above self-interest, society can be forced to act properly regardless of continued intolerance in the minds of many. Eventually, with a new generation, intolerance may subside. But the precondition for tolerance is absolute justice.

White students generally accept these arguments but often have difficulty visualizing what they themselves are going to do. Working to affect the thinking of racist-minded roommates, friends, and relatives, using the books and articles from the course, often leads to personal experiences which, though causing strained relations at times, cause further ideas for specific action to flow. Opportunities to influence people can be found in the largest city or the most remote, rural village. And whites also must learn to fight, even at times by confrontations, for the absolutely equal application of the national creed.

To blacks and whites together I suggest that as they force change in social institutions and work for justice, they will find ways to ally themselves in meaningful coalitions which will truly create a new America. This great nation has accomplished much in its relatively short career. No system of government and no economic structure have produced more nor opened greater opportunities to as many human beings. There is much that is noble

---

[5] Kenneth B. Clark, *Dark Ghetto* (New York: Harper & Row, 1965), p. 229.

and good in this country and well worth keeping. The remaining imperfections demand attention partly because they contrast so terribly with the larger ideal.

Finally, I insist that no one can avoid the situation. No citizen can sit this one out, unless he goes into exile in a foreign land. Either this nation goes forward to a new society or we end up with something very different from the relatively open present. The fact that whites far outnumber blacks does not mean that the majority will win out and retain the past extended into the future. Blacks, aroused by centuries of abuse, may lose in some future armageddon. But America will never be the same again for the civil blood bath and repressive aftermath which will characterize such an era.

As the nation begins the decade of the 1970's no objective observer of the American racial scene can fail to find some signs which are moderately encouraging. But bleakness dominates. As the lengthy 1970 report of the Civil Rights Commission notes, "the great promise of the civil rights laws, executive orders and judicial decisions of the 1950's and 1960's has not been realized." The Commission, chaired by Father Theodore M. Hesburgh of Notre Dame, concludes that we are on a "collision course"[6] with national disaster unless we place every talent and energy to the task of making the Constitution a reality for every citizen.

As has so often been true since the Civil War, white America seems to be tiring of the race question. At a time when equal rights should be receiving the highest priority, the national government has begun to limit its commitment to the equal enforcement of all the laws. From the beginning of the Reconstruction period to the present decade, the same pattern has emerged in each phase of the struggle. At the very point when serious insistence upon constitutional guarantees would make the greatest difference the majority has reduced the amount of this insistence. To paraphrase President Ulysses Grant, the public has become tired of the long hot summers of the 1960's.

In May 1971, more than three years after the issuance of the Kerner Commission Report on civil disorders, the chairman of the Commission told a Senate committee that he did not believe that the facts of the report had been accepted by the majority of the nation's citizens. With unemployment among young blacks approaching 30 per cent, even higher than in 1967 when the Commission made its study, Judge Kerner concluded that a situation as dangerous as any we had faced was upon the nation.

---

[6] Excerpts from the Commission Report in the Rochester, N.Y., *Democrat and Chronicle*, October 13, 1970, p. 9A.

The Nixon administration's "Southern strategy," however well intentioned it may be, has further diminished whatever limited optimism existed in the minds of antiracist citizens of both colors. On the crucial issue of change in the public schools, for example, the administration spent more than a year trying to devise a way around the desegregation guidelines set up by the Health, Education, and Welfare Department during the Johnson era. White supremacists have been encouraged to work hard on measures to postpone further the coming of genuine equality. The election of November 1970 returned George Wallace to power in Alabama and he continues to be a significant figure on the national political scene.

Vice President Spiro Agnew speaks in strong language out of a vast ignorance. The favorable response which he has evoked from the silent white majority, north and south, suggests the dangerous dimensions of the present situation. During the Baltimore riots following the assassination of Martin Luther King, Jr., then Governor Agnew summoned black leaders to a meeting, which he addressed in a petulant tone. He accused some 100 black officials of selling out to demagogues and of taking a cowardly stance in a time of public crisis. Most of the blacks walked out in protest and denounced Agnew for his demeaning approach. "We are shocked," they wrote, "at the gall of the governor suggesting that only he can define the nature of the leadership of the black community. Agnew's actions are more in keeping with the slave system of a bygone era. . . ." They concluded, "Agnew must be made to know that he cannot treat black men and women like children. Agnew must be made to know that all Americans are going to share fully in the fruits of this country."[7]

Yet blacks continue to have difficulty convincing white America that the period of genuine change is upon us. During 1969–1970 twelve black congressmen tried for more than a year to obtain an audience with President Nixon. Finally they succeeded in gaining the president's attention and presented sixty specific recommendations of federal programs to effect social change. They insisted that minority groups had suffered "irreparable harm" during the Nixon administration and called upon the president to make an "unequivocal commitment" to the "cause of equal rights." They set May 17, 1971, anniversary date of the school desegregation decision, as the proper target for presidential response to the recommendations. But Mr. Nixon entered the White House with the support of many white racists and has followed, at least in major part, the policy of "benign neglect" urged upon him by

---

[7] *National Observer*, August 19, 1968, p. 5.

advisors.[8] He seems an unlikely figure to emerge as a champion of equal rights for American blacks. The dialogue continues but little concrete progress has been realized despite the long-standing nature of the social problems included in the report of the caucus of congressional blacks.

All whites in America must come to realize that blacks no longer accept their traditional "place" nor any arguments whatsoever for continued patience on the question of racial equality. As one militant recently put it, "this is real. There is no place to hide, to run: the bullshit has ended, and all the pimps of the mind and action will be dispatched actually or spiritually when the time comes and yes, . . . [it] is indeed coming."[9] The time to grant the birthright is now! If it comes to racial holocaust blacks will heed a call like that of Claude McKay:

> *If we must die, let it not be like hogs*
> *Hunted and penned in an inglorious spot,*
> *While round us bark the mad and hungry dogs,*
> *Making their mock at our accursed lot.*
> *If we must die, O let us nobly die,*
> *So that our precious blood may not be shed*
> *In vain; then even the monsters we defy*
> *Shall be constrained to honor us though dead!*
> *O kinsmen! we must meet the common foe!*
> *Though far outnumbered let us show us brave,*
> *And for their thousand blows deal one deathblow!*
> *What though before us lies the open grave?*
> *Like men we'll face the murderous, cowardly pack,*
> *Pressed to the wall, dying, but fighting back!*[10]

How much better, however, for all Americans, black and white together, to join with Martin Luther King, Jr., in refusing to accept either "the idea that man is mere flotsam and jetsam in the river of life which surrounds him," or the "view that mankind is so tragically bound to the starless midnight of racisim . . . that the bright daybreak of peace and brotherhood can never become a reality."[11]

---

8 Rochester, N.Y., *Democrat and Chronicle*, March 26, 1971, p. 5A, and the *National Observer*, March 9, 1970, p. 2.

9 Tariq Ibn Hassiz, "On That Black Administrator Sitting in Darkness," *Liberator*, Vol. 11, No. 3, March 1971, p. 11.

10 James A. Emanuel and Theodore L. Gross, eds., *Dark Symphony: Negro-Literature in America* (New York: Macmillan, 1968), p. 94. Reprinted by permission of Twayne Publishers, Inc.

11 Lotte Hoskins, ed., *I Have a Dream: The Quotations of Martin Luther King, Jr.* (New York: Grosset & Dunlap, 1968), p. 10.

# Bibliographical Essay

THE bibliographic comments which follow are designed only to inform the reader about the sources most used in this study. They do not encompass all of the works cited in the footnotes, nor do they constitute a comprehensive listing of books available on the subject of race relations in the United States. Two readily available excellent bibliographies appear in Ashley Montagu, *Man's Most Dangerous Myth: The Fallacy of Race* (Cleveland: World Publishing Co., 1964), pp. 429–488, and John Hope Franklin, *From Slavery to Freedom: A History of Negro Americans* (New York: Alfred A. Knopf, 1969), pp. 653–686.

## General Studies: Primary

Gilbert Osofsky, ed., *The Burden of Race: A Documentary History of Negro-White Relations in America* (New York: Harper and Row, 1967) and John Hope Franklin and Isidore Starr, eds., *The Negro in 20th Century America: A Reader on the Struggle for Civil Rights* (New York: Random House, 1967) have been indispensably valuable, containing as they do a wide variety of sources connected with excellent editorial commentary. Albert P. Blaustein and Robert L. Zangrando, eds., *Civil Rights and the American Negro: A Documentary History* (New York: Washington Square Press, 1968) is especially strong in congressional, executive, and judicial materials. These three together have supplied a large percentage of the primary source materials used in this study.

Leslie H. Fishel, Jr., and Benjamin Quarles, eds., *The Black American: A Documentary History* (Glenview, Ill.: Scott, Foresman, 1970) is also valuable for most topics. Joanne Grant, ed., *Black Protest: History, Documents, and Analyses 1619 to the*

*Present* (Greenwich, Conn.: Fawcett, 1969) supplies a wealth of material in a low-cost format.

I. A. Newby, ed., *The Development of Segregationist Thought* (Homewood, Ill.: Dorsey Press, 1968) and Barry N. Schwartz and Robert Disch, eds., *White Racism: Its History, Pathology and Practice* (New York: Dell Publishing Co., 1970) deal with white attitudes. The low-cost format of the latter should make it especially valuable in many high school and college courses which treat white racism.

John H. Bracey, Jr., August Meier, and Elliott Rudwick, eds., *Black Nationalism in America* (Indianapolis: Bobbs-Merrill, 1970) fills a major need for readily accessible materials on black nationalism, the most dynamic concept agitating the intellectual community at the present time. Unfortunately the volume came to hand too late to be of major use in this study.

Three classic autobiographies by twentieth-century American blacks belong in the General Studies category. They are Wm. E. Burghardt Du Bois, *Autobiography* (New York: International Publishers, 1968), James Weldon Johnson, *Along This Way* (New York: Viking, 1943), and Malcolm X, *Autobiography* (New York: Grove Press, 1965).

## General Studies: Secondary

Ashley Montagu, *Man's Most Dangerous Myth: The Fallacy of Race* (Cleveland: World Publishing Co., 1964) is probably the best one-volume treatment of the disease known as racism.

John Hope Franklin, *From Slavery to Freedom: A History of Negro Americans* (New York: Alfred A. Knopf, 1969) supplies an indispensably valuable overview for any understanding of the subject of race relations in the United States. Lerone Bennett, Jr., *Before the Mayflower: A History of the Negro in America, 1619–1964* (Baltimore: Penguin Books, 1966) is a highly readable, relatively brief survey. Both have been constant reference companions in the present study.

George W. Williams, *History of the Negro Race in America from 1619 to 1880* (New York: G. P. Putnam's Sons, 1883) was carefully done and supplies an interesting early example of the work of a black author in the field. Another dated but still useful study is E. Franklin Frazier, *The Negro in the United States* (New York: Macmillan, 1957).

Many books have dealt with the attitudes of blacks and whites toward each other and toward the race problem in the United States. The three which supplied the most penetrating insights for the study at hand were Charles E. Silberman, *Crisis in Black and White* (New York: Vintage, 1964), William H. Grier and Price M. Cobbs, *Black Rage* (New York: Bantam Books, 1969), and J. Saunders Redding, *On Being Negro in America* (Indianapolis: Bobbs-Merrill, 1962). Silberman's study was particularly helpful in starting my thinking in new directions.

Oscar Handlin, *Race and Nationality in American Life* (Garden City, N.Y.: Doubleday, 1957) is basic to an understanding of the racial complexities in the history of the country. Penetrating insights into black life appear in E. Franklin Frazier's two influential works, *Black Bourgeoisie* (New York: Macmillan, 1968) and *The Negro Family in the United States,* rev. ed. (Chicago: University of Chicago Press, 1968). The main thesis of the latter is presently undergoing major revision as a result of studies by scholars who have access to new materials.

W. E. Burghardt Du Bois, *The World and Africa: An Inquiry Into the Part Which Africa Has Played in World History* (New York: International Publishers, 1965) and Frantz Fanon, *The Wretched of the Earth* (New York: Grove Press, 1968) provide valuable insights into the problem of the color line on a world scale.

Although somewhat dated now, Gunnar Myrdal, *An American Dilemma* (New York: Harper & Row, 1944) contains much basic material for understanding race relations in America. Arnold Rose, *The Negro in America* (Boston: Beacon Press, 1962) offers a useful shorter version in a low-cost format.

## 2. *Slavery and Reconstruction*

Allen Weinstein and Frank O. Gatell, eds., *American Negro Slavery: A Modern Reader* (New York: Oxford University Press, 1968) supplies a variety of readings in a low-cost format. Winthrop D. Jordan, *White Over Black: American Attitudes Toward the Negro 1150–1812* (Baltimore: Penguin Books, 1969) breaks important new ground. It is the sort of germinal work which will doubtless inspire a number of fresh studies which together will expand our understanding of modern racism.

Of the many books on American slavery, Kenneth M. Stampp, *The Peculiar Institution: Slavery in the Ante-Bellum South* (New York: Vintage, 1965) offers the most balanced, brief treatment. It gives the antidote to the proslavery classic, Ulrich B. Phillips, *American Negro Slavery* (Baton Rouge, La.: Louisiana State University Press, 1966). Stanley M. Elkins, *Slavery: A Problem in American Institutional Life* (Chicago: University of Chicago Press, 1968) has opened a variety of new vistas which beckon scholars to move beyond earlier molds. Leon F. Litwack, *North of*

*Slavery: The Negro in the Free States, 1790–1860* (Chicago: University of Chicago Press, 1961) gives a highly readable insight into the life of free blacks before the Civil War.

Of the many influential comments from the white supremacist viewpoint, Joseph Arthur de Gobineau, *The Inequality of Human Races* (New York: G. P. Putnam's Sons, 1915) was the most useful in the study at hand. R. W. Shufeldt, *The Negro: A Menace to American Civilization* (Boston: Badger, 1907), and Charles Carroll, *The Negro a Beast* (Miami, Fla.: Mnemosyne Pub. Co., 1900) supply the classic American versions of white supremacist arguments. Madison Grant, *The Passing of the Great Race* (New York: Charles Scribner's Sons, 1916) is more anti-Eastern European and anti-immigrant than antiblack, but the carry-over value is clear. Pseudoscientific racism continues to be popular in America. See especially Carleton Putnam's two widely read polemics, *Race and Reason: A Yankee View* (Washington, D.C.: Public Affairs Press, 1961) and *Race and Reality* (ibid., 1967). Arthur R. Jensen, "How Much Can We Boost I.Q. and Scholastic Achievement," *Harvard Educational Review*, Vol. 39, No. 1, Winter 1969, is really a short book indicative of the continuing scholarly interest in finding ways to shift the blame for culturally imposed limitations from society to the individual.

The Reconstruction period in American history has received a great deal of scholarly attention. Richard N. Current, ed., *Reconstruction: 1865–1877* (Englewood Cliffs, N.J.: Prentice-Hall, 1965) and Robert W. Johannsen, ed., *Reconstruction: 1865–1877* (New York: Macmillan, 1970) supply two useful collections of primary source materials. Joel Williamson, ed., *The Origins of Segregation* (Boston: D. C. Heath, 1968) brings together a variety of secondary comments.

W. E. B. Du Bois, *Black Reconstruction in America* (New York: Atheneum, 1969) still stands as a classic attempt to place the black man in proper historical perspective. John Hope Franklin, *Reconstruction After the Civil War* (Chicago: University of Chicago Press, 1967) supplies an excellent, balanced, brief overview in a low-cost format. Lerone Bennett, Jr., *Black Power U.S.A.: The Human Side of Reconstruction, 1867–1877* (Chicago: Johnson Publishing Co., 1967) is a highly readable account of the role of blacks in southern and national politics during the period. C. Vann Woodward, *Reunion and Reaction: The Compromise of 1877 and the End of Reconstruction* (Boston: Little, Brown, 1951) has stood for a generation as the definitive work on the subject and seems as secure as ever.

The earlier view which demeaned the blacks appeared in Claude G. Bowers, *The Tragic Era: The Revolution After*

*Lincoln* (Boston: Houghton Mifflin, 1929). This classic work has had great influence and is still widely read, although subsequent scholarship has largely undermined it. Hodding Carter, *The Angry Scar: The Story of Reconstruction* (Garden City, N.Y.: Doubleday, 1959) while somewhat more balanced than Bowers, carries a similar, white supremacist message. It too continues to be influential in many schools and some colleges.

The *Life and Times of Frederick Douglass* (New York: Macmillan, 1962) is a classic autobiography by one of the country's most accomplished citizens. Fawn Brodie, *Thaddeus Stevens* (New York: Norton, 1959) gives a vivid account of a leading white who truly favored absolute equality.

## 3. *The Coming of Jim Crow*

Howard Brotz, ed., *Negro Social and Political Thought, 1850–1920* (New York: Basic Books, 1966) and Allen Weinstein and Frank O. Gatell, eds., *The Segregation Era: 1863–1954: A Modern Reader* (New York: Oxford University Press, 1970) contain a variety of useful materials on various aspects of the Jim Crow problem.

C. Vann Woodward, *The Strange Career of Jim Crow*, 2nd rev. ed. (New York: Oxford University Press, 1966) has been properly termed a landmark study in the history of American race relations since Reconstruction. It has been indispensably valuable in developing Chapter 3. The same author's *Origins of the New South, 1877–1913* (Baton Rouge: Louisiana State University Press, 1951) also belongs in the category of classic works. Rayford W. Logan, *The Betrayal of the Negro from Rutherford B. Hayes to Woodrow Wilson,* New Enlarged Edition (New York: Macmillan, 1968), although rather awkwardly put together in places supplies a wealth of insight and information. It too has been exceedingly valuable in the development of several chapters in the work in hand.

Stanley P. Hirshson, *Farewell to the Bloody Shirt: Northern Republicans and the Southern Negro, 1877–1893* (Bloomington: Indiana University Press, 1962) and Farrish G. Wood, *Black Scare: The Racist Respone to Emancipation and Reconstruction* (Berkeley: University of California Press, 1968) deal with important major themes in the post-Civil War generation.

## 4. *The Record of Judge Lynch*

Hugh D. Graham and Ted R. Gurr, eds., *The History of Violence in America,* Report to the National Commission on the

Causes and Prevention of Violence (New York: Frederick A. Praeger, 1969) deals with violence on a large scale, but the racial theme is a significant item. Allen D. Grimshaw, ed., *Racial Violence in the United States* (Chicago: Aldine Publishing Co., 1969) contains a wealth of material covering topics from the early days of slavery to the 1960s.

Ida B. Wells Barnett was the original student of lynch mob terrorism in the United States; some of her writings have been collected and reprinted in *On Lynchings* (New York: Arno Press, 1969). Walter White, *Rope and Faggot: A Biography of Judge Lynch* (New York: Arno Press, 1969, first published by Knopf in 1929) has been extremely valuable in working up Chapter 4. White drew upon the experience represented by the NAACP study *Thirty Years of Lynching in the United States, 1889–1918*, (New York: Crisis Publications, 1919). Arthur F. Raper, *The Tragedy of Lynching* (Chapel Hill: University of North Carolina Press, 1933) also presents shocking evidence of the brutality of race relations in the United States. James E. Cutler, *Lynch Law: An Investigation Into the History of Lynching in the United States* (Montclair, N.J.: Patterson Smith, 1969) and Ralph Ginzburg, *100 Years of Lynchings: The Shocking Record Behind Today's Black Militancy* (New York: Lancer, 1969) both supply an extended record. Ginzburg's study reprints hundreds of newspaper accounts from widely scattered cities.

David M. Chalmers, *Hooded Americanism: The History of the Ku Klux Klan* (Chicago: Quadrangle Books, 1968) is probably the best study of America's most vicious social institution. John M. Mecklin, *The KKK: A Study of the American Mind* (New York: Harcourt, Brace, 1924) focuses on the 1920's. The Klan during the current era has been studied by William Bradford Huie, *Three Lives for Mississippi* (New York: Signet, 1968). This powerful book was valuable in developing portions of Chapter 4. Don Whitehead, *Attack on Terror: The FBI Against the KKK in Mississippi* (New York: Funk & Wagnalls, 1970) supplies an excellent picture of the need for federal action to curb racial violence on the local level.

## 5. *Early Equal-Rights Movements*

August Meier, *Negro Thought in America, 1880–1915: Racial Ideologies in the Age of Booker T. Washington* (Ann Arbor: University of Michigan Press, 1968) presents incisive assessments of the major figures of the era. W. E. B. Du Bois, *The Souls of Black Folk* (Greenwich, Conn.: Fawcett, 1961) is a classic piece of writing which is revealing of the thought of the time in which it was first published (1903) but also surprisingly (even shock-ingly) revealing of the continuing race problem in America. In many ways the problem of white attitudes toward blacks remains much the same as when Du Bois first discussed it and termed the "problem of the twentieth century" the "problem of the color line." Elliott M. Rudwick, *W. E. B. Du Bois: Propagandist of the Negro Protest* (New York: Atheneum, 1968) is the best biography of this most influential American black. See also, of course, Du Bois' *Autobiography*, listed in General Studies. The accommodationist view can be found in Booker T. Washington's greatly influential *Up from Slavery* (New York: Bantam Books, 1956). I. A. Newby, *Jim Crow's Defense: Anti-Negro Thought in America, 1900–1930* (Baton Rouge: Louisiana State University Press, 1968) provides a useful overview of the white-supremacist perspective.

John D. Weaver, *The Brownsville Raid* (New York: Norton, 1970) tells the story of this shameful episode which characterized the Theodore Roosevelt era. Many monographs of this type are needed to fill in the gaps in our knowledge of race relations history.

Charles F. Kellogg, *NAACP: A History of the National Association for the Advancement of Colored People* (Baltimore: Johns Hopkins Press, 1967) is the best scholarly study of the most important equal-rights organization, but Langston Hughes, *Fight for Freedom: The Story of the NAACP* (New York: Norton, 1962) is also very useful. Other early equal-rights organizations need further study.

## 6. *Internal Migration and the Making of the Northern Ghetto*

Carter G. Woodson, *A Century of Negro Migration* (New York: Russell and Russell, 1969) first appeared in 1918 and was properly acclaimed as breaking important new ground. Emmett J. Scott, *Negro Migration During the War* (New York: Arno Press, 1969) came out shortly afterward and supplied further insight into the immense social change then taking place in the United States as a result of the departure of millions of blacks from the rural South. The white problem was about to surface everywhere in the nation. Arna Bontemps and Jack Conroy, *Anyplace But Here* (New York: Hill and Wang, 1968), was originally published with the title *They Seek a City*. This excellent book has been highly valuable in the study at hand, especially in the development of Chapter 6. Edwin S. Redkey, *Black Exodus* (New Haven, Conn.:

Yale University Press, 1969) tells the story of black attempts to emigrate to Africa during the late nineteenth century.

August Meier and Elliott Rudwick, eds., *The Making of Black America,* Vol. II (New York: Atheneum, 1969) contains a wide variety of readings on the "Black Community in Modern America." Robert C. Weaver, *The Negro Ghetto* (New York: Russell and Russell, 1948) is a useful study, as is Kenneth T. Jackson, *The Ku Klux Klan in the City 1915–1930* (New York: Oxford University Press, 1967).

Examples of Northern ghetto life have centered upon New York and Chicago, no doubt because these two cities have received more study over a longer period of time. Gilbert Osofsky, *Harlem: The Making of a Ghetto: Negro New York, 1890–1930* (New York: Harper & Row, 1966) is extremely valuable. It supplied much to my thinking and information in portions of Chapter 6. Kenneth B. Clark, *Dark Ghetto: Dilemmas of Social Power* (New York: Harper & Row, 1967) and James Weldon Johnson, *Black Manhattan* (New York: Atheneum, 1968) are also classic studies.

Allan H. Spear, *Black Chicago: The Making of a Negro Ghetto, 1890–1920* (Chicago: University of Chicago Press, 1967) is immensely well done and was very valuable in the study at hand. St. Clair Drake and Horace R. Cayton, *Black Metropolis: A Study of Negro Life in a Northern City* (New York: Harper & Row, 1962) two volumes, updates a classic work on Chicago which first appeared in 1945.

Claude Brown, *Manchild in the Promised Land* (New York: Signet, 1965) provides a valuable insight into the problems of growing up in a Northern black ghetto, as does James Baldwin, *The Fire Next Time* (New York: Dial Press, 1963). Portions of Malcolm X's *Autobiography* mentioned in General Studies are also revealing on the same theme. Charles S. Johnson, *Growing Up in the Black Belt: Negro Youth in the Rural South* (New York: Schocken Books, 1967) presents a series of insights into the country counterpart of the urban black ghetto.

Modern and continuing ghetto problems are well presented in James B. Conant, *Slums and Suburbs* (New York: Signet, 1964), Sterling Tucker, *Beyond the Burning: Life and Death of the Ghetto* (New York: Association Press, 1968), William Moore, Jr., *The Vertical Ghetto: Everyday Life in an Urban Project* (New York: Random House, 1969), and Karl E. Taeuber and Alma F. Taeuber, *Negroes in Cities* (New York: Atheneum, 1969).

## 7. *World War I and Its Aftermath*

The black role in America's war effort is told in Emmett J. Scott, *The American Negro in the World War* (New York: Arno Press, 1969, first published 1919) and Arthur W. Little, *From Harlem to the Rhine: The Story of New York's Colored Volunteers* (New York: Covici, Friede, 1936). Race relations on the home front are treated in Elliot M. Rudwick, *Race Riot in East St. Louis, July 2, 1917* (Carbondale, Ill.: Southern Illinois University Press, 1964). This outstanding piece of writing was extremely valuable in developing portions of Chapter 7. The Chicago riot and conditions after the war are included in the Report of the Chicago Commission on Race Relations, *The Negro in Chicago: A Study of Race Relations and a Race Riot* (Chicago: University of Chicago Press, 1922).

Sterling D. Spero and Abram L. Harris, *The Black Worker* (New York: Atheneum, 1968) is an immensely worthwhile study which carries the record of union opposition to black advance through the 1920's. Herbert R. Northrup, *Organized Labor and the Negro* (New York: Harper & Row, 1944) and Robert C. Weaver, *Negro Labor, a National Problem* (Port Washington, N.Y.: Kennikat Press, 1946) tell the later story.

E. David Cronon, *The Story of Marcus Garvey and the Universal Negro Improvement Association* (Madison: University of Wisconsin Press, 1969) is an excellent study. For Garvey's views, see Amy Jacques-Garvey, ed., *Philosophy and Opinions of Marcus Garvey* (New York: Atheneum, 1969).

Dan T. Carter, *Scottsboro: A Tragedy of the American South* (Baton Rouge: Louisiana State University Press, 1969) is the definitive work on the subject. It contains great insight into the unbalanced judicial procedures of the period. Patterson's own story appears in Haywood Patterson and Earl Conrad, *Scottsboro Boy* (New York: Macmillan, 1969). Leon Friedman, ed., *Southern Justice* (Cleveland: World Publishing Co., 1967) brings the story of unequal treatment for blacks by public officials, through the 1950's. William M. Chace and Peter Collier, eds., *Justice Denied: The Black Man in White America* (New York: Harcourt Brace Jovanovich, 1970) includes a wide variety of readings. Loren Miller, *The Petitioners: The Story of the Supreme Court of the United States and the Negro* (Cleveland: World Publishing Co., 1967) is a comprehensive account from the country's beginnings through the mid 1960's.

## 8. *World War II and Its Aftermath*

Two books of readings are especially useful for this period. They are Bernard Sternsher, ed., *The Negro in Depression and War: Prelude to Revolution 1930–1945* (Chicago: Quadrangle Books, 1969) and Lettie J. Austin, Lewis H. Fenderson, and Sophia P. Nelson, eds., *The Black Man and the Promise of America* (Glenview, Ill.: Scott, Foresman and Co., 1970). The latter contains a wide variety of materials which cover the full span of American race relations history.

The story of black participation in the war effort may be found in John D. Silvera, *The Negro in World War II* (New York: Arno Press, 1969) and Ulysses Lee, *The U.S. Army in World War II: Employment of Negro Troops* (Washington: U.S. Govt. Printing Office, 1966). The desegregation process is discussed in Richard M. Dalfiume, *Fighting on Two Fronts: Desegregation of the Armed Forces* (Chicago: Quadrangle Books, 1969) and in Richard J. Stillman, II, *Integration of the Negro in the U.S. Armed Forces* (New York: Frederick A. Praeger, 1968).

The most acute instance of continued racial friction on the home front is detailed in Alfred M. Lee and Norman D. Humphrey, *Race Riot: Detroit 1943* (New York: Octagon Books, 1968). See also, Robert Shogan and Tom Craig, *The Detroit Race Riot: A Study in Violence* (Philadelphia: Chilton Books, 1964). Some of the new spirit in black America can be seen in Walter White, *A Rising Wind* (Garden City, N.Y.: Doubleday, 1945) and Roi Ottley, *New World A-Coming: Inside Black America* (Boston: Houghton, Mifflin, 1943). Gerlad Messner, ed., *Another View: To Be Black in America* (New York: Harcourt Brace Jovanovich, 1970) contains a wide variety of readings, but many which bear upon the new spirit of revolt in black America during and after World War II. Carl T. Rowan and Jackie Robinson, *Wait Till Next Year* (New York: Random House, 1960) provides some of the story of change in the world of sports.

White resistance to the new era appears in John B. Martin, *The Deep South Says 'Never'* (New York: Ballantine Books, 1957). Ralph McGill, *The South and the Southerner* (Boston: Little, Brown, 1963) and Lillian Smith, *Killers of the Dream* (New York: Norton, 1949) provide sensitive insights by white authors who disagree with the majority viewpoint in their region.

Change in the world of politics appears in Herbert J. Storing, ed., *What Country Have I? Political Writings by Black Americans* (New York: St. Martin's Press, 1970). A special aspect of the political equation is treated in Wilson Record, *Race and Radicalism: The NAACP and the Communist Party in Conflict* (Ithaca, N.Y.: Cornell University Press, 1966).

## 9. Equal-Rights Revolution of the 1950's and 1960's

The literature of protest has grown so rich that it is difficult to present a select list. Francis L. Broderick and August Meier, eds., *Negro Protest Thought in the Twentieth Century* (Indianapolis: Bobbs-Merrill, 1965) contains a wide variety of background readings. Two excellent personalized histories of the 1950's and 1960's are Louis E. Lomax, *The Negro Revolt* (New York: Signet, 1963) and Lerone Bennett, Jr., *Confrontation: Black and White* (Baltimore: Penguin Books, 1965). Michael Harrington, *The Other America: Poverty in the United States* (Baltimore: Penguin Books, 1966) deals with the question of poverty as a whole including the extent to which poverty in America is racially based. Lewis M. Killian, *The Impossible Revolution? Black Power and the American Dream* (New York: Random House, 1968) and the Editors of Ebony Magazine, *The White Problem in America* (New York: Lancer Books, 1966) get directly to the central question—white attitudes toward blacks.

The beginnings of major social change are presented in Howard Zinn, *SNCC: The New Abolitionists* (Boston: Beacon Press, 1965) and Jack Newfield, *A Prophetic Minority* (New York: Signet, 1967). Individual insights into various phases of the confrontation program are found in Daisy Bates, *The Long Shadow of Little Rock* (New York: David McKay, 1962), Merrill Proudfoot, *Diary of a Sit-in* (Chapel Hill: University of North Carolina Press, 1962), James Peck, *Freedom Ride* (New York: Simon and Schuster, 1962), and Tracy Sugarman, *Stranger at the Gates: A Summer in Mississippi* (New York: Hill and Wang, 1967).

The two giant figures of the period were Martin Luther King, Jr., and Malcolm X. They are well represented in printed works. See especially, for King, *Stride Toward Freedom* (New York: Ballantine Books, 1958) and *Why We Can't Wait* (New York: Signet, 1964). For Malcolm X, in addition to the *Autobiography* mentioned in General Studies, see George Breitman, ed., *Malcolm X Speaks* (New York: Grove Press, 1966) and *The Last Year of Malcolm X: The Evolution of a Revolutionary* (New York: Schocken Books, 1967), by the same author. See also John H. Clarke, ed., *Malcolm X: The Man and His Time* (New York: Macmillan, 1969).

C. Eric Lincoln, *The Black Muslims in America* (Boston: Beacon Press, 1961) tells the story of the organization which has probably provided the central thrust of the new black attitude. Black power has been presented in a wide variety of books. Floyd B. Barbour, ed., *The Black Power Revolt* (New York: Macmillan, 1969) and Sethard Fisher, ed., *Power and the Black Community* (New York: Random House, 1970) are two excellent readers on various aspects of the subject. Attitudes are emphasized in Nathan Wright, Jr., *Black Power and Urban Unrest* (New York: Hawthorn Books, 1967) and in William Brink and Louis Harris, *Black and White: A Study of U.S. Racial Attitudes Today* (New York: Simon and Schuster, 1967).

Powerful, individual insights into the views of the black "militants" can be seen in Eldridge Cleaver, *Soul On Ice* (New York: Delta, 1968) and Robert Scheer, ed., *Eldridge Cleaver: Post Prison Writings and Speeches* (New York: Vintage, 1969). See also, Floyd McKissick, *Three Fifths of a Man* (New York: Macmillan, 1969), Julius Lester, *Look Out Whitey! Black Power's Gon' Get Your Mama!* (New York: Grove Press, 1969), and H. Rap Brown, *Die Nigger Die!* (New York: Dial Press, 1969).

Outcomes of the equal-rights revolution in a variety of acid situations appear in Kerner Commission, *Report of the National Advisory Commission on Civil Disorders* (New York: Bantam Books, 1968), a work which every American, especially those who happen to be white, should study. Memorable accounts of specific riots include Robert Conot, *Rivers of Blood, Years of Darkness* (New York: Morrow, 1967), John Hersey, *The Algiers Motel Incident* (New York: Knopf, 1968), and Ben W. Gilbert, *Ten Blocks from the White House* (New York: Frederick A. Praeger, 1968) for Watts, Detroit, and Washington, respectively.

Literature which deals with solutions has yet to appear in large quantity. Brief statements and viewpoints are scattered through many of the collections of readings. Nathan Wright, Jr., *Let's Work Together* (New York: Hawthorn Books, 1968) offers some useful suggestions, as does Martin Luther King, Jr., *Where Do We Go From Here: Chaos or Community?* (New York: Bantam Books, 1968). Application of the black power concept to political situations is treated in Stokely Carmichael and Charles V. Hamilton, *Black Power: The Politics of Liberation in America* (New York: Random House, 1967). But the entire subject of practical recommendations for action needs attention. Although the bigots and the militants seize the headlines, many blacks and whites are working out solutions in both single and multiracial organizations of many types. The record of success and failure should be made available on the widest possible scale.

# Index